Strategic Finance for Criminal Justice Organizations

Strategic Finance for Criminal Justice Organizations

Daniel Adrian Doss
William H. Sumrall III
Don W. Jones

CRC Press
Taylor & Francis Group
Boca Raton London New York

CRC Press is an imprint of the
Taylor & Francis Group, an **informa** business

CRC Press
Taylor & Francis Group
6000 Broken Sound Parkway NW, Suite 300
Boca Raton, FL 33487-2742

Version Date: 20120224

International Standard Book Number: 978-1-4398-9223-7 (Paperback)

Library of Congress Cataloging-in-Publication Data

Doss, Daniel Adrian.
Strategic finance for criminal justice organizations / Daniel Adrian Doss, William H. Sumrall III, Don W. Jones.
p. cm.
Includes bibliographical references and index.
ISBN 978-1-4398-9223-7 (pbk.)
1. Criminal justice, Administration of. 2. Finance--Decision making. I. Sumrall, William H. II. Jones, Don W. III. Title.

HV7419.D673 2012
364.068'1--dc23 2012005187

Visit the Taylor & Francis Web site at
http://www.taylorandfrancis.com

and the CRC Press Web site at
http://www.crcpress.com

Contents

Preface

This text represents a unique approach to discussing the administration of criminal justice organizations. Unlike many texts that primarily consider qualitative aspects of management, leadership, and organizational theories, this book provides a quantitative perspective solely from the context of financial management decisions. Specifically, this book provides a quantitative consideration of the strategic capital budgeting methods for rendering financial decisions that affect law enforcement entities.

Before any organization can implement its strategy, it must have a clear notion of its vision. Simply, vision is the expression of what the organization hopes to become through the passage of time. Vision is the end state of organizational maturation over years or decades. Vision is the epiphany that strikes organizational leaders and spurs the overwhelming desire to achieve the future state of existence of the organization through time. From an analogy of human children, vision may be best considered as the answer to a simple question: What is it that you wish to be when you've grown up?

Organizations may also be faced with a similar question: What is it that the organization hopes to become through time? The answers are varied, and represent a plethora of unique domains and settings within the law enforcement and criminal justice communities. No solitary answer is perfect because the answers differ for each individual organization. Only the organization itself can provide the answer to this question, and only the organization itself may determine its future courses of actions through which it strives to achieve its fulfilling of vision through time.

These courses of actions, which contribute toward the achieving of a visionary future state, are expressed through a single word: *strategy*. Strategy is the overall method, the long-term plan, through which the pursuits and fulfilling of the visionary state occurs. Strategic notions encapsulate the mission, goals, and objectives of an organization through time. Because strategic periods are often long and occur over years or decades, the facets of strategy may be both complex and varied. Within the strategic environment are known and unknown influences that either facilitate strategic pursuits or become impediments that necessitate contingency courses of actions. The strategic environment is constantly dynamic and manifests a robust set of characteristics that uniquely impact organizations.

These primary, strategic plans and contingency plans demonstrate a myriad of both long-term and short-term projects that, hopefully, provide value for the organization through time. Further, given the contexts of law enforcement, the criminal justice system, and related entities, such considerations of value must also be manifested among society and the local communities that are served by such organizations. Therefore, organizations may develop and pursue a variety of initiatives, through time, that contribute toward the creation of value and capitalize upon growth opportunities.

However, these initiatives are not free. Somewhere, somehow, and in some way, financial compensation must be rendered and invested toward the creation of value and growth; the derivation of organizational, societal, and community benefits; and the pursuit of strategy through time. Therefore, some poor, overworked, underappreciated schmuck must make a decision regarding capital investments that impacts the future of the organization. In some cases, such decisions might have consequences and ramifications for the job security and employment longevity of those who render such decisions. For every decision this person makes, there will be both praise and criticism. Regardless, some organizational leader(s) must render a decision regarding either the pursuance or the discarding of strategic courses of action that necessitate capital investments through time. This person must play roulette with the innards of the organization's piggy bank.

Cash flow is the lifeblood of any organization. If managed wisely, cash flow can invigorate an organization financially, and facilitate the pursuance of organizational goals and objectives toward the fulfilling of the organization's mission through time. If poorly managed, cash flow can devastate and contribute to the dissolution of an organization. Regardless, the cash flow of any entity, whether for-profit or nonprofit in its structuring, is essential to the long-term, strategic success of the organization.

Numerous examples exist regarding the eventual successes that result from sound financial management practices over long-term periods. These examples are found in the computer software industry, the overnight shipping industry, the medical industry, the food and beverage industry, the energy industry, and in a variable array of other industries. However, among these same industries are examples of dismal organizational failures. Through sound financial management practices, good ideas became great, and are representative of common household products and business services. However, through poor financial management, many good ideas never realize their potential.

Within the context of government, which is a nonprofit entity, the use of money is considerable. From the federal context, the use of money may be conceptualized simply through a consideration of the distribution of tax dollars that comprise government spending. According to the National

Priorities Project, the following distribution of tax dollars represents 2009 government spending estimates[*]:

26.5¢	Military spending
20.1¢	Health
13.6¢	Interest on debt
9.8¢	Government use
8.5¢	Income security and labor
7.2¢	Housing and community
3.7¢	Food
3.5¢	Veterans' benefits
2.5¢	Environment, energy, and science
2.0¢	Education
1.3¢	International affairs
1.3¢	Transportation

This distribution provides an understanding of the domains in which tax dollars are expended annually. Further, during 2009, a total of 57 cents of every dollar was borrowed.[†] These considerations, of a single dollar, may be increased by numerous orders of magnitude to represent the workings of the current U.S. expenditures annually. These financial amounts represented approximately "$2.7 trillion federal fund outlays" during 2009.[‡] Given this staggering amount, it is obvious that sound financial management is a salient consideration of government.

The preceding concepts are not limited to the domains of for-profit and nonprofit business endeavors (including government). Instead, they are also applicable to the realms of law enforcement entities and criminal justice organizations. The notions of sound financial management are just as valid within the contexts of criminal justice entities and law enforcement organizations as they are among for-profit and nonprofit business environments.

Contemporary law enforcement agencies are representative of extensions of governments, thereby demonstrating their characteristics of nonprofit financial management functions. However, numerous for-profit prison system corporations, youth programs, and community services organizations are representative of for-profit financial management functions. Given these considerations, the saliency of sound financial management principles impacts law and justice organizations in a fashion that rivals their implementations among entities within the corporate sector. Therefore, funding decisions are of paramount importance among law enforcement and criminal justice organizations.

[*] National Priorities Project, "Where Did Your Tax Dollars Go?" http://www.nationalpriorities.org/auxiliary/taxday2010/NPP-Tax_Day_2010.pdf (accessed September 2, 2010).

[†] Ibid.

[‡] Ibid.

The funding of law enforcement and criminal justice entities varies according to the demographics of their served public markets. Within a variety of academic programs, the only considerations of financial management in the context of criminal justice entities and law enforcement organizations are limited primarily to various discussions of budgeting and tax revenues. Other discussions may pertain to various facets of economic influences that impact funding allocations. Regardless, these topics are concerned with two dominant themes: the past and present of money. However, relatively few discussions consider the strategic future of revenues.

Within the strategic perspective of revenues is the notion of rendering human decisions. Human decisions greatly influence the success of organizations through time. Among the for-profit and nonprofit sectors, strategic decisions must be rendered according to the tenets of maximizing the wealth of shareholders or with respect to the provision of societal betterment. The rendering of these decisions is not arbitrary and involves varying amounts of risk. Regardless, these perspectives must be facilitated through a robust consideration of the problem domain, and must occur through some systematic, methodical process regarding the identification, evaluation, and selection of strategic courses of action.

Rarely are such concepts and themes considered in introductory courses in criminal justice or law enforcement academic programs. Because of the potency of financial management, strategically, the rendering of decisions among criminal justice entities and law enforcement organizations must be seriously considered regarding any potential advantages and disadvantages. This embellishing of the process of rendering decisions may be considered from the perspective of strategic capital budgeting functions.

Among many contemporary criminal justice courses are considerations of annual budgets or considerations of historical cash flows. However, despite discussions of budgeting, few criminal justice programs consider capital investments of cash flows, strategically, through time, to provide some long-term, future benefit for law enforcement and criminal justice organizations. However, among courses in business administration, these notions of long-term financial management are common and are critical to a sound understanding of organizational finance. Within the context of business administration, these notions are encapsulated within discussions of capital budgeting functions. Therefore, a primary purpose of this book is to provide a synopsis of these capital budgeting functions, and to describe and discuss their usefulness within the law enforcement and criminal justice domain.

Because many law enforcement positions are elected, those who occupy these positions represent varied backgrounds. Other positions may be appointed. Regardless, some personnel may have a sound understanding of business finance, whereas others may have absolutely no understanding or knowledge of business finance techniques. Therefore, this book is written for an introductory audience, and explains capital budgeting concepts through the use of practical examples that consider examples of salient decisions that are applicable within the domains of law enforcement and criminal justice organizations.

This book contains discussions and descriptions regarding the basic functions of capital budgeting. Because it is written for a basic audience, the advanced principles of capital budgeting and financial management, necessitating the knowledge of business calculus or graduate statistics, are not included in this text. Instead, only a good understanding of algebraic principles is required to understand the discussions and examples contained herein. Therefore, this book is appropriate for those who wish to gain an introductory knowledge and understanding of capital budgeting applications within the criminal justice and law enforcement domains. Hopefully, such an understanding will contribute to improvements of the skills that are required to robustly render long-term, strategic decisions among such environments.

Regardless of the size of a law enforcement or criminal justice organization, the entity has to concern itself with its finances. This notion is common among all law enforcement and criminal justice environments. Whether such financing is derived from taxation or for-profit revenues, the management of monies is of paramount importance to efficiently and effectively fulfill the goals and objectives of the organization strategically through time. Only through sound financial management principles can law enforcement and criminal justice organizations maximize their impacts of providing quality public services among a myriad of communities and societies.

Therefore, given these considerations, this book serves as a practical guide to explain the basic tenets of capital budgeting principles. Its contents may be of use among both for-profit and nonprofit settings. From the perspective of capital budgeting, the contents contain discussions regarding the salient dimensions of financial management: time, value, cash flow, profitability, and rate.

The purchasing of a building requires time, involves a variety of cash flow attributes, may enhance or detract from revenue streams, may provide some form of profit or calculable value, and may require a mortgage rate or leasing rate. The uses of such assets may serve as a police station, holding facility, or equipment storage facility. Certainly, many other assets may be identified as capital investments ranging from traffic cone sets to patrol cars. Regardless, monetary decisions must be rendered regarding the potential benefits of such items, and such benefits must be examined quantitatively. The use of capital budgeting provides a systematic, methodical tool through which such examinations may occur.

Within the context of capital budgeting, the leaders of law enforcement and criminal justice organizations gain the ability to perform such examinations from multiple perspectives. Many leaders may consider a limited approach to their decisions without regard to a complete consideration of the full capacity of capital budgeting attributes. Therefore, a purpose of this book is to provide an introductory overview of the possible benefits that may be derived from capital budgeting.

The format of this book provides a consideration of economic and financial decisions that pervaded U.S. national history and the currency of the characteristics of such decisions. Although much time has passed since the inception of the nation, the questions of financial management and the economic allocation of resources are relatively unchanged. Within the mathematical context of decision domains, these issues of financial management and resource allocation are salient considerations that impact law enforcement and criminal justice organizations through time. Therefore, a purpose of this book is to provide a set of basic tools through which such decisions may be formulated and rendered. Regardless of the size of the organization, the use of the capital budgeting tools described herein is appropriate for embellishing the considerations of strategic decisions.

It is also important to note some observations regarding the mathematical calculations used in the examples of this text. The example problems were solved using Microsoft Excel. Therefore, some minor rounding differences may be observed if any readers verify the solutions to the problems contained herein using tabular solutions. Similar numerical rounding differences may be observed if verifications of problem solutions are performed using handheld calculators.

Given such notions, it is hoped that the readers of this book shall derive meaningful benefits from its contents. Although this text is a basic introduction to the concept of capital budgeting, it provides resources through which organizational leaders may facilitate long-term, strategic decisions incorporating the elements of time, rate, cash flow, and profitability. Through the integration of these perspectives, it is hoped that the skills of organizational leaders are greatly improved toward the rendering of robust, efficient, and effective decisions strategically.

This section opened with a simple notion of strategic vision expressed through a primary question: What is it that the organization hopes to become through time? The use of capital budgeting techniques may assist organizations in shaping, planning, and achieving strategies through which they may fulfill their visions. Through capital budgeting, organizations may invest in their futures wisely. It is hoped that the contents of this book will assist organizations as they mature and fulfill their independent visions.

Acknowledgments

Thanks to Almighty God for this publication opportunity. Micah 6:8—"He hath shewed thee, O man, what is good; and what doth the Lord require of thee, but to do justly, and to love mercy, and to walk humbly with thy God?"

This work is for my parents, Jerry W. Doss and Margaret S. Doss. When I was little, you always said I should eventually write a book. Well, here it is!

Thank you to my coauthors, Don Sumrall and Bill Jones. Your participation and friendship are greatly appreciated, and I have thoroughly enjoyed this opportunity to collaborate with you.

A very special thank you is rendered to Martha Shirley for her patience and kindness in assisting with our writing project and for her editing skills.

Thank you to the faculty and staff of the University of West Alabama. Your encouragement was essential in keeping our efforts focused when completing this manuscript.

Thank you to the faculty and staff of the Department of Legal Studies at the University of Mississippi. It was during the completion of your graduate program that I conceptualized a vision for this book. It is now a reality—so, simply, thank you.

Thank you to the faculty and staff of the Department of Criminal Justice at the University of Massachusetts (Lowell). It was your graduate program that sparked the idea of blending the topics of business and criminal justice as a research endeavor.

Adrian Doss

Two very significant groups have contributed to my determined motivation to complete this book. First, the book is dedicated to the justice administration professionals who provide in society the safety and security needs for stable living arrangements. Second, my immediate and extended family members have continually provided love, affection, and therefore the personal motivation in my life over many years for the accomplishment of all goals.

Bill Sumrall

I acknowledge the support and encouragement of those who have done so much to help me along the way:

My mentors J. D. "Rip" Fanning, Russell McClanahan, Adrian Doss, and Bill Sumrall, thank you for lighting the path (and for picking me up from time to time!).

My family: Lillie Mae and William Ansel, who adopted that squalling infant and gave him opportunity and love; David and William Lee, who endured that screaming infant as he grew into a sometimes screaming adult; Kay and Thunderbunny, who have endured the crazy hours and panic-riddled midnight writing sessions.

My friends and coworkers, who may someday come to realize that ADHD isn't always a bad thing in a colleague: Amber, Audrey, Jeremy, and especially Charles, Stefan, and Susan, the Three Musketeers, who know that breaking away for lunch is often a good substitute for heavy medication.

To those who serve as volunteers, especially the members of the Mississippi State Guard: the Garners, Clines, Hoovers, and so many others who stand ready to serve and defend without recompense—you give me hope for the human race.

I have come to appreciate the sometimes hysterical laughter of good companions in tense moments, the soft words of correction from those who love me enough to tell me the truth, and the magic of a Bunny's smile.

With thanks to many, and glory to One …

Don Jones

Authors

Daniel Adrian Doss, PhD, is an assistant professor with the University of West Alabama. His background also includes adjunct assistant professor, Embry-Riddle Aeronautical University (Daytona Beach, Florida); assistant professor, Belhaven College (Memphis); and chair of Graduate Business and Management, University of Phoenix (Memphis). His education consists of a PhD in business administration, Northcentral University (Prescott, Arizona); MCJ in criminal justice with an emphasis in homeland security, University of Mississippi; MA in computer resources and information management, Webster University (Webster Groves, Missouri); MBA, Embry-Riddle Aeronautical University; graduate certificate in forensic criminology, University of Massachusetts (Lowell); graduate certificate in nonprofit financial management, University of Maryland (Adelphi); and a BS in computer science with a mathematics minor, Mississippi State University. His professional career consisted of software engineering and analytical positions in both the defense and commercial industries. Corporate entities included full-time and contract positions with FedEx and uMonitor.com; and contract positions, via Data Management Consultants (Biloxi, Mississippi), with Loral Corporation (formerly IBM Federal Systems) and Lockheed-Martin. Additional credentials include lieutenant colonel, Mississippi State Guard; graduate of the Lafayette County Law Enforcement Academy; and graduate of the Law Enforcement Mobile Video Institute. He has also coauthored a variety of books, peer-reviewed journal articles, and conference proceedings. Dr. Doss is a member of both the Delta Sigma Pi and Lambda Alpha Epsilon fraternities. He resides in Mississippi.

William "Bill" Sumrall, EdD, has experience as both an academician and a realtor. He currently is among the faculties of Belhaven College (Memphis) and Park University (Parkville, Missouri). Sumrall has coauthored a variety of peer-reviewed journal articles and conference proceedings. Dr. Sumrall's education consists of an EdD in educational leadership, Arkansas State University (Jonesboro); "all but dissertation" (ABD) status with Mississippi State University (Oktibbeha County) with respect to the degree of doctor of business administration in finance; EdS in higher education, Mississippi

State University; MA in economics, University of Southern Mississippi (Hattiesburg); MBA, Delta State University (Cleveland, Mississippi); and a BS in economics, Louisiana Tech University (Ruston). Sumrall resides in Mississippi. He enjoys restoring antique automobiles and spending time with his family.

Don Jones, EdS, is an ordained minister, collegiate enrollment director, counselor, and military officer. He has also coauthored a variety of peer-reviewed journal articles and conference proceedings. He currently is pursuing doctoral study with Arkansas State University (Jonesboro). His educational background consists of an EdS, Arkansas State University; MBA, University of Phoenix (Memphis); MDiv, Logos University; and a BS, Bethel College (McKenzie, Tennessee). Additional credentials include major in the Mississippi State Guard, where he serves as a military police officer. His most recent active-duty periods consisted of service during Hurricane Katrina and Hurricane Gustav. He enjoys spending time with family and friends, performs a multitude of weddings via his ministry, and resides in Mississippi.

Acronyms and Abbreviations

B/C	benefit cost
BCA	benefit–cost analysis
BOEMRE	Bureau of Ocean Energy Management, Regulation and Enforcement
BRAC	Base Realignment and Closure Committee
BEA	break-even analysis
CCA	Corrections Corporation of America
CEO	chief executive officer
CFO	chief financial officer
CIO	chief information officer
CF	cash flow
COO	chief operations officer
CMV	current monetary value
CV	current value
DHS	Department of Homeland Security
DOD	Department of Defense
DOJ	Department of Justice
DOT	Department of Transportation
ECFA	Evangelical Council for Financial Accountability
EPA	Environmental Protection Agency
EVA	Economic Value Added
FBI	Federal Bureau of Investigation
FDOC	Florida Department of Corrections
FEMA	Federal Emergency Management Agency
FTC	Federal Trade Commission
FTE	full-time employee
FMV	future monetary value
FV	Future Value
FY	fiscal year
GAO	Government Accountability Office
GCN	Gulf Coast News
GNJPM	Good News Jail and Prison Ministry

IIC	initial investment cost
IRR	internal rate of return
LPIG	Lakewood Police Independent Guild
MP	Military Police
MPI	Mississippi Prison Industries
MVA	market value added
NASDAQ	National Association of Securities Dealers Automated Quotations
NPCA	National Parks Conservation Association
NPP	National Priorities Project
NPV	net present value
NRLEA	National Rural Law Enforcement Association
NWTEMC	Northwest Tribal Emergency Management Council
PI	profitability index
PIM	profitability index method
PTM	payback time method
PTT	payback time threshold
PV	present value
PY	partial year
SWAT	special weapons and tactics
TVM	time value of money

Introductory Concepts 1

> The problem is not that people are taxed too little, the problem is that government spends too much.*
>
> **President Ronald Reagan**

1.1 Objectives

The objectives of this chapter are to:

- Understand the use of money as a tool to facilitate the exchange of goods and services
- Understand the basic question of economics
- Understand examples of historical American finance
- Understand examples of historical American economics

1.2 Introduction

During the independent courses of their careers, the authors have experienced a variety of different work environments among an array of employers, independent contractor situations, and service duties. Combined, these professional employment settings represent over 70 years of experience among a variety of different organizations. These environments ranged from grocery stores to global software development settings; from venture capital start-up firms to the settings of nonprofit organizations; from defense-related firms to community service organizations; from small, four-year colleges to universities of Carnegie research standings; from realty shops to sales positions; and from State Guard military units to law enforcement settings. These settings also manifested different organizational purposes involving military police and security forces, systems integration and testing, national defense, overnight package delivery, electronic and wireless software and hardware systems, customer service, and various facets of academia.

* Reagan, Ronald, "Taxed Quotes," Brainy Quote, http://www.brainyquote.com/quotes/keywords/taxed.html (accessed July 15, 2011).

Regardless of the type of environmental setting or purpose that was experienced, or of the type of work that was performed, or of the product or service that was developed, one characteristic was shared among each of these environments: the rendering of a human decision regarding money. Within each of these contexts and cases, issues of money were the financial factors that either precluded organizational demise or that invigorated the monetary heartbeat of organizational life. Cash flow is the lifeblood of any organization. Any financial decisions regarding the use of organizational funds must be seriously considered and soundly evaluated.

1.3 The Concept of Money

Before considering decisions regarding money, or any other form of personal or organizational financial decision, one must understand the basic concept of money with respect to a market environment. The market itself is nothing more than the environment in which a variety of transactions occur through time. Within markets, people provide services and partake of services. They also provide goods and obtain goods. However, among such markets, a central concept that underlies these transactions is that of the existence of a commonly accepted medium for servicing and facilitating such exchanges and transactions. This commonly accepted medium must have some attribution of value associated with its existence and use among societies. Using contemporary terms, this concept is expressed and identified quite simply: money. (See Figure 1.1.)

Although the mentioning of the word money may invoke mental models of shiny coins or colorful, oblong papers demarked with enumerated values and national symbols, money is a concept that pervades practically all societies globally. Historically, with respect to its use among transactions, the concept of money was described by a variety of phrases, terms, words, and names: wampum, pesos, beads, jewels, dollars, pounds, gold, silver, legal tender, skins and furs, bimetallism, script.* Many of these descriptors continue to be expressed during modern times, and are readily recognizable among many contemporary languages. However, they are all commensurate with the notion of a medium of exchange, toward the facilitation and completion of market exchanges, with respect to servicing and satisfying the needs and wants of humans.

Regardless of the society or language, all humans have needs and wants, and these needs and wants are presumed to be unlimited through time. Attempts to satisfy such human needs and wants occurs with respect to the

* Davies, "Money in North American History."

Figure 1.1 Money example of U.S. $1.00 coinage. (Courtesy of the U.S. Mint, http://www.usmint.gov/about_the_mint/coinLibrary/#Pres.)

scarcity of available, viable resources that are commensurate regarding the fulfillment of these human requirements. For the biological purposes of survival, humans both need and want to be warm in winter and cool in the summer. Humans both need and want food and water for survival. Such considerations demonstrate the congruency of needs and wants concerning the biological survival of humans. However, it should be noted that there is a distinct difference between needing something and wanting something. Regardless of this distinction, an exchange medium must exist to facilitate market transactions for the purpose of servicing both human needs and human wants.

A consideration of unlimited human needs and wants versus attempts to satisfy them with scare resources may be contemplated historically. The concept of an exchange mechanism to facilitate the transactions through which human needs and wants were satisfied also may be viewed historically. This concept of a medium for exchange permeates the historical literature of the United States.

1.4 Formative U.S. Transactions

Some of the earliest writings and historical accounts of the United States, from a national perspective, are those of its Congress. Within these writings are found allusions to the economic and financial aspects of various human needs and wants. Further, such historical documentation contains a myriad of discussions regarding the concept of market transactions, and it also alludes to the concept of an exchange medium: money. A historical review of the *Journal of the Senate* yields some interesting commentaries regarding market transactions during the formative period of the nation.

During these formative years, a variety of issues were considered among the members of the Congress. During the year 1791, the *Journal of the Senate* indicated that

> the price of all land sold or granted by the United States, shall be twenty-five routs per acre, except such as may be sold by special contract, and such as may be granted as bounties for military services; the warrants for which last mentioned lands shall be located, surveyed, and patented, in the same manner as warrants issuing from the land-office, in consideration of the payment of money, and the exclusive right of locating such warrants in districts set apart for the army, shall cease from anal after the first day of May, one thousand seven hundred and ninety-four: Provided, always, that any purchaser of lands, when the payment thereof shall be due, may proffer in payment any of the certificates of the funded debt of the United States, at the same rates as the treasurer shall have allowed for such certificates, respectively, in the last purchase which he shall have made thereof prior to such payment.*

Such early records of the nation demonstrate the existence of a market for real estate. Within this passage, allusions to the characteristics of human needs and wants are manifested through the description of the realty transaction. The method of satisfaction, with respect to the expressed scope and limitations of the transaction, is delineated regarding the issue of compensation. The last portion of the statement alludes to the existence of a medium through which the real estate transaction may be facilitated. Obviously, this medium involves the concept of money.

1.5 Nineteenth-Century U.S. Transactions

Perusing historical literature also provides notions that were prominent considerations, nearly a century later, during the latter period of the nineteenth century. Considerations of regional, national, and international markets; exchange mediums; and valuation discussions are found among a variety of historical journal articles. An examination of American historical writings, from the latter half of the nineteenth century yields similar considerations of market characteristics. (See Figure 1.2.)

Again, the *Journal of the Senate* (April 15, 1874) may be examined regarding this historical perspective. Such an examination shows historical

* Library of Congress, *Journal of the Senate,* 1791, Vol. 1, p. 270.

Figure 1.2 Cancelled check in the amount of $7.2 million for the purchase of Alaska, issued August 1, 1868; Records of the Accounting Officers of the Department of the Treasury; Record Group 217; National Archives. With this check, the United States purchased Alaska from Russia. For less than 2 cents an acre, the United States acquired nearly 600,000 square miles. (Courtesy of the National Archives, http://www.archives.gov/global-pages/larger-image.html?i=/historical-docs/doc-content/images/check-for-alaska-l.jpg&c=/historical-docs/doc-content/images/check-for-alaska.caption.html.)

Congressional considerations of compensating the "State of West Virginia for moneys expended for the United States in enrolling, subsisting, clothing, supplying, arming, equipping, paying, and transporting militia forces to aid in suppressing the rebellion; which was read the first and second times, by unanimous consent, referred to the Committee on Military Affairs, and ordered to be printed."*

Again, such a historical consideration alludes to the presence of market environments, alludes to the presence of market transactions, alludes to the consideration of financial reimbursement, and alludes to the economic allocation of resources. These considerations are indicative of human needs and wants, regarding compensation, with respect to a variety of activities that occurred during the U.S. Civil War. The concept of money, as a tool through which the servicing of human wants and needs is facilitated, is expressed through the referencing of "moneys expended" regarding these market activities.† Both the United States and the Confederate States of America used some form of printed and coined money (see Figure 1.3).

Given that nearly a century had elapsed between the respective times of these historical accounts of Congress, the size, scope, and magnitude of U.S. economic growth had increased, and new considerations of finance abounded during the latter portion of the nineteenth century. Such issues involved considerations of financial valuation, the types of coinage of money that

* Library of Congress, *Journal of the Senate*, April 15, 1874, Vol. 69, p. 464.
† Ibid.

Figure 1.3 Example of monetary note issued by the Confederate States of America during the Civil War. (Courtesy of the U.S. National Park Service, http://www.nps.gov/history/museum/exhibits/vick/siege/scans/VICK738ConfederateTwentyDollar.html.)

impacted regions of the United States, and international market issues that spurred debates. Within these contexts, allusions are made to the existences of markets, economic activities, and financial activities. Such characteristics are indicative of the attributes of economic and financial mechanisms that are necessary to service human needs and wants through time.

Andrews considers bimetallism within the regions of Boston and New England, and alludes to robust debates that existed regarding the coinage of silver during this period.[*] Walker considers attributes of the historical period that affected the valuation of money.[†] Edgeworth, from a monetary valuation perspective of appreciation, considers the potential and capacity of money to purchase the "luxuries, conveniences, and necessaries of life."[‡] From the perspective of international trading endeavors, Bastable considers notions concerning a lack of consensus regarding monetary standards internationally and contemplates difficulties associated with various instantiations of money that existed during the period.[§]

[*] Andrews, "The Bimetallist Committee."
[†] Walker, "Value of Money."
[‡] Edgeworth, "Appreciation of Gold."
[§] Bastable, "Theory of International Trade."

Such discussions are well over a century old, and allude to the existence of human wants and needs, allude to the presence of some environment in which exchanges and transactions occurred, and allude to the conceptual methods through which such historical market exchanges and transactions were facilitated. Within these historical writings, the presence of a salient notion is manifested: the concept of money.

1.6 Contemporary U.S. Transactions

This concept of money remained unchanged during the initial portion of the twentieth century. The concept of money provided the mechanism through which the servicing of human needs and wants occurred through time. Again, a review of historical accounts provides discussions of economic and financial issues that were considered among members of Congress. Such an additional, historical review may be considered from the perspective of the latter years of the twentieth century.

A review of the *Congressional Record* provides a perspective of historical issues that were of Congressional debate during the 1990s. Within this instance, discussions concerned the Indian Development Investment Zone Act of 1990. The purpose of this proposed legislation was to generate "economic opportunities" among Native American community settings. These opportunities were hoped to improve conditions among "Indian reservations," because a number of these reservations had been "decimated by a combination of high unemployment rates reaching well over 50 percent and equally troubling poverty rates." Despite the willingness and desire of Native American peoples to work to support themselves, they were unable to do so because of the unavailability of employment opportunities. As a result, a migration of Native Americans occurred, from reservations to "metropolitan areas," for the purpose of seeking employment, which intensified the complexities of the "problems of urban America."*

Again, this portion of the *Congressional Record* alludes to the presence of markets, alludes to the needs and wants of humans, and alludes to financial conditions representing monetary concerns. Within this excerpt, market considerations are represented through allusions to the job market, and aspects of potentially satisfying human wants and needs are manifested through allusions to the desires and necessities of Native Americans supporting themselves. Monetary characteristics are represented through allusions of poverty.

* U.S. Congress, *Congressional Record: 101st Congress.*

The examinations of the *Congressional Record* provide salient examples of the basic concepts of market characteristics, considerations of satisfying the needs and wants of humans, and the medium that facilitates market transactions regarding these human needs and wants. Although these examinations of the *Congressional Record* are not exhaustive, they are demonstrative of the basic principles that influence market transactions. Each of the preceding examples considered some aspect of market transactions with respect to the satisfaction of human needs and wants. Further, as a medium through which such market transactions were facilitated, the concept of money pervaded these examples.

Given that the characteristics of humans are unchanging, that the concepts of human needs and wants remain static through time, and that the conceptual means of exchange, through which the satisfaction of human wants and needs occurs, also is unchanged. This concept of money retains its usefulness and relevance as a modern tool, through which market transactions are facilitated through time regarding the servicing of the needs and wants of humans. Acknowledging the money concept is not unfamiliar among humans regardless of their societal affiliations. A variety of applications exist regarding the potential of money.

1.7 Considerations of the Money Concept

Money is the means through which humans facilitate transactions for goods and services. Money is the means through which humans survive financially and obtain the satisfaction of their needs through time. Money is a financial means through which humans prepare for their anticipated years of retirement. Money is the entity through which humans may service their financial obligations of debt or express their financial gains of monetary profits.

Money may be used as a reward for demonstrating excellent and superior behavior during the course of time or as a perk within an organizational setting. For example, some organizations may issue monetary bonuses for improving the efficiency and effectiveness of business operations or for ceremonial purposes (e.g., Christmas bonuses). Money may also be used with respect to punitive situations. For example, organizations may deny a monetary bonus if personnel do not satisfy or surpass an established sales quota within a specified time. Money may also be used as a motivational tool among a variety of settings. For example, personnel may have the expectations of higher wages, through time, regarding their length of service time within an organizational setting.

Obviously, the concept of money is powerful, and its uses are varied. Money may be earned, saved, and put away for a myriad of purposes. It may also be squandered aimlessly, and wasted upon the futile efforts of shallow and lustful applications. Its benevolent use may be leveraged for the purposes of charitable contributions resulting in a variety of tax deductions. Regardless, the concept of money is a powerful tool through which humans exercise various judgments, in accordance with a host of perceptions and beliefs, with respect to some determination regarding its highest and best use.

Such a determination of this perception of use is summed up with one phrase: we make a decision! Humans specify which course of action is acceptable with respect to the contemplated methods of satisfying needs and wants, and then pursue the activities that are necessary for the completion of the selected course of action. Certainly, there may be limitations regarding the selected course of action (e.g., time, money, resources). Further, there may be a single choice or multiple choices available that will result in the satisfaction of human needs and wants.

Although the aforementioned considerations provide a variety of types of decisions, they only represent a subset of the decision domain. Such questions are only representative of the high-level questioning and considering of alternatives that is paramount to the act of rendering a financial decision. It is important to realize that the rendering of such a financial decision is also a component of a systematic, methodical process, which integrates various attributes of the problem domain and the decision domain, with respect to the specifications of an established model, as the basis of facilitating human decisions.

Further, one may also consider the characteristics of the posed question regarding its categorization, manifested through the amount of knowledge that is known regarding the considered problem domain, and must consider the posed question with respect to its chronological implications. Therefore, all decisions require some understanding of the considered problem domain and involve the completion of processes before the act of rendering a human decision is finalized (see Figure 1.4).

1.8 Categorization of Decisions

The categorization of a decision involves an examination of the characteristics of its respective problem domain and decision domain. Three categorizations exist regarding algorithmic process approaches to facilitate the rendering of human decision outcomes: structured, semistructured, and unstructured. The first category is indicative of a robust knowledge of a problem domain and decision domain; the second category is indicative of a moderately varying, partial knowledge of the problem domain and the decision domain; and the third category is indicative of a highly unknown and

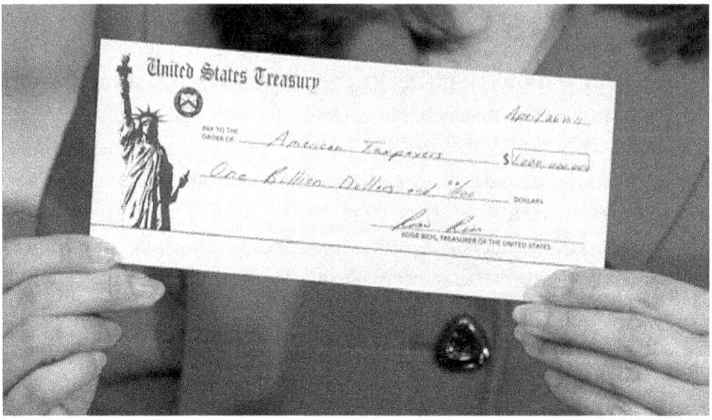

Figure 1.4 Check for the American taxpayers. On Tuesday, April 26, 2011, Treasurer Rosie Rios wrote a ceremonial check to the American taxpayers to highlight the $1 billion that taxpayers will save over the next 10 years as the Treasury moves to electronic payment methods for federal benefits. This compensation resulted from human decisions. (Courtesy of the U.S. Treasury, http://www.flickr.com/photos/ustreasury/5662628156/in/set-72157626469420067/.)

unfamiliar knowledge of the problem domain and the decision domain. The categorization of decisions, with respect to the characteristics of the problem domain, the decision domain, and risk, shows characteristics of strong structures, partial structures, and weak structures. These concepts may be expressed among the following categories:

1. The instance of a strongly structured decision type occurs when a sound knowledge and understanding of the problem domain and decision domain exists. This categorization may demonstrate less risk than the categories of semi-structure and weak structure. Risk reduction occurs because the capacity of rendering a well-informed decision exists with respect to the known aspects of both the problem domain and the decision domain.
2. The instance of a partially structured decision type occurs when a variable knowledge and understanding of the problem domain and decision domain exists. This category may demonstrate greater risk than the category of a strongly structured decision. This category may also demonstrate more risk, equal risk, or less risk than the category of weakly structured decisions. These variations in risk occur because the capacity of rendering a decision exists with respect to variations regarding the quantities of both unknown and known aspects of both the problem domain and the decision domain.

3. Similar to the attributes of a partially structured decision, the instance of a weakly structured decision type occurs when a variable knowledge and understanding of the problem domain and decision domain exists. This category may also demonstrate more risk, equal risk, or less risk than the category of partially structured decisions and strongly structured decisions. These variations in risk occur because the capacity of rendering a decision exists with respect to variations regarding the quantities of both unknown and known aspects of both the problem domain and the decision domain. However, within this category, the unknown facets of the decision domain and the problem domain are quite significant, influences of ignorance and ambiguity may affect the decision process, and a significantly higher consideration of risk, within the context of rendering human decisions, may be manifested.

A myriad of decision types are applicable regarding these categories of decisions. A strongly structured decision demonstrates a robust knowledge of the decision domain and the problem domain. Within the context of law enforcement decisions, such decisions are often made regarding tangible resources and involve the considerations of short-term decisions.

For example, purchasing a law enforcement vehicle may involve known financial attributes that affect the decision regarding the sales transaction. In this instance, the purchase price of the vehicle is known, an interest rate is specified, insurance costs are identified, and the quantity of periods necessary for rendering payments, through time, is specified. Although the exact, future costs of fuel and maintenance may be unknown over time, they may be estimated. Regardless of such estimates, a strong knowledge of influential factors exists.

Another example of a strongly structured decision may be considered from the perspective of the criminal justice decisions that occur among court settings. Within this context, an example may be the awarding of punitive sentences that result from acts of crime. In such instances, decision must adhere to the guidelines and limitations that are established according to the law. The decision itself may involve the verdict of the jury (or judge if a bench trial); the limitations, scope, and magnitude of the types of punishments that are expressed via written laws that are commensurate with the specific crime committed; and the discretion of the judge regarding sentencing. However, although the sentencing guidelines may vary and the discretion of the judge may fluctuate per the personal characteristics and beliefs of the individual human, the primary attributes of the decision domain are known and expressed via the written expression of law.

With respect to the financial aspects of such punitive measures, various financial costs, of this type of structured decision, may involve the specification and payment of any monetary fines that are mandated per the written law, the awarding of fees affiliated with the services of a specific attorney, and any associated court costs. Misdemeanor examples of crimes and the commensurate trial proceedings that incur such costs, with respect variances among local and state laws, may include vehicular speeding, loitering, and littering.

Another example involves the scheduling of law enforcement resources. Shift supervisors may render decisions concerning the specific assigning of officers to a patrol area to a series of identified street blocks. Decisions regarding partners may be identified among the assigning of officers per patrol shifts and assigned patrol areas. Such decisions are indicative of the daily, operational aspects of rendering decisions regarding the allocation and assigning of police resources. Financial aspects of these decisions may include base salaries, potential overtime payments, the costs of vehicular maintenance, and vehicular fuels costs.

Partially structured decisions involve some specific knowledge of the decision domain and some unknown aspects of the decision domain. A good bit of ambiguity may exist regarding the information involved in rendering decisions. This category of decisions may be found among the functions of criminal analysis and various facets of criminal justice administration activities.

The nature of a partially structured decision is indicative of a combination of known facts versus unknown characteristics of the decision domain and the problem domain. Within the context of a criminal justice perspective, rendering decisions regarding the purchasing and the use of new weaponry or new defensive tools that have recently achieved market availability. Some knowledge exists regarding the performances of these items because of manufacturer product testing and pilot-testing among a small group of participants. However, because such items are newly available, they do not manifest a historical performance record over a significant time period from which information may be taken to influence the rendering of decisions. Therefore, the rendering of decisions, within this context, involves considerations of various facets of some known attributes of the decision and problem domains versus the unknown facets of these domains.

Weakly structured decisions involve a knowledge of the decision domain and problem domain that may be imprecise, that may be ambiguous, and that demonstrates significant, unknown characteristics. The solidly known characteristics and well-defined attributes of the decision domain and the problem domain may be few. This type of decision is the most challenging given the potentials of risk regarding the outcomes of decisions that are rendered using such ill-defined information.

Examples of such decisions pervade contemporary facets of terrorism. With respect to the crimes of ecoterrorism, which generally are representative of an infrastructure of leaderless resistance, much difficulty is experienced when attempting to strategically infiltrate ecoterrorist organizations because of the problems associated with identifying and penetrating independent terrorist cells. Further, given such leaderless resistance and the dynamic, separate organizational structures that exist among terrorist groups, gaining a full knowledge of these organizations, their capacities, communications, personnel, logistics, and operations is extremely difficult. Therefore, it may require significant periods of time and significant costs to infiltrate such entities, and may require significant funding to counter the effects of their criminal activities.

Therefore, when attempting to implement antiterrorist and counterterrorist operations, tactics, and strategies, law enforcement and criminal justice decisions may not involve a full knowledge of both the decision and problem domains. Because of these unknown characteristics, the financial attributes of decisions may fluctuate through time. Each terrorist cell represents a unique situation and incurs its own unique costs. As a result, the financial costs that are necessitated to pursue the infiltration efforts of any given terrorist cell may not be sufficient for facilitating the successful penetration of any other terrorist cell or organization.

Although these categories have a common component regarding the ultimate rendering of a human decision, they each represent varying levels of risk. These variances of risk are commensurate with the levels of knowledge that exist regarding the characteristics of the problem domain and the decision domain. Within respect to these domains, risk may be either controlled or uncontrolled. Specifically, risk may be either systematic or unsystematic. Regardless, risk cannot be eliminated completely.

Considerations of such risk in the context of capital budgeting decisions are discussed further in the latter chapters of this text. These types of financial decisions may be considered from the perspective of criminal justice applications. The succeeding chapters of this text elucidate the saliency of these categories and provide examples of each category.

1.9 Chronological and Risk Aspects of Decisions

Now that these categories are established, a consideration of their chronological impacts may be contemplated. Time is a factor, which may not be an immaterial influence, of the rendering of a decision. Time is generally a significant consideration and limitation within the context of the decision process. With respect to the rendering of human decisions, time may be viewed through three perspectives: strategic, tactical, and operational. With respect to business strategies and policies, a consideration of the chronological aspects of decisions may be viewed from the perspective of criminal justice organizations. Therefore, within the context of the criminal justice system and law enforcement entities, considerations of these chronological perspectives may be given as follows:

1. A strategic perspective involves rendering decisions that encompass periods that surpass at least five years. From the perspective of a financial context, the act of leasing a building for thirty years is the result of a strategic decision and is characterized by its long-term commitment. Criminal justice considerations would involve the financial costs of housing prisoners who are incarcerated for significant periods. This category of decision is generally rendered among the executive leadership levels of hierarchical organizational structures. Examples of the financial aspects of strategic decisions would include long-term costs affiliated with food, housing, and prison personnel salaries.
2. A tactical perspective involves rendering decisions that encompass periods somewhere between one to five years. Within the financial context, leasing a police vehicle for two or three years is representative of such decisions. This category of decision is generally rendered among the directorial and middle levels of hierarchical organizational structures. Examples of tactical decisions would include considerations of annual interests costs affiliated with vehicle leases and the costs of property taxes within the context of for-profit corrections environments.
3. An operational decision involves rendering decisions that demonstrate immediate, time-sensitive characteristics. This category of decision is generally rendered among the lowest levels of hierarchical organizational structures. Examples of operational decisions would include the scheduling of work shifts and the assigning of patrol areas. Considerations of affiliated costs may include weekly overtime considerations among personnel.

Risk is a consideration of each chronological perspective. With respect to the rendering of decisions, longer periods of time are indicative of greater amounts of risk. Shorter periods of time are indicative of potentially less risk regarding decisions. However, it is important to note that no decision is without risk. Although the potential of risk may be diminished through a variety of analytical methods and planning efforts, risk potentials may not be completely eliminated. Therefore, each and every decision, regardless of the chronological period and anticipated factors involved, is subject to some aspects of risk through time.

Decisions that incorporate some aspect of risk are not uncommon. Historic examples of decisions involving risk include the launching of the ill-fated space shuttle *Challenger* and the pursuit of the famous D-Day invasion of World War II. Both events involved varying levels of uncertainty regarding their outcomes. The former example is demonstrative of negative outcomes that occur, whereas the latter example demonstrates a positive decision outcome. Despite this dichotomy of outcomes, one factor was present regarding both cases: risk.

Although the financial characteristics of risk may only be estimated before the rendering of decisions, the true costs of such decisions may not be apparent until after a decisions is rendered, after a specific course of action is undertaken, and after an outcome of the decision is manifested. History is the best judge of the effects of decisions, and only through time are true costs identified. This notion may be considered from the perspectives of both the *Challenger* incident and the activities of the U.S. government.

Such costs are not necessarily insubstantial. Estimates of the financial costs associated with the *Challenger* disaster approached figures of $175 million. These financial costs were affiliated with investigating the exploding of the craft. The response and recovery activities, which occurred in the Atlantic Ocean, incurred financial costs of approximately $100 million.* These financial costs only include considerations of activities that occurred after the *Challenger* disaster. They do not include any of the financial costs that preceded the disastrous *Challenger* flight.

The costs of military reorganization are significant. According to the U.S. Government Accountability Office, regarding the fifth round of the Base Realignment and Closure Committee (BRAC), Department of Defense (DOD) activities involved "hundreds of BRAC actions affecting over 800 defense locations," considered the relocation of "over 123,000 personnel," and incurred expenditures of "over $35 billion—an unprecedented amount, given that DOD" expended approximately "$26 billion to implement the four previous BRAC rounds combined when all relevant BRAC actions have been completed."† Obviously, these costs are enormous. They are not insignificant, and the complexities of rendering such financial decisions must not be understated.

Decisions are entities that require time, incorporate some varying amount of risk, and involve considerations of both the problem domain and the decision domain. The integration of these concepts provides the basis of rendering human decisions. Within the context of financial perspectives,

* Vartabedian and Pae, "Cost of *Columbia* Accident Inquiry Is Soaring."
† U.S. Government Accountability Office, "Congressional Committees."

a variety of mathematical models exist that facilitate the rendering of human decisions. However, before one may consider such facets of rendering human financial decisions, one must possess a basic understanding of modeling and simulation concepts.

1.10 An Integrative Perspective

An integrative perspective of decision categories, risk potentials, chronological attributes, reporting formats, and organizational hierarchy provides a multifaceted view of the financial decisions that are manifested among criminal justice organizations. Based on the preceding discussions, Table 1.1 shows such an integrative perspective. Within Table 1.1 are the salient characteristics of financial decisions. The characteristics of time define the nature of a decision regarding its appropriateness as strategic, tactical, or operational with respect to its considered period. Longer periods of time are indicative of higher risks, whereas lesser periods of time are indicative of fewer risks. Therefore, strategic decisions are much riskier than tactical and operational decisions, and operational decisions pose significantly less risk than strategic and tactical decisions. Longer periods of time are characterized by greater facets of unknown attributes within the decision domain, whereas shorter periods of time are representative of fewer unknown attributes thereby coinciding with commensurate levels of risk within the context of rendering operational decisions.

Shorter periods of time are indicative of decisions that involve immediate courses of actions and outcomes. Therefore, the very nature of these decisions is representative of structured context. In contrast, longer periods of time are indicative of decisions that involve long-term periods, over many years, which are representative of variety of unknown factors that may be manifested through time. This situation is characteristic of an unstructured decision domain. Decisions that are neither immediate nor long-term are symbolic of a fluctuating amount of risk and time, and are thereby demonstrative of decision domains in which partial elements of influential factors may be identified.

Table 1.1 Integrative Perspective

Decision	Period	Risk	Structure	Format	Level
Strategic	5+ years	High	Weakly structured	Executive summary	Executive leadership
Tactical	Less than 5 years	Moderate	Partially structured	Basic synopsis	Directorial and middle levels
Operational	Immediate	Low	Strongly structured	Detailed	Lowest supervisors

Humans are the entities that render decisions. Although a variety of tools exist to assist humans in rendering decisions, it is the human who finalizes and selects a choice, pursues a course of action, and experiences the consequences and ramifications of a decision. Humans exist among the strategic, tactical, and operational levels of organizational infrastructure, and must render decisions that are both appropriate and commensurate with their responsibilities. Therefore, humans must consider the reporting aspects of decisions, through various methods, which are commensurate with the organizational aspects of information and the appropriate contexts of decisional activities.

Long-term, strategic financial decisions may involve the use of executive summaries as an overview of an extended, thorough financial analysis. Tactical decisions may require the use of various summary reports that provide a synopsis of analytical financial assessments. Operational, short-term decisions may involve the use of specific reporting tools (e.g., expense reports, reimbursement forms). Regardless, information must be presented with respect to the nature of the considered decision and must be commensurate with the expectations of those who are responsible for rendering decisions.

The conceptual aspects of rendering financial decisions must be coherent and must be viewed from a perspective that facilitates the human capacity of rendering a decision based upon some form of analysis. Therefore, humans must form cognitive models and mental models of the financial decision domain. Hence, constructs must exist to assist humans with respect to exploring various facets of the financial decision domain. For the purposes of this text, these constructs are identified as models and simulations.

1.11 Models and Simulations

Models may be considered as expressions of reality regarding some specific entity, whereas simulations may be thought of as an embellished model that portrays various behavioral aspects of the considered entity. Through the use of models and simulations, the characteristics of a financial system may be explored, defined, specified, and understood through time. The interpretations of the outcomes of such explorations provide necessary information within the process of rendering human decisions.

The use of a model may delineate relationships among variables regarding the long-term financial aspects of a capital investment. Within simulation applications, changes among the variables of a model may be tested to determine a variety of potential decision outcomes through time. Humans may evaluate these simulated outcomes as either acceptable or unacceptable within the context of rendering a financial decision.

A mathematical model may be used to delineate the relationships among variables, and simulation surpasses this concept by allowing an examination of facilitating human conjecture regarding possible outcomes with respect to changes that occur among the relationships and among variables that comprise such modeling constructs. Such notions introduce the concepts of scenario analysis and simulation analysis.

Examples of questions that may be investigated through such methods are varied. From the criminal justice perspective, such conjectures may include issues regarding where to locate a for-profit prison, with respect to changes among personnel costs, changes among tax rates, changes among insurance costs, changes among risk values, and changes among building costs. This use would find relevance among applications of regional planning. An additional use may include the mathematical evaluations of threat assessments concerning determinations of probable costs associated with potential terrorist attacks. This use would find relevance among intelligence analysis applications. Both examples are indicative of long-term, strategic planning initiatives.

Although the preceding examples consider the legal aspects of financial decisions among criminal justice entities, there also is an antithesis regarding such uses of money. In this instance, one must acknowledge the presence and existence of black markets. Such markets exist for the purposes of illegally satisfying the needs and wants of humans.

1.12 Black Market Decisions

Examples of familiar black markets include transactions involving pirated software and movies; transactions involving narcotics and pornography among markets in which such items may be illegal; transactions involving the selling of human organs (e.g., kidneys, eyes); transactions involving both gambling and prostitution where such activities are deemed illegal; transactions involving the smuggling and trading of disallowed items across national boundaries; and transactions involving the financing of terrorist organizations through practices of money laundering (Figure 1.5).

Although individual instances of such illegal market activities may involve short-term or immediate time considerations, there exists a strategic aspect regarding these black markets. The rendering of long-term, strategic decisions with respect to the commensurate attributes of black market human wants and needs is common regarding the functioning of organized crime entities and terrorist organizations.

Such black markets are varied. Diverting goods and services from legitimate markets into illegal markets is a practice that provides a plethora of

Figure 1.5 Black market money. Hundreds of alleged Sinaloa Cartel members and associates were arrested in nationwide takedown of Mexican drug traffickers. "Operation Xcellerator" took over 23 tons of narcotics off America's streets and seized more than $59 million in drug money. (Courtesy of the U.S. Drug Enforcement Administration, http://www.justice.gov/dea/images_major_operations.html#xcellerator.)

resources among criminal entities. Gundlach, Bradford, and Wilkie consider the diversions of handguns from legitimate markets into illegal markets.[*] Kurniawanti and Setiabudi consider the use of software tools to commit financial fraud.[†] Coffin considers the smuggling of financial resources between the United States and Mexico among petroleum market transactions.[‡] Heber considers the use of illegal laborers within the construction and building trades.[§] Moyle examines tiger poaching among Chinese markets.[¶] Similarly, Wyatt examines black markets that involve Russian animal trading.[**] Dumitrescu, Neacsu, and Zamfirescu examine the influences of illegal markets toward the establishing of legal market environments.[††] Despite red roses being legitimate products among many nations, the buying and selling of such roses are considered as illegal transactions within Islamic environments of the Middle East because of the religious and government banning

[*] Gundlach, Bradford, and Wilkie, "Countermarketing and Demarketing."
[†] Kurniawanti and Setiabudi, "The Crooked Credit Analyst."
[‡] Coffin, "Black Gold, Black Market."
[§] Heber, "Networks of Organised Black Market Labour."
[¶] Moyle, "Black Market in China."
[**] Wyatt, "Illegal Wildlife Trade."
[††] Dumitrescu, Neacsu, and Zamfirescu, "Underground Economy."

of Valentine's Day among such nations.[*] Balatski discusses the purchasing of Russian academic credentials that followed the downfall of the Soviet Union.[†] Certainly, black market transactions also involve the bootlegging of entertainment products, tobacco products, and liquor products.

Many other examples exist that involve weaponry and drug trafficking. Elliott and Neirotti examine facets of Cuban tourism with respect to black market influences and characteristics.[‡] Priddle and Santos examine financial aspects of Chinese lending activities and exchanges of currency.[§] Strakes examines various characteristics of illegal arms trading among global black market environments.[¶] Kaliadin examines the negative potential of weapons of mass destruction among black markets, and examines control schemes to avoid the entries of such weapons and their means of deliveries among black markets.[**] Fitzpatrick considers Iranian efforts to procure nuclear resources and technologies.[††] Within the United States, Cook et al. examine Chicago weapons trading among domestic black market settings.[‡‡] Prunckun examines the pricing of heroin among Australian black market environments, and considers the impacts of such pricing among law enforcement activities and operations designed to curtail drug trafficking.[§§]

These preceding black market examples provide only a miniscule consideration of the overall set of activities and transactions that comprise and occur among illegal market environments. Certainly, almost an innumerable and incalculable quantity of transactions and activities occur among a myriad of illegal markets. However, these examples are demonstrative of market transactions that are pursued to satisfy the needs and wants of humans. Humans select to secure goods and services either legally or illegally, and such procurement occurs among market settings. Again, some medium of exchange exists to motivate and facilitate these illegal transactions.

1.13 Legal Market Decisions

However, a variety of legal markets exist through which goods and services may be procured and exchanged through time. Again, an innumerable array of examples exists of such legal activities. Visiting a department store and

[*] "Saudis Ban Valentine Day Roses."
[†] Balatski, "Dissertation Trap."
[‡] Elliott and Neirotti, "Challenges of Tourism."
[§] Priddle and Santos, "Chinese Economy."
[¶] Strakes, "Illicit Arms Transfers."
[**] Kaliadin, "Weapons of Mass Destruction."
[††] Fitzpatrick, "Lessons Learned."
[‡‡] Cook et al., "Underground Gun Markets."
[§§] Prunckun, "Does Price Really Matter?"

buying clothing or going to the movies for a Friday night date are certainly examples of such legal activities. Such activities are common among modern society. The goods and services rendered and procured among such markets environments are legal entities.

Within the context of criminal justice, a variety of legal market activities are manifested. From a marketing perspective, Reynecke and Fourie consider the use of a variety of resources, including financial, that may be leveraged to facilitate the successful provision of public service.[*] Historically, Ames considers the 1973 Japanese expenditures of approximately "two billion dollars" to provide police resources as tools through which public service could be rendered. According to Ames, examples of such activities included obtaining "vehicles, boats, and weapons," "communication equipment and systems," and various other costs associated with human resources.[†] Similarly, Frank considers the use of financial investment and spending, among law enforcement entities, with respect to population growth. Within this context, Frank alludes to the resources that must be purchased and developed (e.g., new or larger jails).[‡]

Other financial investments among market environments may be examined within the context of criminal justice entities. Fleischner, Von Hippel, and Barton consider police financial investments that support educational initiatives, technology familiarization, and mentoring programs.[§] Based on the *Annual Budget of the United States Government*, examples of a variety of recent law enforcement market expenditures and transactions regarding community-oriented policing involved financial spending to provide "Law Enforcement Armor Vests," quantities of "resource officers" among schools, programs to counter drug trafficking, training grants, border security, and "technical assistance" activities.[¶]

Again, such examples are only a subset of the market transactions and exchanges that occur legally. Further, given the contexts of law enforcement and criminal justice functions, such expenditures and transactions serve the purposes of preventing crime and maintaining good order among communities and within society. However, these examples are demonstrative of market transactions that are pursued to satisfy the needs and wants of humans. Again, market settings are involved among the examples. Commensurate with the preceding discussions, some medium of exchange exists to motivate and facilitate these legal transactions. Certainly, the rendering of a human decision regarding financial investment impacts the use of such expenditures through time.

[*] Reynecke and Fourie, *Police Management Beyond 2000.*
[†] Ames, *Police and Community in Japan.*
[‡] Frank, *Public Financial Management.*
[§] Fleischner, Von Hippel, and Barton, *Homebound Security.*
[¶] U.S. Government, *Annual Budget of the United States Government.*

1.14 Integrative Observations

This point in the discussion, regarding both the legal and illegal venues of market transactions, yields some basic considerations of the rendering of financial decisions by humans. These tenets may be given as follows:

1. A primary query of resource allocation exists, economically, through the questioning of how the unlimited wants and needs of humans may be satisfied and serviced with respect to the availability, limitations, and allocations of scarce resources. This concept applies to both legal and illegal markets and economic systems.
2. Within this primary query are manifested three themes regarding investigative subqueries concerning the characteristics of what should be produced, the quantities of production, and for whom such production should occur through time. Again, this concept applies to both legal and illegal markets and economic systems.
3. Both the primary question and its subqueries are indicative of the satisfying of human needs and wants through time with respect to human decisions regarding allocations of limited, scarce resources. The entity, in which occurs a variety of transactions and attempts to satisfy these human needs and wants, necessitates an environment that facilitates a myriad of transactions. This entity is the market environment. Market environments serve both legal and illegal purposes.
4. Within market environments, through time, provisions of goods and services and the obtaining of goods and services are both represented through transactions. The concept, which facilitates these transactions, is the existence of a commonly accepted medium for servicing such exchanges and transactions. This commonly accepted medium has some attribution of value associated with its societal acceptance and use, is present within both legal and illegal markets, and is referred to as money.
5. Humans use money to facilitate the servicing of their needs and wants among market environments. Therefore, humans must render financial decisions regarding such use of money. These financial decisions may be classified as strongly structured, partially structured, and weakly structured decisions, and each category demonstrates varying considerations of risk. Again, both black markets and legal markets demonstrate some amount of risk with respect to decisions.
6. The rendering of financial decisions, regardless of the category of decision involved, occurs through time. The effects and courses of actions resulting from human decisions also are manifested through time. This perspective of time involves considerations of strategic, tactical,

and operational periods. Longer periods of time are representative of greater risks, whereas shorter periods of time may manifest fewer risks. Time is a characteristic of both black markets and legal markets.
7. The preceding concepts lend themselves to the notions of scenario analysis and simulation analysis, through time, regarding the rendering of financial decisions. Applications of such modeling and simulation are varied, and are useful among a variety of functions. Examples of these functions include strategic financial planning and costs associated with terrorism threat assessments. Again, such concepts are applicable among both legal and illegal markets.

Within the context of this text, decisions will be viewed primarily from the perspective of financial managers. Based on the preceding concepts, the satisfaction of human needs and wants, through the allocation of resources, economically, will be considered from the perspective of rendering financial decisions that have strategic impacts. Thus, a long-term approach is given to the use of financial resources among criminal justice and law enforcement environments.

This approach differs from those of other texts. Many other texts examine monetary aspects of criminal justice entities from the perspectives of accounting and budgeting. However, from the perspective of investing monies in projects and endeavors, with respect to the desire to maximize the benefit received from such investment, these perspectives are incommensurate with the basic tenets of finance strategically.

Accounting is primarily concerned with the history of monetary activities through time. Examples of monetary activities affiliated with the concept of accounting include the calculation and payment of taxes regarding preceding years. Accounting is a historical perspective, regarding costs and cash flows, of the transactions that occurred among markets.

Budgeting is primarily concerned with the immediate and near-term periods of monetary activities. Examples of budgeting may include activities affiliated with quarterly or annual expenditures. Given this perspective, budgeting is primarily concerned with the activities of the present time. Budgeting is a current perspective, regarding costs and cash flows, of the transactions that occur among markets.

However, the concept of finance is different. Finance considers the future of money. Finance explores the potential uses of money to influence strategic, long-term decisions through time. Given these notions, an understanding and knowledge of finance provides humans with powerful tools through which the processes of rendering decisions may be strengthened and embellished. Therefore, the concept of finance necessitates the rendering of decisions to produce future organizational benefits. The methods that support this future outlook are known as capital budgeting methods.

1.15 Capital Budgeting Concepts

Because of the purpose of demonstrating primary, monetary capital budgeting methods through which financial decisions may be rendered, the particular capital budgeting of this text involves a consideration of various decisions that impact criminal justice entities. This theme generally involves specified quantities of cash flow amounts and specified risk percentages through time, thereby demonstrating estimates of risk regarding the influencing of human decisions.

The secondary forms of analysis involve scenario analysis and simulation analysis. Within this context, another theme of this text will involve an examination of risk, through time, that impacts a variety of decision outcomes. Primarily, the uses of scenario analysis and sensitivity analysis are considered from the perspectives of criminal justice organizations. Discussions regarding these concepts are contained within the succeeding chapters of this text.

The tools provided within the succeeding chapters approach financial decisions from a variety of perspectives and involve some element of risk. They also are representative of the economic concerns of resource allocation and the financial concerns of investing minimal capital in the hopes of gaining the best reward, through time, of investment decisions. Specifically, the methods listed in Table 1.2 are considered among the succeeding chapters of this text.

The notion of capital budgeting may incite mental models of financial budgeting regarding the current or short-term allocations and uses of funds. However, this notion is incorrect because of the strategic characteristics of capital budgeting. Capital budgeting is not synonymous with the traditional concept of budgeting that is commonly manifested among criminal justice environments. Instead, capital budgeting involves the rendering of a human decision, through the use of quantitative, analytical financial tools, with respect to time. This financial decision must demonstrate the manifestation of human judgment about the highest and best use of monies for the purpose of securing the strongest and most robust benefit financially, with respect to the ability of the organization to successfully serve its intended public market efficiently and effectively (Figure 1.6). Given these considerations, capital budgeting involves

Table 1.2 Decision Methods

Method	Description
Payback method	Provides a time-based perspective of rendering decisions.
Internal rate of return	Provides a rate-based perspective of rendering decisions.
Net present value	Provides a cash-based perspective of rendering decisions.
Profitability index	Provides a profitability perspective of rendering decisions.

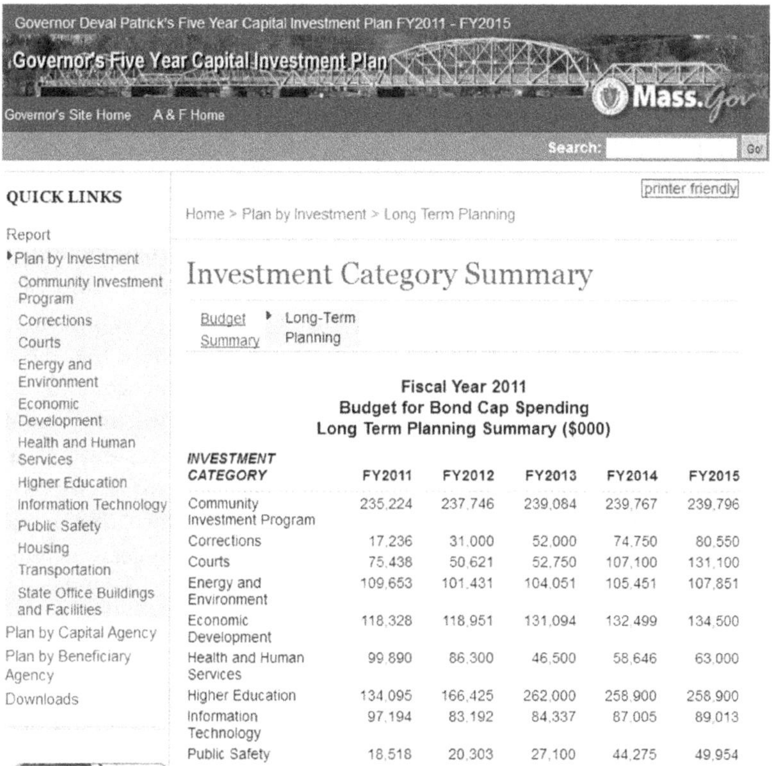
Governor Deval Patrick's Five Year Capital Investment Plan FY2011 - FY2015

Governor's Five Year Capital Investment Plan

Mass.Gov

Governor's Site Home A & F Home

Search: Go

QUICK LINKS

Report
- Plan by Investment
  - Community Investment Program
  - Corrections
  - Courts
  - Energy and Environment
  - Economic Development
  - Health and Human Services
  - Higher Education
  - Information Technology
  - Public Safety
  - Housing
  - Transportation
  - State Office Buildings and Facilities
- Plan by Capital Agency
- Plan by Beneficiary Agency
- Downloads

printer friendly

Home > Plan by Investment > Long Term Planning

Investment Category Summary

Budget Summary ▸ Long-Term Planning

Fiscal Year 2011
Budget for Bond Cap Spending
Long Term Planning Summary ($000)

INVESTMENT CATEGORY	FY2011	FY2012	FY2013	FY2014	FY2015
Community Investment Program	235,224	237,746	239,084	239,767	239,796
Corrections	17,236	31,000	52,000	74,750	80,550
Courts	75,438	50,621	52,750	107,100	131,100
Energy and Environment	109,653	101,431	104,051	105,451	107,851
Economic Development	118,328	118,951	131,094	132,499	134,500
Health and Human Services	99,890	86,300	46,500	58,646	63,000
Higher Education	134,095	166,425	262,000	258,900	258,900
Information Technology	97,194	83,192	84,337	87,005	89,013
Public Safety	18,518	20,303	27,100	44,275	49,954

Figure 1.6 Capital budgeting and decisions for the state of Massachusetts. Although a variety of financial application domains may be considered, this screen capture shows investments for public safety, corrections, courts, and health and human services. These entities are affiliated with the criminal justice system and law enforcement entities. (Courtesy of the State of Massachusetts, http://www.mass.gov/bb/cap/fy2009/rec/hpdefault.htm.)

a long-term, strategic perspective of rendering human decisions. Hence, such decisions should neither be taken lightly nor deemed insignificant.

These methods may be used independently or collaboratively to embellish the rendering of human financial decisions. The capital budgeting methods, consisting of the perspectives of the payback period (i.e., time), rate (i.e., internal rate of return), cash value (i.e., net present value), and profit (i.e., profitability index) generally show a common outcome among most decisions. The latter methods of decisions involving scenario analysis, sensitivity analysis, and leasing versus purchasing provide a view of decisions that involve greater complexity through time. Regardless, it is assumed that an examination of these techniques will provide a good overview and basic understanding of tools that facilitate the rendering of strategic, human financial decisions, through time, that impact criminal justice and law enforcement entities.

1.16 Chapter Comments and Summary

This chapter serves as the basis for describing the basic tenets of rendering financial decisions. Specifically, it shows that historic attributes of human needs and wants continue to persist during contemporary periods, and that such needs and wants are unchanging. The relationships among economic systems, markets, and concepts of exchange mediums to facilitate transactions among humans are considered within this chapter. These notions are salient with respect to decisions that influence the use of money. The characteristics of such decisions remain constant through time.

The human act of rendering a decision is a powerful event that has the potentials of immediate, short-term, and long-term consequences and ramifications through time. Human decisions may prosecute war or they may ensure peace; they may result in lifetime commitments or separations; and they may facilitate the rise or downfall of nations. Human decisions are propagated through time, and their effects may be experienced among many succeeding generations. Therefore, the rendering human decisions must occur with solemn regard to the considerations of the effects of the decisions considered and must integrated as much information as possible regarding the problem domain.

Human decisions occur among legal markets and illegal markets. With respect to both cases, human decisions encapsulate an innumerable series of transactions among a variety of market systems and environments. Examples of illegal transactions include commonly identified crimes of prostitution, drug trafficking, fraud, and money laundering. Examples of legal transactions concerning criminal justice and law enforcement include the purchasing of patrol cars, the building or expansion of jail facilities, community service programs, and officer training programs. Certainly, many more examples within both categories may be identified. However, in both cases, the legal and illegal markets serve the needs and wants of humans with respect to the availability of scarce resources. In both cases, the tenets of economic supply and demand affect the pricing characteristics of transactions.

Such decisions may be viewed from strategic, tactical, and operational perspectives. Regardless of the period considered, the potentials of risk cannot be completed eliminated. Within the context of rendering financial decisions, this text is primarily concerned with strategic decisions via the use of capital budgeting methods. These capital budgeting methods include the net present value, the internal rate of return, the profitability index, and the payback period. Additional tools include scenario and sensitivity analysis.

1.17 Terminology

Accounting
Alternatives
Budgeting
Capital budgeting
Complexity
Costs
Decision
Economics
Economic question
Economic system
Exchange
Finance
Internal rate of return
Market
Model
Money
Needs and wants
Net present value
Operational
Payback period
Partially structured
Profitability index
Risk
Simulation
Strategic
Strongly structured
Tactical
Weakly structured

1.18 Thought and Discussion Questions

1. The *Congressional Record* provides a variety of historical accounts of financial and economic issues that challenged the nation through time. Search through the *Congressional Record*, and locate three situations that challenged the U.S. economically and financially. In each case, what were the considered needs and wants of humans? In each case, what were the financial mechanisms that were involved in these issues? In each case, what were the potential courses of actions that were possible? In each case, what were the possible advantages and disadvantages of pursuing these courses of actions? Further, what types of decisions were involved with respect to the selected courses of actions?
2. Human needs and wants are manifested among a variety of legal markets. Identify a criminal justice market that serves legal purposes. Within the context of this market, what are some of the legal human needs and wants that are serviced? What are the characteristics of the market itself? What types of decisions are rendered among the participants of this market?
3. Human needs and wants are manifested among a variety of illegal markets. Identify a black market that serves illegal purposes. Within the context of this market, what are some of the illegal human needs and wants that are serviced? What are the characteristics of the

market itself? What types of decisions are rendered among the participants of this market? What types of decisions are rendered among law enforcement entities to counter the activities of this market?

4. Capital budgeting involves rendering decisions that impact organizations for long-term periods. Given each of the discussed capital budgeting tools, identify criminal justice examples that would be an appropriate use of each tool. Further, for each example, identify and explain the types of market risk that may affect the strategic concerns of capital budgeting.

Bibliography

Ames, Walter. *Police and Community in Japan*. Berkeley, CA: University of California Press, 1981.

Andrews, E. Benjamin. "The Bimetallist Committee of Boston and New England." *Quarterly Journal of Economics*, 8 (1894): 319–327.

Balatski, E. "The Formation of a 'Dissertation Trap.'" *Russian Politics & Law*, 46 (2008): 67–91.

Bastable, Charles. "On Some Applications of the Theory of International Trade." *Quarterly Journal of Economics*, 4 (1889): 1–17.

Coffin, Bill. "Black Gold, Black Market." *Risk Management* 56 (2009): 12–13.

Cook, Philip, Jens Ludwig, Sudhir Venkatesh, and Anthony Braga. "Underground Gun Markets." *Economic Journal*, 117 (2007): F588–F618.

Davies, Roy. "Money in North American History: From Wampum to Electronic Funds Transfer." October 9, 2008. Accessed September 16, 2010: http://projects.exeter.ac.uk/RDavies/arian/northamerica.html.

Dumitrescu, Constantini, Razvan Neacsu, and Nicole Zamfirescu. "Underground Economy, Disturbatory Facto in National Economy Development." *Annals of DAAAM and Proceedings*, Jan (2009): 989–990.

Edgeworth, Francis. "Appreciation of Gold." *Quarterly Journal of Economics*, 3 (1889): 153–169.

Elliott, Sheryl and Lisa Neirotti. "Challenges of Tourism in a Dynamic Island Destination: The Case of Cuba." *Tourism Geographies*, 10 (2008): 375–402.

Fitzpatrick, Mark. "Lessons Learned from Iran's Pursuit of Nuclear Weapons." *Nonproliferation Review*, 13 (2006): 527–537.

Fleischner, Justine, Kain Von Hippel, and Frederick Barton. *Homebound Security: Migrant Support for Improved Public Safety in Conflict-Prone Settings*. Washington, D.C.: Center for Strategic and International Studies, 2009.

Frank, Howard. *Public Financial Management*. Boca Raton, FL: CRC Press, 2006.

Gundlach, Gregory, Kevin Bradford, and William Wilkie. "Countermarketing and Demarketing Against Product Diversion: Forensic Research in the Firearms Industry." *Journal of Public Policy & Marketing*, 29 (2010): 103–122.

Heber, Anita. "Networks of Organised Black Market Labour in the Building Trade." *Trends in Organized Crime*, 12 (2009): 122–144.

Kaliadin, Aleksander. "In Search of an Effective Coercive Strategy to Deter the Use of Weapons of Mass Destruction." *Russian Social Science Review*, 49 (2008): 77–93.
Kurniawanti, Ika and Hendry Setiabudi. "The Crooked Credit Analyst." *Internal Auditor*, 66 (2009): 67–69.
Library of Congress. *Journal of the Senate*, 1791, Vol. 1, p. 270. Accessed July 17, 2010: http://memory.loc.gov/cgi-bin/ampage?collId=llsj&fileName=001/llsj001.db&recNum=263&itemLink=D?hlaw:1:./temp/~ammem_qg4W::%230010264&linkText=1.
Library of Congress. *Journal of the Senate*, April 15, 1874, Vol. 69, p. 464. Accessed July 18, 2010: http://memory.loc.gov/cgi-bin/ampage?collId=llsj&fileName=069/llsj069.db&recNum=462&itemLink=D?hlaw:20:./temp/~ammem_pPQD::%230690463&linkText=1.
Moyle, Brendan. "The Black Market in China for Tiger Products." *Global Crime*, 10 (2009): 124–143.
Priddle, Gerald and Michael Santos. "Informal Sector in Chinese Economy: A Study of Currency Exchange and Informal Banking." *International Journal of Business Research*, 8 (2008): 1–12.
Prunckun, Hank. "Does Price Really Matter? The Relationship between Heroin Price and Purity in Australia and the Ramifications for International Drug Enforcement." *Global Crime*, 8 (2007): 367–380.
Reynecke, Frick and Marius Fourie. *Police Management Beyond 2000*. Lansdowne: Juta and Co., 2001.
"Saudis Ban Valentine Day Roses." *Middle East Quarterly*, 16 (2009): 46.
Strakes, Jason. "Illicit Arms Transfers: Linking Weapons Characteristics and Strategic Applications." *Defense and Security Analysis*, 24 (2008): 61–64.
U.S. Congress. *Congressional Record: 101st Congress*. Accessed September 17, 2010: http://thomas.loc.gov/home/LegislativeData.php?&n=Record&c=101.
U.S. Government. *Annual Budget of the United States Government—Appendix: Fiscal Year 2003*. 107th Congress—Second Session. House Document, 159(2), January 23, 2002–November 22, 2002. Washington, DC: U.S. Government Printing Office, 2003.
U.S. Government Accountability Office. "Congressional Committees." Accessed July 21, 2010: http://www.gao.gov/new.items/d10725r.pdf.
Vartabedian, Ralph and Peter Pae. "Cost of *Columbia* Accident Inquiry Is Soaring." *The Los Angeles Times*, March 15, 2003. Accessed July 21, 2010: http://articles.latimes.com/2003/mar/15/nation/na-probe15.
Walker, F. A. "Value of Money." *Quarterly Journal of Economics*, 8 (1893): 62–76.
Wyatt, Tanya. "Exploring the Organization of Russia Far East's Illegal Wildlife Trade: Two Case Studies of the Illegal Fur and Illegal Falcon Trades." *Global Crime*, 10 (2009): 144–154.

Concepts of Decisions 2

The tax on capital gains directly affects investment decisions, the mobility and flow of risk capital ... the ease or difficulty experienced by new ventures in obtaining capital, and thereby the strength and potential for growth in the economy.*

President John F. Kennedy

2.1 Objectives

The objectives of this chapter are to:

- Understand the concept of rendering human decisions
- Understand the psychological aspects of decisions
- Understand the concept of objective decisions
- Understand the impediments of rendering objective decisions
- Understand various methods of improving the rendering of decisions

2.2 Introduction

Humans may render decisions individually, within groups, or among organizational settings. Humans are imperfect creatures, and the ability of humans to render decisions is influenced by such imperfections. Heuer indicates that, historically, human decisions were perceived from the notion that it was necessary only to "open one's eyes, look at the facts, and purge oneself of all preconceptions and prejudices in order to make an objective judgment." However, contemporary perceptions have changed and acknowledge the realization that bias exists within the context of rendering human decisions. Heuer recognizes this concept through observing that contemporary analysis entities do not approach decisions with "empty minds," and begin to approach decisions "with a set of assumptions about how events normally transpire in the area for which they are responsible."†

* Kennedy, John, "Decisions Quotes," Brainy Quote, http://www.brainyquote.com/quotes/keywords/decisions.html (accessed July 11, 2011).

† Heuer, *Psychology of Intelligence Analysis*.

From the perspective of criminal justice and law enforcement entities, these notions are relevant. The financial costs of intelligence functions are enormous given the necessity of maintaining homeland security efforts nationally and internationally. However, despite such costs, it is imperative that the economic functioning, financial functioning, and business functioning of the nation are unimpeded. Therefore, decisions regarding the funding of a myriad of programs and initiatives must be contemplated vehemently and meticulously to provide the best decision possible (Figure 2.1).

Despite the need to render such potent and important decisions, such financial decisions are often influenced by tangible and intangible elements of the decision domain and by the characteristics of humans. Therefore, the objectivity of decisions must be considered from a variety of perspectives. These notions are not limited only to the concerns of national security and intelligence functions. Instead, they apply to all facets of criminal justice organizations and law enforcement entities.

2.3 Objective Decisions

The aforementioned considerations are important aspects of understanding objective decisions. Objectivity is the "expressing or dealing with facts or conditions as perceived without distortion by personal feelings, prejudices, or interpretations" and is "limited to choices of fixed alternatives and reducing subjective factors to a minimum."[*] Heuer considers objectivity from the complements of awareness and perception, from the influences of preconceptions, the influences of alternatives among multiple hypothesis considerations, the limitations of human cognitive attributes and mental modeling, and considerations of the criteria and characteristics of the decision domain itself. These concepts all influence the objectivity of human decisions.[†]

The writings of Heuer present some interesting observations regarding objectivity. Within the composition, it is the opinion of this author that three considerations of objectivity are salient. First, "objectivity is achieved by making basic assumptions and reasoning as explicit as possible so that they can be challenged by others and analysts can, themselves, examine their validity." Based on the writings of Heuer, it is the opinion of this author that this observation provides an interesting consideration of objectivity in that it shows the necessity of maintaining the visibility of "assumptions and reasoning," concerning both the analyst and peers, without their dismissal. Second, Heuer indicates that "objectivity is gained by making assumptions explicit so that they may be examined and challenged, not by vain efforts to eliminate

* *Merriam-Webster Online Dictionary*, "Objectivity."

† Heuer, *Psychology of Intelligence Analysis*.

Figure 2.1 Contemplating decisions. FEMA Administrator Craig Fugate (left) talks with Armond Mascelli, VP Disaster Services Operations, American Red Cross (center), and Alex Dornstauder, Deputy Director for Homeland Security, U.S. Army Corps of Engineers (right), before a briefing for congressional staff on the upcoming 2011 spring flood season. (Photo by Aaron Skolnik/FEMA. Courtesy of the U.S. Department of Homeland Security, http://www.dhs.gov/ynews/gallery/.)

them from analysis." Again, based on the writings of Heuer, this observation provides an interesting consideration of objectivity in that it shows the necessity of maintaining the visibility of "assumptions" without their dismissal. Third, Heuer indicates that "significant biases in the evaluation of intelligence estimates are attributable to the nature of human mental processes, not just to self-interest and lack of objectivity, and that they are, therefore, exceedingly difficult to overcome." Given this notion of Heuer, despite the necessity of visibility regarding "assumptions and reasoning," there exist impediments that inhibit the manifestation of objectivity within the intelligence function.*

The writings of Heuer demonstrate the fallibility of humans. Humans are imperfect creations, and are subject to any number of biases and weaknesses, both physically and mentally, when experiencing various facets of decision processes. Although the human mind is formidable, various levels of complexity hamper the process of rendering decisions. Criminal justice entities and law enforcement entities are comprised of humans. Therefore, the decisions rendered among these environments are subject to the imperfections of humans. Given this notion, a variety of factors affect the objectivity of rendering human decisions.

* Heuer, *Psychology of Intelligence Analysis.*

2.4 Impeding Factors

A variety of impeding factors may impact the objectivity and rendering of human decisions. Based on the writings of Lidwell, Holden, and Butler[*]; Heuer[†]; Gordon[‡]; and Mullen and Roth[§]; examples of such impediments include groupthink, bounded rationality, cardinality, satisficing, stress, decision capacities and styles, cognitive biases, value hierarchies, and the characteristics of the decision domain (e.g., decision risk, organizational politics). Although many other impediments exist, these considerations show the types of influences that impede the rendering of human decisions among criminal justice and law enforcement functions. Despite the diminishing of the potency of human decisions, methods exist through which the effects of impediments may be countered.

2.5 Group Decisions: Cardinality and Groupthink

Cardinality is another characteristic of impediments that influence decisions. The cardinality of decisions may either be manifested through the use of individuals or groups to render decisions. Gordon primarily considers the rendering of decisions from the perspective of organizational groups. Within this context, impediments are manifested because a longer time frame is required to render a decision, because groups often render decisions that may be "extreme," because groups often "ignore individual expertise, opting instead for group consensus, and because of the potential of groupthink to taint rendered decisions."[¶]

According to Gordon, groupthink may occur when group members "avoid a critical evaluation of alternatives so that they can preserve a sense of group unity and consensus," and that efforts to achieve such consensus avoid "being too critical in their judgment of other group members' ideas."[**] Sims[††] indicates that groupthink deteriorates "mental efficiency, reality testing, and moral judgment," and manifests dysfunctions regarding the rendering of group decisions. According to Sims[‡‡] and Gordon,[§§] the symptoms of groupthink include perceptions of invulnerability, rationalization, illusions

[*] Lidwell, Holden, and Butler, *Universal Principles of Design.*
[†] Heuer, *Psychology of Intelligence Analysis.*
[‡] Gordon, *Organizational Behavior.*
[§] Mullen and Roth, *Decision Making.*
[¶] Gordon, *Organizational Behavior.*
[**] Ibid.
[††] Sims, *Ethics and Corporate Social Responsibility.*
[‡‡] Ibid.
[§§] Gordon, *Organizational Behavior.*

of morality, stereotyping of others, peer pressure among group members, self-censoring, demands of unanimity, and protective mind-guarding. All groups are susceptible to the mindsets and influences of groupthink, and a variety of moral and ethical consequences are affiliated with the implementation of flawed decisions. Such influences contribute toward the rendering of decisions that are contrary to "enlightened, self-interest" and are "counterproductive."*

Notable examples of groupthink pervade history. The Enron debacle was an example of the effects of groupthink because of the decision characteristics manifested among its organizational leadership. Tyson (1998) considers the 1961 Cuban Bay of Pigs invasion as an example of groupthink and indicates that all of the symptoms of groupthink were manifested among "Kennedy, Rusk, McNamara, and the other top-ranking policy makers."† These examples, respectively, are representative of business intelligence applications and government intelligence applications. Sims cites Watergate and various amounts of unsuccessfulness of Vietnam War operations as additional examples.‡ (See Figure 2.2.)

No organization is insusceptible to the influences and consequences of groupthink. From the perspective of law enforcement and criminal justice entities, groupthink may be manifested among a variety of settings. Internally, groupthink may pervade the organizational settings of criminal justice entities. Further, groupthink may originate external to the criminal justice organization, and the organization must deal with the consequences of such mindsets. Various incidents highlight these notions.

An example of internal groupthink is found within the Philadelphia Police Department. During 1985, this department decided to attack a neighborhood using incendiary weaponry. The results of its actions were dismal and continue to plague the city. According to Moore, "Five children and six adults, members of a small radical collective called MOVE, died; 61 homes in a middle-class neighborhood were destroyed." This action also spawned raging fires that further destroyed the area. Moore indicates that the estimated costs of this event resulted in "$42 million in financial settlements, investigation and rebuilding" efforts. Moore also indicates that an additional "24 homeowners won a $12 million suit against the city for the botched rebuilding and repairs of their homes" during 2005.§

External examples of groupthink may gain national notoriety. The members of the Heaven's Gate cult, during 1997, committed mass suicide in the hopes of a joyful rendezvous with an alien spacecraft. This event resulted

* Sims, *Ethics and Organizational Decision Making.*

† Tyson, *Working with Groups.*

‡ Sims, *Ethics and Organizational Decision Making.*

§ Moore, "1985 Bombing in Philadelphia Still Unsettled."

Figure 2.2 View of Nixon's departure as seen from the President's helicopter. President Richard Nixon ultimately resigned as President of the United States as a result of the Watergate incident. (From NixonLibrary.gov, http://www.nixonlibrary.gov/virtuallibrary/gallery11.php.)

in the deaths of 39 individuals.* This example is indicative of the extreme dangers of groupthink. This event shows the dangers of losing the benefit of individual thought and reasoning while conforming unquestionably to the philosophies of the cult.

Cardinality is indicative of rendering decisions either as individuals or as groups. Individual decisions involve the responsibility of a single person rendering a decision. This situation necessitates strong skills of critical analysis and the ability to independently demonstrate the competency to contemplate alternative courses of actions within a decision domain, and select the option that provides the highest and best outcome for the organization. In contrast, group decisions may involve a greater diversity of talents, opinions, and perspectives, but may be influenced through the dangers of groupthink. Therefore, when rendering decisions, care must be taken to recognize potential pitfalls and to avoid disastrous outcomes.

* "One Year Later, Heaven's Gate Suicide."

These notions are certainly relevant within the context of law enforcement and criminal justice organizations. Community-oriented policing proponents advocate the empowerment of individual officers within their duty stations and patrols. This empowerment facilitates the independence of the personnel to react and respond to a myriad of community situations ranging from community service to situational responses to criminal activities. Within this context, law enforcement personnel must demonstrate the ability to render decisions as individuals during the course of their duties. Therefore, strong critical analysis skills and the ability to evaluate situations are paramount to the rendering of decisions.

However, traditional paradigms of policing are different and do not espouse such intensities of empowerment among personnel. Traditional policing mindsets involve a structured, regimented approach to rendering decisions through time. Individual officers may not have the authority and freedom to render decisions as independent entities. Therefore, multiple actors may be involved in the processes of analyzing situations, performing evaluation, and rendering a decision. Hence, the potential of groupthink to influence such decisions is present among such traditional models.

2.6 Bounded Rationality and Satisficing

Another impediment is bounded rationality. Gigerenzer[*] indicates that bounded rationality involves rendering decisions in accordance with an "optimization under constraints" of the decision domain. Similarly, according to Heuer, bounded rationality is "recognized widely, though not universally, both as an accurate portrayal of human judgment and choice and as a sensible adjustment to the limitations inherent in how the human mind functions."[†] Brecher and Harvey[‡] embellish the clarifications of Gigerenzer and Heuer, and indicate that bounded rationality "largely involves a process of judgment."

Griffin and Moorhead indicate that bounded rationality involves the consideration that "although individuals may seek the best solution to a problem, the demands of processing all the information bearing on the problem, generating all possible solutions, and choosing the single best solution, are beyond the capabilities of most decision makers," and that the outcomes of such decisions are less than ideal.[§] According to Taudes, an example of decision outcomes involving bounded rationality is the volatility of the stock market, which demonstrates the decisions and actions of traders. The effects

[*] Gigerenzer, *Rationality for Mortals.*
[†] Heuer, *Psychology of Intelligence Analysis.*
[‡] Brecher and Harvey, *Conflict, Security, Foreign Policy.*
[§] Griffin and Moorhead, *Organizational Behavior.*

of bounded rationality are manifested because "the market price does not converge to the equilibrium price, but rather oscillates around it."*

This concept of market price oscillation is relevant among entities within the criminal justice system. A variety of entities within the criminal justice system represent for-profit businesses. Direct entities include for-profit corrections programs and systems. Indirect entities may include the for-profit vendors that supply various facets of these direct entities. Examples may include food services, and power and utilities companies. Because they are classified as for-profit entities, their stocks may be traded among a variety of markets and may involve numerous stock trades daily. It is the market that affects the valuation and stock pricing of such entities.

Another impediment is satisficing. According to Daft, satisficing is the selection of the "first solution alternative that satisfies minimal decision criteria" in which alternatives are unexamined regardless of the presence of "better solutions are presumed to exist." Daft differentiates between satisficing and bounded rationality through observations that bounded rationality involves the considerations of limits or boundaries regarding rational behavior, including potential alternatives, whereas satisficing involves an incomplete consideration of the characteristics of such constraints and fulfills only the immediate, "minimal decision criteria" without any consideration of alternatives.†

From a commercial finance perspective, Daft considers the Quaker Oats acquisition of Snapple as an example of satisficing because the event did not encompass a robust consideration of market alternatives and was quickly fashioned toward "thwarting" the threat of a Quaker takeover by its competitors. This event was an example of satisficing because Quaker did not consider market alternatives, and it immediately leveraged Snapple's debt to dissuade interested competitors from considering the acquisition of Quaker.‡

2.7 Stress

Stress also impedes the rendering of human decisions. According to Mullen and Roth, stress inhibits the rendering of human decisions cognitively. When stressed, because of the human inclination to "take action," the act of "reflective thought" may be hampered. During such instances, humans may "take actions that provide the short-term advantage of stress reduction at the expense of our long-term goals," and may render "counter-productive" decisions.§ (See Figure 2.3.)

* Taudes, *Adaptive Information Systems.*

† Daft, *Management.*

‡ Ibid.

§ Mullen and Roth, *Decision Making.*

Figure 2.3 Military police perform missions and render decisions among stressful environments. U.S. Army 1LT Andrew Williams radios status updates during a neighborhood patrol with Iraqi police officers in Haswah, Iraq, January 13, 2009. Williams is assigned to the 4th Infantry Division's Charlie Troop, 1st Squadron, 10th Calvary Regiment, 2nd Brigade Combat Team. (U.S. Navy photo by Petty Officer 2nd Class James Wagner. Courtesy of the U.S. Department of Defense, http://www.defense.gov/dodcmsshare/homepagephoto/2009-01/hires_090113-N-1509W-100b.jpg.)

According to the National Transportation Safety Board (NTSB), "decision-making can be degraded when individuals are under stress because they selectively focus on only a subset of cues in the environment" and may "impede an individual's ability to evaluate an alternative course of action, resulting in a tendency to proceed with an original plan even though it may no longer be optimal." As an example of decisions that were impaired by the effects of stress, the NTSB cites the accident of American Airlines Flight 1420 that crashed after it overran a runway in Little Rock, Arkansas, in 1999. According to the NTSB, this accident resulted in the deaths of 11 individuals and caused over 105 injuries.*

2.8 Decision Style and Capacity

Decision capacities and styles are also impediments to the rendering of human decisions. According to Gordon, these characteristics encompass the "basic abilities to perform the components of the rational decision-making process, including situational analysis, and objective setting as well as the generation, evaluation, and selection of alternatives." Gordon includes

* National Transportation Safety Board, "Aircraft Accident Report."

cognitive complexity (i.e., the "human ability to tolerate ambiguity") and values hierarchies (i.e., the human preferences of tasks and issues) within the scope of decision capacities and styles. Further, Gordon considers heuristics within the scope of decision capacities and styles and cognitive complexities. An example of impeded decisions, regarding capacities and styles, would result from an individual rendering decisions among domains in which his personal and professional skills and knowledge are incommensurate with the requirements of the decision domain.*

According to Gordon, regarding cognitive complexity, when framing and evaluating problems, impediments among decisions may be manifested through the biases of availability, representativeness, and adjustment. These factors influence the framing of problems because "individuals tend to take fewer risks regarding choices they frame in a positive fashion, and tend to take more risks about choices they frame negatively." From the perspective of business intelligence decisions, among organizations, Gordon cites the 1980s Coke Classic debacle as an example of such impeded decisions.†

2.9 Risk

The considerations of risk are characteristic of most decision domains. According to Griffin and Moorhead, decision domains involve varying amounts of certainty versus uncertainty (i.e., risk), and involve various extraneous factors that may impede the rendering of robust decisions (e.g., organizational politics).‡ According to Jordaan, decision domains are permeated with varied probabilities, varied subjectivity, and varied objectivity.§ Because of such attributes, decision domains demonstrate risk considerations that may be structured, unstructured, or semistructured.¶ Donohue et al. cite the routing of air traffic and air transportation decisions as examples of contemplations that involve structured, unstructured, and semistructured considerations.** Evaluating risk is a significant component of any decision domain. Figure 2.4 shows some of the factors that must be contemplated with respect to decision risk.

* Gordon, *Organizational Behavior.*
† Ibid.
‡ Griffin and Moorhead, *Organizational Behavior.*
§ Jordaan, *Decisions under Uncertainty.*
¶ Donohue et al., *Air Transportation Systems Engineering.*
** Ibid.

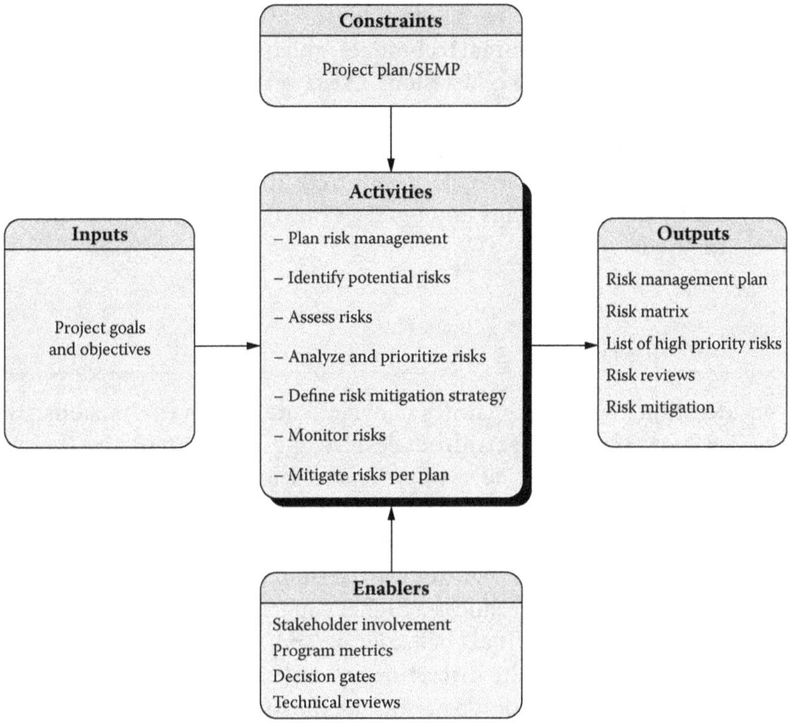

Figure 2.4 Risk management involves a variety of considerations that influence the rendering of human decisions. This image shows various attributes of the decision domain that must be considered during periods of risk evaluation. All decisions, whether structured, unstructured, or semistructured, involve some amount of risk. (Courtesy of the U.S. Department of Transportation, Federal Highway Administration, http://www.fhwa.dot.gov/cadiv/segb/views/document/sections/Section3/3_9_4.htm.)

2.10 Countering Impediments

The aforementioned impediments impact decisions uniquely. Each organization demonstrates a myriad of characteristics that define its uniqueness as a decision domain. Each human possesses a unique ability to render decisions. Humans are fallible and imperfect, and are susceptible to any of the identified impediments. Because organizations are comprised of humans, they are also susceptible to the limitations of human capacities to render decisions. However, regardless of human imperfections regarding the rendering of decisions, various methods of countering impediments exist.

Such countering methods include group dynamics, brainstorming, consensus techniques (e.g., the nominal group technique, the Delphi technique, and Strawman maps), and the use of groupware. Olson and Wu (2008) also consider the Delphi and nominal techniques, and include a systems approach for improving the rendering of decisions.[*] Also, various artificial intelligence tools and other quantitative methods (e.g., scenario analysis, sensitivity analysis, simulation analysis) may be used to improve the robustness of decisions. Although perfect decisions may not result from the use of such methods, it is expected that improvements among decisions will occur through the use of these methods.

2.11 Group Dynamics

A consideration of group dynamics may facilitate improved decisions. The dynamics of group settings introduce leverages the cumulative knowledge, skills, and capacities of group members to generate synergy. Such leveraging facilitates decisions that are of "higher quality than the sum of individual decisions" and is the result of individuals contributing "additional knowledge and skills" within the decision domain. A consideration of group dynamics also introduces a higher capacity of innovation through multiple facets of "attitudinal, behavioral, and cultural" characteristics when considering "difficult, discretionary tasks." Group dynamics also incorporate some level of consensus among the members of the group, and "more readily leads to acceptance of the decision."[†] Based on the writings of Henry about law enforcement applications, relevant examples are the use of task forces among law enforcement entities within the context of the Compstat paradigm.[‡]

2.12 Brainstorming

Brainstorming also facilitates improvements among decision environments. According to Olson and Wu, the concept of brainstorming "involves redefining the problem, generating ideas, and seeking new solutions" through the creation of a "climate of free association through trading ideas and perceptions." Improvements, among decisions, are generated because "better ideas are expected from brainstorming than from individual thought because the minds of more people are tapped."[§] Similarly, Gordon indicates that brainstorming involves the generation of "large numbers of ideas or alternatives

[*] Olson and Wu, *Enterprise Risk Management.*
[†] Gordon, *Organizational Behavior.*
[‡] Henry, *Compstat Paradigm.*
[§] Olson and Wu, *Enterprise Risk Management.*

relating to a decision without evaluating their merits," and may result in the generation of "unexpected and potentially useful possibilities for attacking a problem."[*] As an intelligence example, Treverton considers the merits of brainstorming from the perspective of intelligence-led policing via the examination of preventive strategy to counter the activities of European organized crime.[†]

2.13 Nominal Group Technique

The nominal group technique is another method of improving decisions. According to Gordon, this technique involves brainstorming succeeded by a "rank order series of ideas as a way of resolving differences in group opinion," and that the contributions of ideas may occur anonymously.[‡] The potency of the technique improves with group size and variations among skills, knowledge, and capacities of the individual comprising the group. According to Olson and Wu, this method enhances brainstorming because it tends to "yield more unique ideas, more total ideas, and better quality ideas."[§] Within the context of intelligence analysis, Murray considers the use of this technique among intelligence operations in embellishing operational security, with respect to the attributes of cognition and deception necessary during the planning and implementation of intelligence operations.[¶]

2.14 Delphi Technique

The Delphi technique also embellishes decision environments. According to Gordon, this method involves the use of "repeated administration of rating scales to obtain opinions, first unfocused and then refocused, about a decision," and that each iteration of the rating scales involves an increased quantity of respondents.[**] Olson and Wu embellish this definition through indicating that "anonymous ideas are exchanged for either a given number of rounds, or until convergence of ideas" occurs.[††] Applications of this technique may be used among forecasting environments. According to Elwyn, Greenhalgh, and MacFarlane, earliest origins of the technique originated during the 1940s among U.S. military settings and the RAND Corporation

[*] Gordon, *Organizational Behavior.*
[†] Treverton, "Addressing Complexities in Homeland Security."
[‡] Gordon, *Organizational Behavior.*
[§] Olson and Wu, *Enterprise Risk Management.*
[¶] Murray, *Protecting Critical Information and Technology.*
[**] Gordon, *Organizational Behavior.*
[††] Olson and Wu, *Enterprise Risk Management.*

to improve understanding of "future technological capabilities that might be of interest to them" and to "study predictive methods in relation to intercontinental warfare."[*]

Both the nominal group and Delphi techniques contribute toward consensus regarding the improvement of decisions.[†] A third consideration of consensus involves the use of Strawman maps. According to Gordon, the use of Strawman maps improves decisions through the involvement of "clustering and categorizing of similar ideas to ultimately result in a solution" regarding "complex problems that have interconnected elements, and many sequential steps."[‡] This concept has implications regarding intelligence functions within the contexts of social network theory and crime mapping applications. According to Gill, the usefulness of such concepts is manifested through the mapping of activities associated with unlawful organizations and terrorists.[§] Similar observations are given by Henry regarding crime-mapping activities using the Compstat paradigm.[¶]

2.15 Groupware

Groupware also contributes toward the improvement of decisions (Figure 2.5). According to Gordon, groupware facilitates the virtual "sharing of ideas" regardless of physical location.[**] Within the context of the intelligence function, Waltz indicates that the use of groupware establishes "collective goals and commitments around a common intelligence problem," enhances the sharing of "individual contributions of knowledge," and "collaboratively" contributes toward the rendering of decisions regarding problem solutions.[††] According to Stahl, considerations of intelligence functions may involve research aspects of "conversation analysis" and "video analysis" to facilitate potential improvements among decisions.[‡‡]

2.16 Systems Approach

A systems approach may be considered for the improvement of decisions. According to Olson and Wu, such analysis is an "approach intended to

[*] Elwyn, Greenhalgh, and MacFarlane, *Groups*.
[†] Ibid.
[‡] Gordon, *Organizational Behavior*.
[§] Gill, "Theories of Intelligence."
[¶] Henry, *The Compstat Paradigm*.
[**] Gordon, *Organizational Behavior*.
[††] Waltz, *Knowledge Management*.
[‡‡] Stahl, "Groups, Group Cognition, and Groupware."

Figure 2.5 Using groupware facilitates organizational communications. SPC Robert Anderson with the 328th Engineer Company uses a computer at the Fort McCoy Mobilization Soldier Computer Center. Groupware provides several functions that allow organizational members to share information across geographic regions and organizational components. (Photo by Tom Michele, Fort McCoy. Courtesy of the U.S. Army, http://www.army.mil/media/157286.)

improve the prospects of success by examining similar undertakings that have failed with the intent of avoiding those things that caused failure," and the methods of rendering of decisions involves "studying the process as a system, to enable modeling the system so that cause and effect relationships can be understood."*

Gray and Larson provide an example of this form of analysis through considerations of failures resulting from Operation Eagle Claw during 1979 in which the United States responded to the Iranian attack upon a U.S. embassy. The use of such analysis facilitated a comparison of the actual events that transpired versus the planned events that were anticipated.† Through such analysis, the United States learned a variety of lessons from the failure, and determined a myriad of suggestions for future improvements of strategy, tactics, and operations.

A variety of mathematical tools exist to improve the rendering of human decisions. Human decisions may be improved through the use of artificial intelligence tools, scenario analysis, simulation analysis, and other quantitative methods. Similar notions are expressed by Blank and Tarquin about decisions involving the strategic allocation of resources, cost–benefit calculations, capital budgeting, sensitivity analysis, and scenario analysis.‡

* Olson and Wu, *Enterprise Risk Management*.

† Gray and Larson, *Project Management*.

‡ Blank and Tarquin, *Engineering Economy*.

2.17 Neural Networks

The use of neural network artificial intelligence software embellishes decisions because of its mimicking of human cognition. Murray indicates that "people learn through rearrangements in the connections between their brain cells (neurons), and this type of software tries to imitate the way the human brain works" through methods of "trial and error to refine its predictions and is claimed to be superior in accuracy to statistical techniques such as linear regression."* Further, Murphy indicates that the use of such tools "have produced a better forecast of U.S. Treasury bill rates one year ahead than either the futures market or leading economists."† From the perspective of intelligence analysis, Hall and Citrenbaum indicate that the use of neural networks may improve an understanding of enemy networks and the characteristics of their functions.‡

Specifically, Hall and Citrenbaum indicate that enemy insurgents "hide by blending in with the population and its everyday movement and activity." Despite such complexities, Hall and Citrenbaum state that specifications of enemy attributes may be determined, and that such enemy entities may be "dealt with."§ Although the use of neural networks occurs through the use of software, humans render the ultimate decisions. The use of software does not replace the human capacity of rendering decisions but provides a tool through which human decisions may be strengthened (Figure 2.6).

2.18 Scenario and Sensitivity Analysis

Quantitative tools also contribute toward the strengthening of human decisions among intelligence functions. Among these tools are the methods of scenario and sensitivity analysis. According to Dess, Lumpkin, and Eisner, scenario analysis is an "in-depth approach to environmental forecasting that involves experts' detailed assessments of societal trends, economics, politics, technology, or other dimensions of the external environment."¶ According to Blank and Tarquin, sensitivity analysis involves a determination of how decisions "might change based on varying estimates, especially those that may vary widely."** Through the use of these methods, intelligence analysts may speculate potential outcomes regarding changes in variables in the

* Murray, *Protecting Critical Information and Technology.*
† Murphy, *Competitive Intelligence.*
‡ Hall and Citrenbaum, *Intelligence Analysis.*
§ Ibid.
¶ Dess, Lumpkin, and Eisner, *Strategic Management.*
** Blank and Tarquin, *Engineering Economy.*

Figure 2.6 Simulation of defending against cyberattacks. Seniors Tera Corbari (left) and Steven Smiley check over a computer network in Thayer Hall with Colonel Jeff Girard (standing) during the Cyber Defense Exercise. U.S. Military Academy cadets studying computer science participated in the exercise to test their computer skills against the National Security Agency, which tried to hack in and disable the network. (Courtesy of the U.S. Army, http://www.army.mil/media/60907.)

problem domains, and consider potential impact when crafting strategies that impact operations and policies.

One may consider the applications of these tools within the context simulations that influence decisions among intelligence functions. Within this context, Murphy indicates that the use of war games is an appropriate application of such methods. With respect to the human rendering of decisions, Murphy states that "military planners try to improve their understanding of what will happen in actual campaigns (and hone commanders' skills in responding to changing circumstances)."[*]

[*] Murphy, *Competitive Intelligence.*

2.19 Integrative Perspective

The aforementioned qualitative and quantitative tools are not the only methods that serve to counter impediments regarding the rendering of human decisions. However, they do not replace the human element of rendering of decisions, but they contribute toward the strengthening of human decisions. Other methods include forecasting models (e.g., regression), competitive analysis (e.g., strengths, weaknesses, opportunities, threats, etc.), metrics analysis of performance (e.g., efficiency and effectiveness), trade-offs and compromises; and a myriad of other tools.*

Regardless of the methods or tools used to facilitate the strengthening of human decisions, one element remains constant: the human. Humans are imperfect, and, despite the use of tools to counter the effects of decision impediments, humans remain susceptible to influences that impact their rendering of decisions. Hall and Citrenbaum, despite the use of such tools, warn that impediments persist within the context of rendering decisions. Humans may lack expertise and skills regarding all of the facets of the decision domain; each human has limitations regarding the uniqueness of cognitive capacity; various effects of dissonance may occur; the effects of preconceptions and misconceptions may occur; and defects may exist within perceptions and understandings of the attributes of the decision domain.†

Based on the cumulative, aforementioned discussions concerning the countering of impediments, with respect to Heuer's notions regarding the necessity of maintaining the visibility of "assumptions and reasoning" and his notions regarding "significant biases" of impediments, it is the conclusion of this author that biases and impediments shall always exist regarding the rendering of human decisions.‡ The processes, procedures, and tools that facilitate the rendering of human decisions and contribute toward the diminishing of impediments may enhance efficiency, enhance effectiveness, enhance validity, and strengthen of the act of deciding, but humans shall always be susceptible to some form of influence or weakness within the context of rendering decisions. Therefore, with respect to the rendering of human decisions within a financial domain, it is imperative that humans remain vigilant to strive toward objectivity while being mindful of the observations of Heuer§ about human fallibilities and the impediments of the decision environment. Although financial decisions are subject to the imperfections

* Dess, Lumpkin, and Eisner, *Strategic Management*; Blank and Tarquin, *Engineering Economy*; Henry, *Compstat Paradigm*; Gray and Larson, *Project Management*.

† Hall and Citrenbaum, *Intelligence Analysis*.

‡ Heuer, *Psychology of Intelligence Analysis*.

§ Ibid.

of humans, one must be mindful of human imperfections that may bias or influence the rendering of decisions.

2.20 Chapter Comments and Summary

This chapter introduces the concept of rendering decisions. The rendering of decisions may have long-term, strategic ramifications and consequences among law enforcement and criminal justice entities. This perspective of decisions is manifested among a variety of environments ranging from the erection of prison facilities and police stations to deciding which vendor is awarded a contract to supply food services among corrections settings. Therefore, the financial characteristics of such decisions and periods of time are strategic in nature.

Decisions are rendered by humans. Although humans may use a variety of tools to facilitate their decisions, the ultimate rendering of decisions is performed by humans. Therefore, humans must be vigilant to understand the characteristics of the considered problem domain. Humans must also recognize and acknowledge the potential ramifications and consequences of their decisions. Further, the leaders and managers of law enforcement and criminal justice organizations must render decisions that provide long-term, strategic benefits for both the organization and society.

Given these notions, the financial decisions of law enforcement and criminal justice organizations are serious, and their significance must not be understated. However, despite the importance of such decisions and the best efforts of humans to render the best possible decisions within a problem domain, a variety of impediments exist that impact the rendering of human decisions.

This chapter considered impediments that impact group and individual decisions (e.g., groupthink, satisficing, bounded rationality). These impediments may originate via the limitations of human cognition, or they may be manifested as components of the problem domain itself. Although impediments may impact the rendering of human decisions, there are methods through which impediments may be countered. The countering of such impediments involves a variety of factors (e.g., group dynamics, Delphi technique).

In this chapter are examples of decisions that tainted the reputation and perceptions of law enforcement and the criminal justice system. A primary example was the Philadelphia incendiary bombing during 1985. Although an examination of such events may demonstrate impediments of human decisions, their deeper connotations are indicative of long-term diminishments of perceptions of law enforcement and the criminal justice system. Given these historical accounts of tarnished decisions, one lesson is prevalent: when rendering decisions, personnel must learn from historical errors, avoid previous mistakes, and attempt to avoid future pitfalls.

2.21 Terminology

Artificial intelligence
Bias
Bounded rationality
Brainstorming
Cardinality
Cognitive bias
Cognitive model
Consensus techniques
Decision
Decision capacity
Decision risk
Decision style
Delphi method
Group dynamics
Groupthink
Impediments
Improvements
Intelligence
Intelligence analyst
Intelligence function
Limitations
Mental model
Neural network
Nominal group technique
Objectivity
Politics
Risk
Satisficing
Scenario analysis
Sensitivity analysis
Simulation analysis
Strawman map
Stress
Systems approach
Value hierarchies

2.22 Thought and Discussion Questions

1. Define the terms *mental model* and *cognitive model*. Once defined, identify and discuss the relationship between these two concepts. Within your response, identify a practical example of rendering decisions within the criminal justice system that involves the use of both conceptual and mental models.
2. Identify an example of a decision that was rendered within the context of criminal justice and law enforcement. Identify and discuss the characteristics of the decision domain. Within your response, identify and discuss impediments that may have affected the rendering of the decision. Further, provide a discussion of the effects of these decisions.
3. Based on the response provided to the second question, identify and discuss the methods that were used to counter the effects of impediments.

Bibliography

Blank, Leland and Anthony Tarquin. *Engineering Economy*. (6th ed.). New York, NY: McGraw-Hill Publishing, 2005.

Brecher, Michael and Frank Harvey. *Conflict, Security, Foreign Policy, and International Political Economy: Past Paths and Future Directions in International Studies*. Ann Arbor, MI: University of Michigan Press, 2005.

Daft, Richard. *Management*. (8th ed.). Mason, OH: Thomson-Southwestern Publishing, 2008.

Dess, Gregory, G.T. Lumpkin, and Alan Eisner. *Strategic Management: Text and Cases*. (4th ed.). New York, NY: McGraw-Hill Publishing, 2008.

Donohue, George, Andes Zellweger, Herman Rediess, and Christian Pusch. *Air Transportation Systems Engineering*. Reston, VA: American Institute of Aeronautics and Astronautics, 2001.

Elwyn, Glyn, Trisha Greenhalgh, and Fraser MacFarlane. *Groups: A Guide to Small Group Work in Healthcare, Management, Education, and Research*. Abington, UK: Radcliffe Medical Press, 2001.

Gigerenzer, Gerd. *Rationality for Mortals: How People Cope with Uncertainty*. New York, NY: Oxford University Press, 2008.

Gill, Peter. "Theories of Intelligence: Where are We, Where Should We Go, and How Might We Proceed?" In *Intelligence Theory: Key Questions and Debates*, edited by Gill, P., Marrin, S., and Phythian, M., 208–226. New York, NY: Routledge, 2009.

Gordon, Judith. *Organizational Behavior: A Diagnostic Approach*. (5th ed.). Upper Saddle River, NJ: Prentice Hall Publishing, 1996.

Gray, Clifford and Erik Larson. *Project Management: The Managerial Process*. (2nd ed.). New York, NY: McGraw-Hill, 2003.

Griffin, Ricky and Gregory Moorhead. *Organizational Behavior: Managing People and Organizations*. (9th ed.). Mason, OH: Thomson-Southwestern, 2010.

Hall, Wayne and Gary Citrenbaum. *Intelligence Analysis: How to Think in Complex Environments*. Santa Barbara, CA: ABC-CLIO, 2010.

Henry, Vincent. *The Compstat Paradigm: Management and Accountability in Policing, Business, and the Public Sector.* Flushing, NY: Looseleaf Law Publications, 2003.

Heuer, R. *Psychology of Intelligence Analysis*. Center for the Study of Intelligence: Central Intelligence Agency, 1999. Accessed June 23, 2010: https://www.cia.gov/library/center-for-the-study-of-intelligence/csi-publications/books-and-monographs/psychology-of-intelligence-analysis/PsychofIntelNew.pdf.

Jordaan, Ian. *Decisions under Uncertainty: Probabilistic Analysis for Engineering Decision*. Cambridge, UK: University of Cambridge Press, 2005.

Lidwell, William, Kritina Holden, and Jill Butler. *Universal Principles of Design*. Boston, MA: Rockport, 2010.

Merriam-Webster Online Dictionary. "Objectivity." Accessed June 28, 2010: http://www.merriam-webster.com/dictionary/objectivity.

Moore, Martha. "1985 Bombing in Philadelphia Still Unsettled." *USA Today*, May 11, 2005. Accessed July 30, 2010: http://www.usatoday.com/news/nation/2005-05-11-philadelphia-bombing_x.htm.

Mullen, John and Byron Roth. *Decision Making: Its Logic and Practice*. Savage, MD: Rowan and Littlefield, 1991.

Murphy, Christopher. *Competitive Intelligence: Gathering, Analysing and Putting It to Work*. Burlington, VT: Gower, 2005.

Murray, Thomas. *Protecting Critical Information and Technology: Fourth National Operations Security Conference*. McClean, VA: DIANE Publishing, 1993.

National Transportation Safety Board. "Aircraft Accident Report: Runway Overrun during Landing, American Airlines Flight 1420, McDonnell Douglas MD-82, N215AA, Little Rock, Arkansas, June 1, 1999." 2001. Accessed June 25, 2010: http://www.ntsb.gov/publictn/2001/AAR0102.pdf.

Olson, David and Desheng Wu. *Enterprise Risk Management*. Danvers, MA: World Scientific, 2008.

One Year. "One Year Later, Heaven's Gate Suicide Leaves Only Faint Trail." CNN, March 25, 1998. Accessed July 30, 2010: http://www.cnn.com/US/9803/25/heavens.gate/.

Sims, Ronald. *Ethics and Corporate Social Responsibility: Why Giants Fall*. Westport, CT: Praeger, 2003.

Sims, Ronald. *Ethics and Organizational Decision Making: A Call for Renewal*. Westport, CT: Quorum Books, 1994.

Stahl, Gerry. "Groups, Group Cognition, and Groupware." In *Groupware: Design, Implementation, and Use* edited by Fuks, H., Lukosch, S., and Salgado, A., 1–16. New York, NY: Springer, 2005.

Taudes, Alfred. *Adaptive Information Systems and Modeling in Economics and Management Science*. Morlenbach, Germany: Springer, 2005.

Treverton, Gregory. "Addressing Complexities in Homeland Security." In *The Oxford Handbook of National Security Intelligence* edited by Johnson, L., 343–358. New York, NY: Oxford University Press, 2010.

Tyson, Trevor. *Working with Groups*. (2nd ed.). South Yara, Australia: MacMillan, 1998.

Waltz, Edward. *Knowledge Management in the Intelligence Enterprise*. Norwood, MA: Artech House, 2003.

3 Financial Management Decisions

If I decide to be indecisive, that's my decision.*

Roger McGough

3.1 Objectives

The objectives of this chapter are to:

- Understand the concept of rendering financial decisions
- Understand the consequences of financial decisions
- Understand the concept of strategic decisions
- Understand the concept of capital budgeting
- Understand the concept of making capital budgeting decisions

3.2 Introduction

The concept of financial management invokes a variety of mental images. Such imagery may involve considerations of retirement planning, the management of a financial portfolio of investment funds, the monthly balancing of a checkbook, or the disbursing of funds for a myriad of purposes. Other mental imagery may include thoughts of mortgage and rental payments, vehicle loan payments, insurance payments, or credit card payments. Some folks may imagine the frustrations and joys of planning both professional and personal budgets monthly or quarterly. Although these concepts are indicative of money management, one must question their significance regarding the notion of rendering long-term financial management decisions.

The initial considerations are commensurate with strategic aspects of financial management. Retirement planning and managing investment portfolios involve the rendering of financial decisions that incorporate significantly large periods of time. Based on the discussions of the preceding chapters, these considerations are strategic because they encompass periods

* McGough, Roger, "Decision Quotes," Brainy Quote, http://www.brainyquote.com/quotes/keywords/decision_14.html (accessed July 11, 2011).

of greater than five years. With respect to retirement planning, such periods may even span forty (or more) years.

There are other decisions that span similar periods. Such strategic endeavors include the constructing and maintaining of highways and roadways, the development and implementation of communications infrastructures (e.g., telephone lines), the development and implementation of electrical power grids, and the erection and maintenance of buildings. Certainly, other examples may be identified. Each of these entities requires the rendering of human decisions that impacts the development, implementation, and maintenance of constructs that may survive for many generations. However, each of these constructs also requires financing with respect to varying, strategic periods of time.

Within the context of the criminal justice system, affiliated organizations, and other affected entities, similar interests of strategic decisions requiring financial contemplations may be identified. Such strategic elements consist of the erection and maintenance of prison facilities and police stations; the development and nurturing of community-oriented policing programs; and the development, integration, and use of regional information sharing networks and infrastructures. Again, each of these entities requires the rendering of human decisions that impacts the development, implementation, and maintenance of constructs that may survive for many generations. Again, each of these constructs also requires financing with respect to varying, strategic periods of time.

Such financing is the result of human decisions, and these decisions may be indicative of the selecting of a specific option from an array of possible courses of actions. Organizations may have insufficient funds to pursue all of their potential courses of actions and must find some projects to be preferable, whereas other projects may be discarded. This notion is commensurate with the three primary economic subquestions that were introduced within the first chapter. The act of selecting involves considerations of the service or product to produce, the quantity in which production should occur, and the identification of the serviced market and its characteristics. Therefore, given these concepts, the financing of such decisions represents a long-term commitment to satisfy the needs and wants of humans with respect to the scarcity and availability of resources through time.

Because of this commitment, the considered periods of time, and its allocation of necessary resources, the rendering of strategic financial decisions is a serious action that implies a variety of ramifications. Managers and leaders must ensure that their discretion and judgment are facilitated through considerations of the best possible knowledge of the decision domain. Decisions must be rendered, as robustly as possible, with respect to any existing constraints of the problem domain. Decisions must also be rendered with respect the long-term benefit of the organization, its stakeholders, and society. These

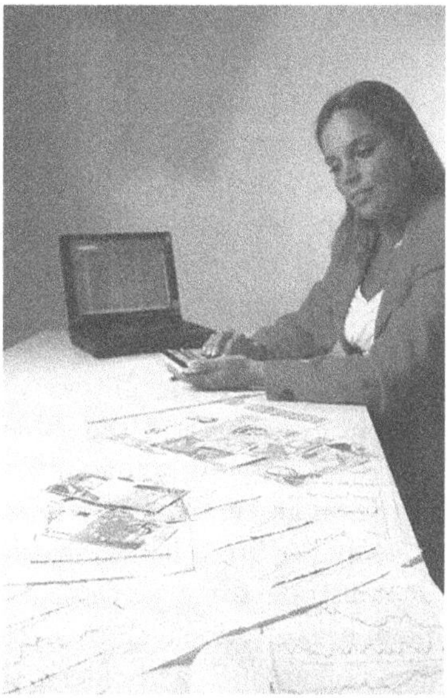

Figure 3.1 Financial decisions involve a fiduciary obligation and responsibility to render decisions that are in the best interests of the law enforcement organization, its stakeholders, and society. (Courtesy of the U.S. Department of Labor, Bureau of Transportation Statistics, http://www.stats.bls.gov/oco/ocos301.htm.)

decisions and relationships are manifested among a variety of organizational environments. Therefore, leaders and managers have a fiduciary obligation to render decisions that are representative of the best interests of their stakeholders and society (Figure 3.1).

3.3 The Attributes of Financial Relationships

This fiduciary obligation is intangibly expressed through the crafting and nurturing of relationships. When considered from the for-profit perspective, these relationships exist primarily between the leaders of an organization and the shareholders of the organization (if any). However, when considering the additional characteristics of nonprofit firms, these relationships also extend to the stakeholders of the firm. Although this cursory description services a notion of the principal–agency relationship, one must consider the roles and attributes of these entities to gain a deeper understanding of the nature of such relationships.

The leaders of the organization are responsible for rendering decisions that are in the best interests of the organization, its shareholders, and its stakeholders. Such decisions are strategic and impact the obligations of the long-term financing obligations and investments of the organization through time. The individuals who render such decisions may hold positions as chief executive officer, chief financial officer, chief operations officer, and a variety of other executive positions. From the perspective of traditional economic and financial thought, such individuals are responsible for rendering decisions that contribute toward the maximization of the wealth of equity shareholders.

Shareholders and stakeholders are not synonymous terms. Although similar, these terms denote two separate notions in the relationship between an organization and the recipients of its service. Shareholders are representative of the individuals that invest their money in the firm, with the hopes of future financial benefits and returns, in exchange for some percentage of equity ownership in the organization. Such ownership may include voting rights with respect to influencing the decisions and leadership of the organization.

The concept of stakeholders differs from that of shareholders. The notion of a stakeholder is indicative of any entity that has a vested interest in the long-term, strategic success of the firm. Obviously, shareholders are stakeholders because they demonstrate some percentage of equity ownership through their purchasing of organizational stock(s). However, not all of the stakeholders of an organization are its shareholders. The concept of a stakeholder involves the acknowledging of any entity that has a vested interest in the overall successfulness of the organization. Basically, in order for a stakeholder to have some level of success among its separate operations, the successfulness of the primary organization must be apparent and realized through time.

Stakeholders of a firm may exist among a variety of entities. From an individual perspective, one may consider the personnel who perform a variety of tasks within a for-profit youth program or a for-profit correctional facility. Although these individuals may not own the stock of the organization that employs them, they are employed by the organization itself. They are stakeholders because they are employed by the organization. Periodically, they receive a paycheck from their employer and may use such funds to satisfy the requirements of their individual costs of living. In order to continue their lifestyles financially, they depend upon the continued financial success of their employer as a solvent organization. In turn, these personnel may contribute to their local economies through the purchasing of a variety of goods and services (e.g., groceries, automobiles, utilities). This relationship is indicative of a stakeholder relationship between a primary firm and its personnel.

This notion of economic participation also highlights another perspective of stakeholder entities. A variety of subcontractors and vendors of service may supply needed resources within the environments of the primary organization. Such services may be manifested through subcontracted medical services, janitorial and cleaning services, laundry services, food services, accounting and financial consultancies, and a myriad of other venues. For small businesses, such contracts may represent the bulk of their clientele. Therefore, they have a strong, vested interest in the successfulness of the primary organization as a means of ensuring their own successfulness through time. This condition is indicative of a stakeholder relationship between organizations.

These relationships show two primary categories of the stakeholder relationship. The first category is manifested between a primary organization and its personnel. This relationship exists regarding both the full-time hires and the contractual personnel of a primary organization. The second category is representative of the stakeholder relationships between organizations whose facets of successfulness are integrated.

Within the primary firm, the decisions rendered affect a variety of entities. These entities may be the personnel of the organization, its providers of services, the members of its served market, or any other entity that is dependent upon its overall successfulness through time. These decisions also impact the shareholders—the owners—of the organization. Therefore, the rendering of financial decisions must not be lightly considered and must be weighed heavily regarding any potential consequences and ramifications through time.

The rendering of such decisions involves a fiduciary obligation to identify and pursue courses of actions for the purposes of providing the highest and best benefits through time. Although such notions are indicative of a perfect scenario, the potential of imperfection exists within the domains of such decisions. Certainly, the discussions of Chapter 2 are pertinent regarding the impediments of rendering human decisions. However, an additional consideration must be acknowledged: the potential of humans to yield to temptation.

Although the fiduciary obligation exists to render decisions that are in the best interests of the organization, its shareholders, or its stakeholders, humans may render decisions that serve their own interests while sacrificing these fiduciary obligations. When this situation occurs, various instances of white-collar crime, financial fraud, embezzlement, blackmail, and a host of others crimes may be manifested. The damages among entity relationships, personal relationships, and reputations may be irreparable. As a result, the members of any served markets may be wary of pursuing good-faith investments that would normally provide benefit for the organization financially. Notable examples include the failures of both WorldCom and Enron. During the time of this writing, allegations of misconduct were voiced against Representative Charles Rangel. Each of these scenarios is indicative of violations of the sanctity of the trust between leaders and their served public and private entities.

The Enron example shows significant criminal activity through which the personnel of the corporation, its stakeholders, and the public were defrauded. Figure 3.2 depicts the workings of the Enron fraud. Within the first relationship of the transaction, in exchange for an upfront cash payment, Enron agreed to pay Delta Energy Corporation a financial amount

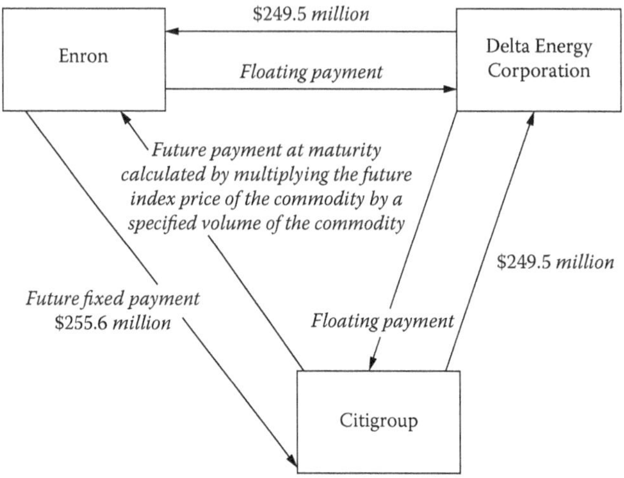

Figure 3.2 The Enron fraud represented a three-point mechanism through which financial maliciousness occurred. Not only did the fraud impact the corporation, but it also affected the energy sector. It also impacted the good faith of market investors regarding potential investments in energy corporations. (Courtesy of the U.S. Securities and Exchange Commission, http://www.sec.gov/litigation/admin/34-48230.htm.)

that was to be determined by multiplying the future index price of the referenced commodity by the contract volume. The amount of the future payment between Enron and Delta varied with respect to fluctuations regarding the future index price (i.e., "spot price"). Under the terms of the agreement, if the spot price fell below a certain level, Delta Energy Corporation would be entitled to less than its $249.5 million upfront payment. This price risk was eliminated via another concurrent transaction.

The second relationship, regarding the processing of the prepay transaction, occurred in which Citigroup funded the Delta Energy Corporation payment to Enron. Citigroup made a $249.5 million upfront payment to Delta on June 28, 2001. This date represented the same day that Delta made its $249.5 million upfront payment to Enron. The commodity price risk regarding Delta Energy Corporation was passed to Citigroup via a methodology in which the future floating payment from Enron to Delta exactly mirrored the future floating payment from Delta to Citigroup. Simply, the same amounts and payment schedule existed among the transactions.

The third relationship, between Enron and Citigroup, involved Enron paying Citigroup an amount of $255.6 million six months after June 28, 2001. Citigroup then passed the commodity price risk back to Enron. This transaction completed the instantiation of the fraudulent financial cycle. The former chief executive officer of Enron, Jeffrey Skilling, received a prison sentence because of this fraudulent scheme. He was convicted of fraud, insider trading, and conspiracy crimes.

In Mississippi, a significant example involves a consideration of the Lumberton Police Department. According to GulfCoastNews.com, during the years following Hurricane Katrina, Maurice Hammond, the former Lumberton chief of police, was sentenced to thirty months of incarceration that were to be succeeded by three "years of supervised release after his prison term," and was mandated to repay "$29,438, which included the cost to set up and maintain the FEMA travel trailer he wrongfully received." This punitive measure resulted because he provided "false claims to FEMA, false statements to FEMA and the Small Business Administration," and committed "wire fraud in applying for and receiving Hurricane Katrina disaster assistance funds." This situation demonstrated Hammond's violation of "the trust of both the public he was to serve and the law enforcement community."* Further, these events, situations, and punitive outcomes represent a solid example of the principal–agency conundrum.

Such situations represent a conundrum regarding decisions that involve the sanctity of these trustful relationships, which must be present to facilitate organizational successfulness through time. This situation occurs because of humans yielding to their own temptations, and sacrificing the greater good of the organization, its shareholders, and its stakeholders for their personal gain through time. Therefore, some controls must be present to diminish the risks and potentials of such situations occurring.

Three control mechanisms may be deployed to facilitate proper conduct among organizational leaders. These controls involve the use of reward systems, punitive measures, and debt tasking. Although these controls may diminish the risks of misconduct, they do not guarantee and ensure that misconduct shall not occur among the various factions of organizational leadership. Humans are imperfect, and they are susceptible to the temptations of servicing their selfish desires. However, control mechanisms may influence the behavior of humans to facilitate their compliance with their obligations and responsibilities as organizational leaders.

The use of reward systems provides a motivational aspect through which the performance of humans may be influenced. Personnel may be rewarded for rendering decisions that are in the best interests of the organization, its shareholders, and its stakeholders. Examples of such rewards may be annual or periodic payment bonuses, contractually specified percentages of profits, professional promotions, and the earning of additional vacation time and other leave time. It is anticipated that such reward mechanisms may offset the desire to use organizational funds illegally, unethically, and immorally.

* GulfCoastNews.com, "Ex-Lumberton Police Chief."

The use of punitive measures provides a motivational aspect through which the performance of humans may be influenced. Personnel may be penalized for rendering decisions that are not in the best interests of the organization, its shareholders, and its stakeholders. Examples of such punitive measures include termination of employment, loss of benefits, reprimands, lawsuits, and possible incarceration. Further, personnel may realize that criminal records may significantly decrease their future employability and realize the disadvantages that are associated with tarnished reputations (both professionally and personally). It is anticipated that such punitive mechanisms, and the fearfulness of their consequences, may offset the desire to use organizational funds illegally, unethically, and immorally.

The use of debt tasking may also influence the behavior of humans. The concept of this control mechanism is simple: to diminish the amount of available cash flows that could be used to service the personal desires of human leaders within the organization. For example, an organization may assume a greater amount of debt, over time, through the purchasing or leasing of vehicles, the erecting of buildings, or the retaining of service providers, and so forth, thereby necessitating periodic payments of money in exchange for such goods and services. Therefore, any available payment funds are tasked with specific purposes of servicing such debts, and cannot be used for any other purposes. Hence, the quantities of available cash resources are reduced, thereby diminishing the capacity of organizational funds being misused.

The preceding discussions demonstrate the basic characteristics of financial relationships that pervade organizations. Organizational decisions have the potential of influencing these relationships either positively or negatively. Regardless, any rendered decisions must be commensurate with the best interests of the organization, its shareholders, and its stakeholders. Although impediments exist that affect the rendering of human decisions, many flawed decisions are the result of humans yielding to the temptations of serving their own interests while sacrificing the best interests of the organization. Therefore, financial relationships must also integrate some control mechanisms to influence the rendering of decisions, thereby improving the potential of pursuing courses of actions that benefit the organization strategically.

Now that a basic consideration of financial relationships and decisions is manifested, it is obvious that such relationships are pervaded by strategic decisions of a financial context. However, before one may contemplate a financial decision regarding the use of financial resources, these financial resources must either currently exist in the organization or be readily obtainable. Therefore, considerations of the methods of financing organizations are salient concepts that preclude the rendering of financial decisions strategically.

3.4 Methods of Financing Organizations

Before one renders any decision regarding the use of funds, it is often helpful if the funds are available. This notion necessitates the posing of a simple question: How does a firm gain its financing through time? Simply, the response to this question involves considerations of primary methods of financing organizations through time: (1) debt, (2) equity, (3) loans and credit, (4) taxation, (5) grant funds, (6) goodwill and charitable donations, (7) insurance, and (8) confiscation of funds. Each of these methods is an appropriate method of obtaining the financial monies that are necessary for pursuing capital investment projects strategically.

3.4.1 Bond Debt

The use of debt is a method through which organizations may obtain funding. Although an initial consideration of debt invokes thoughts and understandings of the financial obligations of an organization, this perception of the debt concept is not commensurate within the context of financing organizations via the use of debt. Financing an organization via the use of debt involves a consideration of bonds. Bonds are an instrument of investment through which the members of a market purchase the debt of the organization.

Conceptually, the members of a serviced market provide their money to an organization in return for the promise of the organization to provide both future compensations of the principal value loaned and an interest payment for the use of their funds. The organization becomes indebted to the providers of such financial resources. In essence, the members of the serviced market loan their monies to the organization. This construct is manifested through the use of the bond financial instrument. From a financial perspective, the stakeholders of an organization include the holders of the debt of the organization.

In this instance, the holders of bonds, or bondholders, are stakeholders. The success of the firm, in due time, is paramount to its ability to compensate the bondholders who provide financial resources to facilitate the financing of the organization. Although members of a serviced market may provide such financial resources, the bond investment is not indicative of equity ownership regarding the organization.

As a method of financing capital projects, bonds may be issued among a variety of organizations. During 2007, the citizenry of Waco, Texas, accepted and approved a combination bond investment instrument that totaled a value of $63 million and involved a rate of 4.615326%. The use of such funding was to purchase a medical building and to convert it into a police headquarters.

Approximate costs of this capital investment totaled $13 million.* The use of such bond instruments provided the necessary monies to pursue capital projects, including the renovation of a new police headquarters building. The use of city bonds is not uncommon because many other cities use similar methods of financial law enforcement capital projects.

However, not all facets of bond instruments are identical. Ratings are important attributes that affect bond investments and their market perceptions of quality. According to Standard & Poor's, the following ratings are appropriate for bond investments†:

AAA, AA, A—Respectively, these categories are indicative of extremely strong, very strong, and strong potentials of satisfying financial obligations. These three categories represent the highest ratings.

BBB, BB, B—These categories are indicative of some level of adequacy regarding an ability to satisfy financial obligations. These three categories represent the second highest ratings, and involve greater amounts of risk than investments that are higher rated.

CCC, CC, C—These categories are indicative of higher vulnerabilities regarding an ability to satisfy financial obligations. These three categories represent the third highest ratings, and involve greater amounts of risk than investments that are rated within the two higher categories.

D—This rating is indicative of a default status regarding an ability to satisfy financial obligations. It is the lowest category, and represents significantly higher risk than the three higher categories.

These ratings are indicative of risk and market attractiveness. Market investors may be attracted to bond offerings that have higher ratings because they may perceive that less risk is involved over the period of the investment, and that less risk is involved with realizing a future return regarding their investment. These market perceptions may diminish in conjunction with lower ratings. The lower the rating, the greater the risk that market investors may determine potential investments to be unattractive or unacceptable through time. Similarly, with higher ratings, the probability is higher that the entity that issues the bonds will have the capacity to satisfy its debt obligations through time. In contrast, lower ratings are indicative of higher risk perceptions regarding the ability of the issuing entity to fulfill and satisfy its financial obligations. Figure 3.3 shows a bond document.

* City of Waco, "Bond Election Update."

† Standard & Poor's, "Credit Ratings Definitions."

Figure 3.3 Cities often issue bonds as a debt form of financing. This image shows a bond that was issued by the City of West Seattle, Washington. (Courtesy of the City of West Seattle, Washington, http://www.seattle.gov/CityArchives/Exhibits/annexation/panel5_image9.htm.)

3.4.2 Stock Equity

Investments that are indicative of the equity ownership of an organization are manifested through the concept of stocks. The use of stocks is another method through which the financing of an organization occurs through time. Market investors exchange their monies for a percentage ownership of an organization. Again, such equity ownership may imply various voting rights, depending on the types of purchased stocks, thereby possibly influencing the rendering of organizational decisions.

Market investors provide financing via the purchasing of stock equity in the hopes of receiving future returns regarding their invested monies. However, because of market influences and market perceptions that affect the valuation of stocks through time, no guarantees exist that stock investors will receive such future benefits. Further, many stocks offer and pay dividends periodically. Further, organizations are not mandated to pay dividends to the holders of their stocks. Therefore, in exchange for the use of their funds, situations exist in which stockholders may not receive any periodic financial payments (i.e., dividends), and no guarantee exists that investors shall reap a financial gain during any future transactions involving the sales and purchases of their stock shares. Therefore, considerations of risk, over time, influence considerations of equity ownership financing.

For-profit organizations are commonly affiliated with such forms of financing. Within the context of the criminal justice system, these entities are representative of for-profit prison systems. In the United States, the Corrections Corporation of America is a leading provider of for-profit prison systems and services. The leadership and management of this organization has a fiduciary obligation to render decisions that contribute toward the wealth maximization of its shareholders, and to render decisions that are in the strategic, best interests of the organization. The strategic growth, over time, of this company is manifested through its modern instantiation of demonstrating "65 correctional and detention facilities, including 44 facilities that we own, with a total design capacity of approximately 87,000 beds in 19 states and the District of Columbia." During the year 2009, this organization manifested total revenues of $1,669,963,000 and a stockholders' equity value of $1,442,546,000.*

Given these considerations regarding its financial amounts, this organization demonstrates a strong potential, as a for-profit mechanism, through which prison services and operations occur. Because it is a for-profit entity, its stock may be openly traded. Through the use of such stock equity, the corporation gains financial funding that supports its operations, growth, and value creation through time. Figure 3.4 shows a stock certificate indicating corporate equity ownership.

3.4.3 Loans and Credit

Another method of financing organizations involves the use of loans and credit. This concept is one that pervades modern society among a variety of fashions. Individuals may pursue loans and credit for the purchasing of houses, automobiles, educational pursuits, and an array of other short-term and long-term uses. Similarly, organizations may pursue loans and credit for the purposes of furthering their long-term, strategic operational interests. The concepts of principal, interest, repayment, and fees influence these forms of organizational financing through time.

* "Corrections Corporation of America."

Figure 3.4 Historical example of a stock certificate. Stock certificates are indicative of equity ownership in a corporation. (Courtesy of the U.S. Department of Justice, http://www.justice.gov/atr/public/hearings/single_firm/docs/219389.htm.)

Within the context of law enforcement agencies, these notions are relevant. Within the United States, such methods of financing are not prevalent unless one considers the use of such items as tools to support costs such as fuel expenditures or travel. However, within the Virgin Islands, such tools may be used to fund capital improvement projects. According to Charles, during 2002 "capital improvement loans of $2 million to the V.I. Justice Department and $500,000 to the Police Department" were approved by the Public Finance Authority of the government. Such funds provided the necessary resources for "jail annex" construction and the implementation of police radio communications systems.*

The use of such methods is not necessarily a primary form of financial support among public, government law enforcement entities, given the necessities of repaying the principal amount with interest costs. However, among other entities, such as nonprofit corporations and for-profit corporations, the uses of loans and credit may be valid components of their financial structures. The presence of such debt is shown in the annual report of the Corrections Corporation of America. During 2009 the corporation demonstrated an association with Lehman Brothers Commercial Bank as a source of financial funds. The report states "Lehman had funded $2.3 million in borrowings and $1.1 million in letters of credit that remained outstanding," and that "the loan balance will be repaid on a pro-rata basis to the extent that LIBOR-based loans are repaid on tranches Lehman previously funded."†

These examples provide salient considerations of the use of credit lines and loans as tools through which funding may be obtained among both

* Charles, "Finance Authority."

† "Corrections Corporation of America."

for-profit and nonprofit settings. In both cases, the purposes of the intended uses were for the betterment of the organizations and the creation of some form of value through time. The use of financial loans and credit lines do require repayment of both the principal value and the interest value.

3.4.4 Taxation

For public organizations, financing may be accomplished through taxation revenues. Federal, state, and local tax dollars may be used to provide funding that supports the efforts of a variety of entities within the criminal justice system. Tax dollars are used to fund law enforcement organizations and penal institutions. The use of tax dollars is not an uncommon method of funding law enforcement entities and elements of the criminal justice system that are government agencies.

The use of tax dollars spawns a variety of considerations regarding the allocation of public resources. Recently, Hayes indicates that the Jersey City, New Jersey, budget contained an amount of "$95.5 million to the Police Department and $66.3 million to fire and emergency services, not including benefits or pension payments."[*] The use of such tax dollars may not be an automatic function of law enforcement entities and the criminal justice system. In some instances, referendums and voting must occur to acknowledge and approve the specific uses of such funds. Such considerations are commensurate with the tenets of public budgeting and finance.

From the perspective of policing, an examination of a small-town, city budget provides a listing of the items that are relevant applications of public tax dollars. According to the City of Tupelo, the 2010 budget components of the police department totaled $10,038,170. Specific costs included personnel costs of $7,183,907; supply costs consisted of $600,250; services costs consisted of $1,887,248; and capital expenditures consisted of $366,765.[†]

Similarly, an examination of larger, urban city budgets provides another perspective of the uses of tax dollars to support law enforcement agencies. In Memphis, Tennessee, policing expenditures adopted for the year 2011 include $207,485,130 for personnel services; an amount of $18,385,943 for materials and supplies; $83,000 for capital outlays; an amount of $2,581,200 for transfers out; and a total expenditures in the amount of $228,535,273. A program revenue amount of $2,562,456 contributes to yield a net expenditures amount of $225,972,817.[‡]

The use of taxation dollars among law enforcement entities and within the criminal justice system provides the police resources that are necessary

[*] Hayes, "City Council."
[†] City of Tupelo, "Tupelo Mississippi City Budget 2010."
[‡] City of Memphis, "Police Services."

for maintaining order and preventing crime. The use of such funds certainly is applied toward the operations of such entities, but may also be used to facilitate a variety of preventive measures including facets of community-oriented policing. This notion is corroborated by Davis et al. According to Davis et al., community-oriented policing programs "developed into a set of different federal grants that had cost American taxpayers $7.5 billion by the end of fiscal year (FY) 2000."*

Regardless of the uses of these tax dollars among law enforcement entities and within the criminal justice system, organizational leaders must be mindful that such funds are derived from the served populace. This notion pertains to any publically support law enforcement entity that incorporates the use of tax dollars within its budget regardless of the size of the organization. Therefore, any capital budgeting project initiatives must be in the best interests of the served citizenry, the served community and society, and the best interests of the organization.

3.4.5 Grant Funding

Government and nonprofit organizations may obtain funding through avenues of grant opportunities. The use of such methods provides revenues that may support prisoner rehabilitation programs, educational outreach programs among inmates, or maybe elements of community-oriented policing paradigms. The origins of grant funding and charitable donations are manifested among entities that comprise both the public and private sectors.

Considerations of grant funding may be examined from the perspective of community-oriented policing initiatives. According to the U.S. Department of Justice (DOJ), regarding its fiscal year 2010 budget request, a variety of grant funds were specified to provide needed financial monies to support policing initiatives. According to the DOJ, such grant funding enables "state and local police agencies to increase the number of officers available for targeted patrols and other strategies designed to prevent and reduce crime during the economic downturn."† (See Figure 3.5.)

In this budget request, appropriations are specified for a variety of purposes. An amount of $336 million exists for new capital project investments that include hiring grants, community policing development and training programs, salaries and expenses, and integrity uses that improve community perceptions of law enforcement agencies. The request also includes specifications of monies for the programs of the Office of Justice. These programs include an amount of $160.8 million for recidivism reduction (i.e., Second Chance Act), $15 million for the National Crime Victimization Survey,

* Davis et al., "Facts about COPS."

† U.S. Department of Justice, "FY 2010 Budget Request."

Figure 3.5 Awarding of Grant Monies. USDA Rural Development State Director Clyde Holloway presents $50,000 Rural Business Opportunity Grant to Pointe Coupee Parish Police Jury to develop a community master plan for unincorporated areas. The ceremonial check is accepted by Melanie Bueche, president of the Pointe Coupee Parish Police Jury. (U.S. Department of Agriculture, http://www.rurdev.usda.gov/la/photo%20gallery/pointecoupeeparishpolicejurymasterplan10-2007.htm.)

$10 million for improvements in forensics (i.e., Coverdell Grants), $20 million for substance abuse programs, $9 million toward social facets of the court system regarding mental health issues of offenders, $25 million for community-based violence prevention initiatives, $6.8 million for salaries and expenses, and $65 million regarding the Crime Victims Fund. Other funding elements include $13.8 million within the federal prison system.* These examples are demonstrative of the grant funding that is available to supplement and assist law enforcement entities and components of the criminal justice system.

A variety of other funding specifications may be considered from the perspectives of such grant monies. Through the use of such funds, law enforcement agencies gain the ability to recruit, train, and retain personnel; provide specialized training courses (e.g., SWAT, bomb tech); gain better integration among a variety of communities; and demonstrate strength of force regarding preventive measures that potentially diminish criminal activities.

An applied use of such grant funding is manifested through the activities of the Durham County, North Carolina, Sheriff's Department. According to the department, the use of grant funding was implemented to attend

* U.S. Department of Justice, "FY 2010 Budget Request."

"community meetings," disseminate "surveys to citizens asking about their concerns," the completion of "fingerprinting and photographing of children at Northgate Mall and churches with the KIDCARE ID kits," participation during "surveillance operations where citizens had complained of drug activity in their community and in areas where burglaries had been taking place." These initiatives were generated through the use of a "Community Oriented Policing" grant.*

These examples of grant funding and its uses are demonstrative of the use of taxpayer dollars to supporting grant opportunities via government entities. However, other sponsors and sources of grant funding opportunities are not indicative of government entities. The National Rural Law Enforcement Association (NRLEA) is an example of such an entity. The NRLEA supports law enforcement agencies, especially those that exist within rural settings, with respect to a variety of administrative and funding tasks.

According to the NRLEA, its funding opportunities include a collaborative approach to implementing a "full reporting system for citizens to file non-emergency non-suspect police reports online 24/7/365," and additional functionality includes "a warrants system, missing persons, most wanted, crime finders and much more including a city alert system which can also be used for many other areas of need." This initiative demonstrates a collaborative partnership because "NRLEA will supply $3225.00 leaving a cost to any agency at $275.00 per year" regarding the overall $3500 cost of the system.†

Regardless of whether grant funding is obtained from government or private sources, its use may be critical among smaller law enforcement entities. Through the use of grant funding, law enforcement agencies gain the resources necessary to purchase operational items (e.g., vests) and to provide training courses (e.g., police academies, continuing education). However, as with all financial management decisions, any decisions regarding the use of grant monies must be in the best interests of the served citizenry, the served community and society, and the best interests of the organization.

3.4.6 Goodwill and Charitable Funds

Similar to grant funding, many activities within the criminal justice system may be the benefactors of goodwill and charitable donations. The uses of such funds may provide both tangible and intangible benefits. Within the context of prison ministry, such organizations include the Good News Jail and Prison Ministry (GNJPM). This nonprofit organization provides ministerial services and chaplains among incarcerated offenders both domestically and internationally.

* Durham County Government, "Sheriff's Community-Oriented Policing Effort."
† National Rural Law Enforcement Association, "Grants-Funds."

According to the GNJPM, its mission is "to provide spiritually mature, equipped, and motivated Christian chaplains to serve in correctional facilities nationally and internationally," and its purpose is "to meet the spiritual needs of both inmates and staff through ministry that includes evangelism, discipleship, and pastoral attention, while facilitating other religious faiths within the guidelines established by law and the individual correctional facility."[*]

The programs of the GNJPM provide a Christian, spiritual worldview approach to "teach inmates how their world and life view relates to every area of life," and emphasizes the necessities of spiritual acknowledgement among all facets of life. These programs also include biblical correspondence courses that may be completed by inmates.[†] However, the implementing and maintaining of such programs requires the use of financial funding through time. Also, further growth of this outreach ministry also requires funding through time.

The characteristics of goodwill and charity are salient considerations regarding the activities of such nonprofit ministries among prison settings. Such funds may originate among a variety of external sources including both individuals and organizations. According to the Evangelical Council for Financial Accountability (ECFA), recent financial revenues of the GNJPM consisted of various cash donations totaling $12,586,103. These financial funds are representative of "gifts made by cash, check, or credit card," and include "gifts of marketable securities, net revenue from special events, private foundation grant revenue and pledges receivable." Excluded are funds involving "government grants, gifts of privately-held securities or noncash (for example, real estate, clothing and furniture) gifts."[‡]

Prison ministries are not the only considerations of goodwill and charity funding. Various, other programs, initiatives, and organizations exist among law enforcement communities and environments that benefit from the uses of such funding. The Lakewood Police Independent Guild (LPIG), in the state of Washington, provides a charity fund in which the beneficiaries are the family members of officers who died during the performance of their duties. A total of nine orphaned children are specifically served through this charity fund. According to Wurts, "because of the generosity of the Lakewood community and beyond, on February 2, 2010, the LPIG Charitable Fund deposited $2,129,968.42 into the Lakewood Fallen Four Officers Children's Trust Fund." Further, because of the magnitude of volunteerism, "99.8% of all donations went directly into the

[*] Good News Jail and Prison Ministry, "Fifty Years Providing Chaplains."

[†] Ibid.

[‡] Evangelical Council for Financial Accountability, "Good News Jail & Prison Ministry."

Rhode Island Military Family Relief Fund

The Rhode Island Military Family Relief Fund was established to provide emergency financial assistance to Rhode Island Reserve Component members and/or their families impacted by mobilization and deployment if they have suffered a casualty or have an emergency financial need as a result of being deployed/mobilized for 30 or more days in support of the Global War on Terrorism (GWOT), a contingency operation or in support of Homeland Security. Applications must be received within one year of returning from deployment for need-based grants.

Funds are received via individual or corporate donations. Other sources are through tax donations from Rhode Island tax returns in accordance with RI General Laws section 44-30-2.9. All funds received by the Rhode Island Military Family Relief Fund go directly to helping Reserve Component Members and/or their families.

For more information or to apply for assistance, contact your First Sergeant, Commander, full-time staff at the unit or contact Rhode Island National Guard (RING) Family Assistance.

RING Family Assistance
1051 North Main Street
Providence, RI 02904
(401) 275-4194 or (877) 440-7994

The RI Military Relief Fund was sponsored by Lt Governor Charles Fogarty and signed by the Governor of Rhode Island on July 2, 2004 to assist Rhode Island Reserve Component members and their families in times of crisis caused by mobilization and deployment, when the situation can reasonably be expected to be remedied with a one-time grant that is either need or casualty based.

The Rhode Island Military Family Relief Fund is not a State Agency or Federal entity. The Rhode Island Military Family Relief Fund Board of Directors sets policy and has the responsibility to oversee the operation of the program and approve all grants. The Board members are comprised of the following: The Adjutant General of Rhode Island, a representative from the Lieutenant Governor's Office, the Rhode Island National Guard State Family Program Director, and the Chief Financial Officer for the Office of Adjutant General, Executive Military Staff. Other members may consist of the following representatives: the Rhode Island Air or Army National Guard, the US Army Reserve in Rhode Island, the US Air Force Reserve in Rhode Island, the US Naval Reserve in Rhode Island, the US Coast Guard Reserve in Rhode Island, and the US Marine Corps Reserve in Rhode Island.

The lead reserve component representative is the Rhode Island Army National Guard who has the responsibility to handle the day-to-day administrative requirements of the operation. Funds are administered through a separate account maintained by the Office of The Adjutant General, Executive Military Staff.

Figure 3.6 A variety of relief funding opportunities exist, including those for military personnel. (Courtesy of the Rhode Island National Guard, http://states.ng.mil/sites/RI/publicaffairs/Pages/RhodeIslandMilitaryFamilyReliefFund.aspx.)

fund."* This example highlights the importance and saliency of goodwill and charity funding and services among law enforcement communities. Through the use of such funds, law enforcement entities, and their separate auxiliaries, guilds, and support groups, are better able to serve the members of their local communities. Similarly, military police personnel and their families may also benefit from similar organizations and funds (Figure 3.6).

* Wurts, "Lakewood Police Independent Guild."

Another consideration of goodwill and charity funding is demonstrated through the auxiliary of the Oklahoma State Lodge of the Fraternal Order of Police. This organization provides scholarships to the "family members of law enforcement officers." It also provides a "$500 death benefit" that is "paid to a member's family usually within 48 hours of the member's death." However, the organization experiences an average of "25 members' deaths annually."[*] Again, similar to the Lakewood organization, this organization provides financial funding that supplements the activities of law enforcement entities.

However, it must be noted that the potential exists for fraudulent organizations to attempt to secure such funds. Warnings against such fraudulent organizations are voiced by the Federal Trade Commission (FTC). According to the FTC, it is imperative to verify the validity of any solicitation of monies with the agencies for which such monies are intended to serve. Through such verification, fraudulent solicitations and misrepresentations may be avoided.[†] Recent events concerning such aspects of fraud and misrepresentation have been highlighted among a variety of news reports.

According to Valentine, during 2010 such fraudulent activity occurred in Tampa, Florida, and involved two individuals fraudulently soliciting funds on behalf of the "Disabled Police Officers of America." Both individuals were incarcerated at the Hillsborough County Jail, and both faced charges of "organized fraud, petty theft, and two counts of unlawful use of a badge."[‡] Similarly, in Mississippi during 2008, a cease and desist order occurred against CJW, Incorporated, because its civilian representatives identified themselves as law enforcement personnel when attempting to solicit funds on the behalf of a legitimate Hinds County Fraternal Order of Police Lodge.[§]

Although the risk of fraud exists, charity and goodwill funding is a valid and worthy method of funding activities and initiatives among law enforcement and criminal justice communities. These funds serve a variety of purposes ranging from providing educational benefits to the grievous tasks associated with death benefits. However, such funds are dependent upon the benevolence and goodwill of both individual and organizations, and must be managed appropriately.

3.4.7 Insurance Policies

An additional method of financing is manifested through the purchasing and maintenance of business insurance policies. Although such policies

[*] Oklahoma Fraternal Order of the Police, "Oklahoma State Lodge."

[†] Federal Trade Commission, "Facts for Consumers."

[‡] Valentine, "Two Accused of Using Police Charity."

[§] Office of the Mississippi Secretary of State Securities and Charities Division, "Summary Cease and Desist Order."

may not immediately interject available cash funds into the organizational environment, such instruments may be necessary to provide funds during periods when the organization experiences various setbacks or conditions that would generate insurance compensations. Additional examples include payments that would occur when physical organizational infrastructure is damaged or destroyed because of natural disasters or operational accidents.

In 2010, a tornado ravaged and destroyed the Millbury, Ohio, police station and several police vehicles. The use of insurance funds provided the financial resources through which such infrastructure could be rebuilt. The estimated costs of such rebuilding efforts were approximately $1.7 million dollars.* This incident represents a situation in which the use of insurance funding may be appropriately used to provide financial resources during the period succeeding disasters and catastrophes.

Such insurance policies are also applicable regarding the potentials of legal actions against law enforcement entities. This type of incident occurred regarding a lawsuit involving the City of Santa Fe. Aulds indicates that the City of Santa Fe and its insurance providers settled a lawsuit in the amount of $125,000. According to Aulds, "procedures were not followed when one of the officers pressed a handcuff key into a pressure point beneath Robles' [the suspect's] ear." This settlement was the result of disputes regarding the conduct of both the plaintiff and the defendants during the course of an arrest. The defendants, both police officers, alleged that Robles, the plaintiff, had "attacked them, and he was charged with two counts of felony assault on a police officer." The testimony of the officers indicated that they stopped Robles because of their belief that he was "someone else for whom they had an arrest warrant." In contrast, regarding the defense of Robles, it was argued that he was grieving during the aftermath of his father's death, had missed the dosage of his medication for "schizophrenia," and did not hear the commands of the officers. When reviewed, video footage of the arrest showed that little resistance was offered by Robles during the arrest.†

The costs of such settlements of lawsuits or the loss of a lawsuit may be quite high. The use of insurance policies may provide funding through which financial monies are provided. The preceding example demonstrates the use of insurance, as a liability mechanism, through which financial compensation was supplied and rendered. However, the potential of insurance fraud also exists regarding such incidents. In some cases, municipalities may not possess insurance contracts as protective measures against any litigation that arises. Regardless, the use of insurance contracts provides preventive and protective measures involving litigation and during the impacts of natural disasters.

* *WKBN News*, "Police Station Ruined."

† Aulds, "City Settles Lawsuit."

3.4.8 Confiscation, Seizure, and Forfeiture of Assets

Often, the financing of law enforcement entities may occur through the confiscation or seizure of assets that were used during actual instances of crime. The financial amounts of such forfeited assets are staggering. According to Burnett, between 2004 and 2008 the "amount of assets seized by local law enforcement agencies across the nation enrolled in the federal program—the vast majority of it cash—has tripled, from $567 million to $1.6 billion. And that doesn't include tens of millions more the agencies got from state asset forfeiture programs." Burnett also indicates that "Texas, with its smuggling corridors to Mexico, public safety agencies seized more than $125 million" during 2007.*

Seized and confiscated financial assets are used to embellish law enforcement funding needs among federal, state, and local agencies. These forfeitures often occur in conjunction with drug interdiction law enforcement programs and operations. Guilford County Sheriff's Office, North Carolina, is a prime example of this concept. The Guilford County Sheriff's Office highlights its recent initiatives as follows:

> The Guilford County Sheriff's Office Vice and Narcotics Section reports the seizure of drugs with a street value of $12,356,283.45 during the last year (2009). The seizures were of such drugs as marijuana, cocaine, crack cocaine, methamphetamine, heroin, MDMA, Psilocybin, Oxycodone, Aderall, Percocet, Hydrocodone, Oxycontin, Methadone, Diazepam, Duragesis and Meperdine.
>
> During this same period, the Sheriff's Office Vice and Narcotics Section took cash and property from the drug dealers amounting to $628,639.04. This amount includes $421,061.04 in US Currency. Sheriff BJ Barnes states: "Taking this amount of drugs and drug money off the street makes a large impact on the drug dealers in our area. I'm very proud of the men and women of the Vice and Narcotics section. Though they are understaffed, their efforts make a difference in our Sheriff's Office and to our community.
>
> During my terms as Sheriff, through their efforts, they have confiscated $3,114,788.76 that has been turned over to the Sheriff's Office to help fight crime. This is money the taxpayer did not pay, money used to buy equipment such as computers, surveillance equipment, bulletproof vests, drug sniffing dogs, vehicles and drug education programs for our kids. These expenditures amount to $2,519,832.67 of confiscated drug money given us by the court to protect the citizens of Guilford County and we will continue to penalize the drug dealer by taking their goods and money for the benefit of our citizens.†

The Guilford County example shows the public benefit of such seized assets. They are used to procure resources that are often necessary to support

* Burnett, "Seized Drug Assets"

† Barnes, "2009 Drug Arrest."

the operational functions of law enforcement agencies and to obtain tactical resources. Through the use of such funds, strategic initiatives, such as Guilford's drug education program, may be strengthened to potentially generate long-term outcomes and influences that affect the stakeholders of the law enforcement organization.

Seized assets may be sold or auctioned to generate cash flows for law enforcement entities. With regularity, such events occur throughout the United States as methods of funding various facets of law enforcement entities. They must occur commensurately in accordance with federal, state, and local laws, directives, policies, and regulations. An example of this notion is found within the legislation of the State of Minnesota. The following excerpt of Minnesota law shows an example of such guidelines:

> The property may be sold if it is not otherwise required by law to be destroyed and is not harmful to the public; it may be kept for official use by the law enforcement and prosecuting agencies; or it may be forwarded to the federal Drug Enforcement Administration. If the forfeited property is a firearm, the law enforcement agency has the following options:
>
> - If the firearm is an antique, the agency may sell it at a public sale
> - If the firearm is an assault weapon, the agency must either destroy it or keep it for official use
> - If the firearm is neither of the foregoing, the agency may destroy the firearm, keep it for official use, or sell it to a federally licensed firearm dealer
>
> The law also provides that if the Hennepin or Ramsey county board disapproves of the sale of forfeited firearms, the local sheriff must comply with that directive. Before administratively forfeited property may be sold, a county attorney must certify that: (1) an evidence or seized property receipt was provided; (2) the seizing agency served timely notice of the intent to forfeit; and (3) probable cause for the forfeiture exists. Property may not be sold to an employee of the seizing agency or to an employee's family member. If property representing proceeds of a designated offense is sold, the proceeds must be applied first, to satisfy valid liens and forfeiture sale expenses and second, to pay court-ordered restitution. If other forfeited property is sold, the proceeds also must be used first to satisfy valid liens and forfeiture sale expenses. The remaining sale proceeds from both types of property are distributed according to the following formula:
>
> - 70 percent to the law enforcement agency
> - 20 percent to the prosecuting agency
> - 10 percent to the state general fund
>
> A special formula applies to the distribution of proceeds from the sale of vehicles forfeited for prostitution violations. In these cases, proceeds are distributed as follows:

- 40 percent to the law enforcement agency
- 20 percent to the prosecuting agency
- 40 percent to the city treasury for distribution to neighborhood crime prevention programs

A special formula also applies to the distribution of proceeds from the sale of property forfeited for trafficking of persons. In these cases, proceeds are distributed as follows:

- 40 percent to the law enforcement agency
- 20 percent to the prosecuting agency
- 40 percent to the commissioner of public safety for distribution to trafficking crime victim service organizations

Each law enforcement agency or the prosecutor must give a written record of each forfeiture incident to the state auditor. The report must be made monthly and include the amount forfeited, the statutory authority for the forfeiture, the date of the forfeiture, a brief description of the circumstances involved, and whether the forfeiture was contested. The report also must include the number, make, model, and serial number of firearms seized by the agency. For DWI and drug forfeitures, the report must indicate if it was initiated as an administrative or judicial forfeiture. Finally, the report must indicate how the property was disposed or if it was returned to the property owner. The state auditor must, in turn, report annually to the legislature on the nature and extent of forfeitures during the preceding year.*

The use of forfeited assets and funds is leveraged to provide benefit for law enforcement organizations and the societies that they serve. However, they are debatable within American society regarding constitutionality and the potential for abuse. According to Witt, examples of such alleged abuse or alleged misapplication of forfeiture involve incidents in which questions of civil rights are involved and instances involving disproportionate charges filed versus the recorded quantities of seizures and forfeitures. Such incidents may occur purposefully as aggressive uses of law to embellish the "shrinking operating budgets" of law enforcement entities.† Because of such alleged civil rights issues and alleged quantitative discrepancies, law enforcement agencies may be the subject of legal proceedings thereby necessitating increased budgetary costs to defend themselves and their personnel during court proceedings. Therefore, when using forfeited assets as a method of law enforcement funding, careful and watchful adherence to any applicable laws, regulations, and policies must occur during the processes and procedures of forfeiture.

* Pirius, "Minnesota's Forfeiture Laws."

† Witt, "Highway Robbery?"

3.5 Value-Added Concepts

The financing of firms provides the most important tool that organizations use to propagate their existence through time: cash. The flow of cash, efficiently and effectively, within an organization is the factor that instantiates its organizational survival and financial solvency through time. This notion involves the perpetuation of the growth of the firm, and capitalizing upon any opportunity that generates both tangible and intangible value for the firm. Through the use of various financing methods, value may be created for an organization through time.

Although strategic decisions impact the long-term interests of an entity, the overall performance metrics and potentials of an organization must be considered through time. Two perspectives may be manifested regarding strategic financial management decisions and the overall performance of an organization: (1) market value-added (MVA) concepts and (2) economic value-added (EVA) concepts. From the perspective of financial management contexts, Botten indicates that MVA involves an external assessment of performance, whereas EVA involves an internal assessment of performance.*

The notion of MVA provides a perspective regarding the overall economic contribution and performance of an organization through time. Mathematically, the concept of MVA is expressed through the manifestation of any differences between the market value of an organization and contributions of investor capital that facilitate the financing of the organization. Both the market value and sources of investor capital are entities that are external to the organization.

The notion of EVA also provides a perspective regarding the overall economic contribution and performance of an organization through time. However, the concept of EVA is commensurate with the manifestation of any investment surplus that occurs through time, and is judged from an assessment of the internal, financial characteristics of an organization. The basic concept of EVA "includes all factors that affect productivity." Mathematically, EVA is expressed as the subtraction of "all economic costs (land, cost of goods, compensation for shareholder capital, taxes, and information management) from profits after taxes" that yields the "true economic surplus" that may be used for investment purposes.†

From the perspective of for-profit entities, both the concepts of MVA and EVA are applicable. The leaders and managers of organizations are responsible for creating and developing organizational value through time. Therefore, any financial management decision must be inclusive of the notion of value.

* Botten, *Enterprise Strategy.*

† Strassman, *Information Productivity.*

Hence, financial management decisions must be indicative of potentially adding value, through time, for the organization and its shareholders, and such value creation must occur in conjunction with expectations of maximizing the wealth of shareholders through time.

From the perspective of nonprofit and government entities, the notions associated with the maximizing of the wealth of shareholders are immaterial because such organizations are not for-profit organizations. However, considerations of EVA are appropriate among nonprofit and government entities. Although such organizations do generate a traditional profit, they also must be managed effectively and efficiently regarding the accomplishing of their missions. The use of EVA principles may contribute toward optimized decisions, efforts, and activities fulfilling the societal obligations and missions of government agencies and nonprofit organizations, thereby inducing cash savings through time.

These concepts may be viewed from the for-profit and nonprofit aspects of the criminal justice system. For example, decisions within the criminal justice system often influence the use of prisoners as laborers among a variety of government and commercial settings. Prison labor provides an abundant labor force that may receive low wages in exchange for the provision of goods and services, through time, that may be sold among a variety of markets. The leveraging of such prisoner workers facilitates opportunities for value creation and development among law enforcement settings and within the criminal justice system.

Prison labor also provides chain-gang personnel that often perform roadway litter control and sanitation services. Regardless, these decisions invoke some aspect of value. Within the for-profit context, such value generation must be commensurate with the expectation of maximizing the wealth of shareholders through time and improving organizational value. Within the nonprofit context, such value generation must be commensurate with the expectations of efficient and effective organizational performance, societal contribution and betterment, and the accomplishing of organizational mission.

3.6 Contexts of Prisoner Labor

Within the context of the criminal justice system, the types and quantities of rendered decisions are varied. Within the context of financial management, a variety of correctional programs demonstrate the use of both public and private monies for a myriad of projects and programs. Many financial decisions that impact the criminal justice system are not without debate. Financial decisions regarding the use of prison labor generate a myriad of discussions regarding ethics, financial profits, and economic interests. Financial

Figure 3.7 Prison labor may be used to generate revenues to support the operations of prison environments. (Courtesy of the Bureau of Prisons, http://www.bop.gov/inmate_programs/unicor.jsp.)

decisions regarding the contracting of for-profit prisons and corrections systems foster a myriad of arguments demonstrating both opinions of advocacy and dissent. Prison labor can be used in state service or among for-profit environments. Noteworthy examples of both contexts have pervaded recent news reports.

Advocacy of prison labor may be considered from the perspective of financial cost savings (Figure 3.7). According to Scott, the use of Clayton County, Georgia, inmates provides resources through which county services and work tasks are accomplished. Scott indicates that prison labor provides approximately 180 prisoners per day among work details, compensates inmates at a rate of $20.00 daily, and such resources contribute toward annual county savings of about "$1.8 million a year—after housing and other costs are factored in—that it would otherwise spend on county payroll." The use of prison labor, through its affiliated pay scale, provides cost savings, and it alleviates the need to hire additional personnel. These savings are manifested because the costs of using prison labor are half as much as the costs of a regular employee when costs of medical benefits are examined.*

Dissenting opinions, regarding the use of prison labor, may be considered from the perspective of the 2010 oil spill that occurred in the Gulf of Mexico.

* Scott, "Atlanta Counties."

The use of prison labor was leveraged to participate during cleaning and restoration efforts during the aftermath of this catastrophe. Both ethical and financial considerations are salient concerns of this decision. Johnson considers the profits of BP versus the wages compensated to prisoner laborers. According to Johnson, the use of prison labor may facilitate compensation rates "as little as 10 cents an hour rather than paying locals real wages," and that tax monies may be used to pay any medical costs of prisoners that are manifested because of prisoner laborers being exposed to the toxicity of the impacted environment.[*]

The ethical dimensions of such financial decisions about the use of prisoners as laborers are debatable. Kang considers these ethical dimensions and indicates that the United States "violates its own international legal commitments both by allowing private companies to use prison labor and by allowing labor to occur within privately run prison facilities." Further, Kang indicates that this situation is demonstrative of a hypocritical dichotomy whereas U.S. foreign policy dissuades the use of such laborers versus domestic, national practices of employing prison laborers.[†]

Derrick, Scott, and Hutson consider the effects of prison labor through the use of economic modeling. During recent decades, questions concerning whether the impact of prisoner labor would offset the labor opportunities for non-prisoners abounded. With respect to this context, using an immigration model, a consideration of prisoner laborers versus non-prisoner laborers indicates that "little impact on the labor market or the overall economy" is manifested through the use of prisoner laborers.[‡] Therefore, the writings of Derrick, Scott, and Hutson suggest that concerns regarding such labor offsets are unfounded.

The financial considerations associated with compensating the costs of incarceration are also salient aspects of decisions regarding the use of prison labor. Scott and Derrick indicate that the use of prisoner laborers "provides positive cash flow from the economic activities" that contribute toward the funding of the prison environment.[§] Although such funding of the prison environment may occur, considerations of the labor impacts among local economies must also be considered. Further, Scott and Derrick observe that displacement does not occur among local labor forces via the use of prisoner laborers, because such "goods and services" generated could have been produced out-of-state or internationally.[¶] Similar to the observations of Derrick,

[*] Johnson, "BP Uses Prison Labor."
[†] Kang, "Forcing Prison Labor."
[‡] Derrick, Scott, and Hutson, "Prison Labor Effects."
[§] Scott and Derrick, "Prison Labor."
[¶] Ibid.

Scott, and Hutson,* the writings of Scott and Derrick† show little evidence regarding the potential of displacement among local labor forces.

Given these observations, financial decisions may involve the use of prisoner labor to achieve the generation of a variety of services and goods. Economically, the resource management characteristics of this labor system provide an available supply of laborers to satisfy a variety of tasks and little, if any, displacement of local workers occurs between non-prisoner and prisoner laborers. Financially, given the costs of incarceration, the use of prisoner labor provides a mechanism through which the costs of incarceration may be reduced through time. Ethically, debates are manifested that either advocate or refute the use of prisoner laborers. However, regardless of the debates, financial considerations, or economic dimensions, the use of prisoner laborers involves the rendering of an organizational decision among leaders, and any such decisions must be rendered with respect to the long-term, best interests of the organization.

3.7 Contexts of Work-Release Programs

Financial decisions regarding labor may also be viewed from the perspective of work-release programs. Labor opportunities are not confined to solely the environments of prisons. Incarcerated people may also perform a variety of functions among local and county regions. For prisoners whose behavior demonstrates a modicum of decorum and who have earned some amount of trust, other labor opportunities exist. Therefore, the leaders of law enforcement organizations and personnel of the criminal justice system may choose to allow the participation of prisoners within work-release programs. These programs provide an opportunity for such incarcerated persons to earn wages while serving the amount of time that is mandated within their incarceration sentences. Further, work-release programs provide a method through which offenders may repay any mandated restitution expenses, the costs associated with court fees, and the costs associated with incarceration.

Examining work-release programs provides a view of their financial components and benefits. According to the Florida Department of Corrections (FDOC), work-release programs provide a 45% subsistence" among state facilities; provide a 55% subsistence among contract facilities; mandate that "10% of net pay goes toward restitution or court ordered payments"; and mandate that "10% of net pay goes to family assistance, including child support."

* Derrick, Scott, and Hutson, "Prison Labor Effects."

† Scott and Derrick, "Prison Labor."

Further, within Florida, the FDOC indicates that "10% of net pay is mandatory for the inmate's savings account," a weekly amount of $100 is counted "toward the inmate's personal incidental," and any remainder is invested into the inmate's savings account.* From a financial perspective, the inmate gains the opportunity to begin earning money that will be beneficial during the remaining period of confinement and upon release, and such programs also assist in defraying the costs of incarceration.

Similar observations are manifested regarding the work-release program of Caddo Parish, Louisiana. According to the Caddo County Sheriff's Department, a variety of benefits are derived from work-release programs. There is no cost for taxpayers to support the work-release programs of this parish, they support revenue streams for the sheriff's department, and participating offenders are responsible for financially compensating for their "own room and board, transportation, and meals." Benefits are also manifested among employers. The work-release programs facilitate a $2400 tax credit to employers, and inmates may work up to twelve hours in a twenty-four hours period within a six-day workweek.†

These examples highlight the saliency of financial decisions regarding work-release programs. Through work-release programs, financial benefits are multiple: the law enforcement agency benefits from providing laborers within local communities and local employers benefit from the use of incarcerated laborers. Work release provides a method through which the costs of incarceration may be offset, provides a cash flow for the law enforcement agency, provides money for inmates, and provides various tax savings for employers. Further, through the use of work-release programs, inmates may begin the processes of socialization and integration into society that embellish their release and transition during stages of postconfinement periods.

Financial decisions about work-release programs must also be cognizant of the best interests of both the law enforcement agency and the employer. Through the use of work-release programs, strategic benefits are manifested, financially and economically, through time with respect to the needs and wants of the employer, the law enforcement agency, and the inmate. When performed collaboratively and amiable, work-release programs provide a means through which the financial management of law enforcement organizations and criminal justice entities may be embellished and strengthened.

* Florida Department of Corrections, "Frequently Asked Questions."

† Caddo Parish Sheriff's Office, "Caddo Parish Work-Release Program."

3.8 Contexts of Recidivism

The concept of recidivism involves the notion that an inmate once released into society after the specified period of incarceration is completed will again commit some form of crime that necessitates an additional period of incarceration. According to the U.S. Department of Justice, research indicates that "two-thirds of ex-offenders released in 1994 came back into contact with the criminal justice system within three years of their release."* Such quantities of recidivists have tremendous financial implications within the criminal justice system, among law enforcement agencies and among taxpayers within a variety of settings.

The financial dimensions of recidivism may also be considered within the context of rendering decisions among law enforcement entities and within the criminal justice system. The use of inmate laborers among work-based programs may contribute toward reduced rates of recidivism among participating offenders after they are released into society following the completion of their sentenced period. Further, through reductions among rates of recidivism, the financial burdens associated with incidents of crime and offenders may also be reduced. Therefore, when considering capital investments decisions about the use of inmate labor programs may be strategically beneficial. These notions are not unfounded. Similar financial aspects of recidivism may be considered from the perspective of correctional education programs.

According to Steurer, Smith, and Tracy, regarding a 1997 study exploring recidivism, the use of educational programs during periods of incarceration may reduce the potential of repeated incarcerations by 29%. With respect to the State of Maryland, an expenditure of $11,700,000 for the implementation of "correctional education" provided a savings of $23,280,000.† These values represent approximately a 2:1 ratio regarding the implementation of educational programs versus the reincarceration of recidivist offenders. Further considerations of financial savings were observed regarding values affiliated with individuals who were not recidivists. In this instance, Steurer and Smith indicate that the "educational programs saved the state over 24 million dollars per year, twice the state's investment in its correctional education program."‡

Given these observations, Steurer and Smith also indicate that that additional financial benefits may be manifested through cost savings "not only in reduced costs of incarceration, but also in costs of the police, judicial, and social service systems," and that people "who no longer commit crime

* U.S. Department of Justice, "FY 2010 Budget Request."

† Steurer, Smith, and Tracy, "Three State Recidivism Study."

‡ Steurer and Smith, "Education Reduces Crime."

and choose to work in lawful jobs pay taxes and support their families."* These notions are salient because they demonstrate the potential of offenders to return to society as viable, legal contributors within the financial and economic systems. Because they do not commit additional crimes, no costs associated with their behaviors are incurred among law enforcement agencies and within the criminal justice system. Further, the costs of insurance agencies become unnecessary, which compensate the victims of crime or that raise insurance premiums because of criminal activities.

3.9 Integrative Financial Management

Among the preceding discussions are a variety of topics that all contribute toward the strategic facets of financial management. Financial management involves the rendering of a human decision regarding the future use and investment of money. Further, depending on the structure of the organization, financial managers must remain mindful of the best interests of the firm, the shareholders, and the stakeholders who must be considered within the contexts of financial decisions. Therefore, all decisions rendered must be inclusive of the potential of manifesting value through time. (See Figure 3.8.)

The rendering of decisions is situational and dependent upon the characteristics of the decision domain. Therefore, countless combinations of financing and revenue streams may be examined to generate strategic value through time. No decision is perfect; though some are better than others. Again, individual situations affect perceptions of the decision environment that influence human decisions. Therefore, each of the concepts within the preceding discussions impact and affect human financial decisions.

3.10 Chapter Comments and Summary

This chapter considers the basic concepts of managerial finance from the perspective of rendering long-term, strategic decisions. Examples of such decisions involve the erection of prison facilities, the developing and implementing of communications infrastructures, activities of intelligence entities; and contemplations of the costs associated with the pursuits of various policing paradigms (e.g., community-oriented policing, organizational collaborations). From the perspective of the current War on Terror, such decisions incite costs ranging in the billions of U.S. dollars, and are indicative of the seriousness of decisions with respect to any associated consequences and ramifications.

* Steurer and Smith, "Education Reduces Crime."

Figure 3.8 President George W. Bush holds up a computer with the E-Budget for the cameras during a Cabinet meeting, Monday, February 4, 2008. Later, the President said, "I submitted the budget today to Congress—it's on a laptop notebook, an e-budget. It saves paper, saves trees, saves money. I think it's the first budget submitted electronically. And it's a good budget. It's a budget that achieves some important objectives. One, it understands our top priority is to defend our country, so we fund our military, as well as fund the homeland security. Secondly, the budget keeps our economy growing." (Photo by Joyce N. Boghosian, http://georgewbush-whitehouse.archives.gov/infocus/budget/2009/index.html.)

Therefore, the rendering of human decisions is a powerful action that may affect a myriad of societies, organizations, and individuals. The rendering of strategic decisions encompasses lengthy periods that may transcend generations. Hence, decisions must be rendered with respect to the overall vision, mission, goals, and objectives of the organization thereby providing courses of actions that are commensurate with the best interests of the organization.

This consideration of best interests applies not only to the organization itself but also to the stockholders and stakeholders of the firm. Although a perfect world scenario would demonstrate consistency of decisions that contribute to these best interests, reality dictates that decisions are not always rendered in conjunction with the best interests of the firm. The characteristics of the decisions domain, the imperfection of humans, and the fallibility of humans contribute to the rendering of such flawed decisions.

Regardless, the leaders of organizations have a fiduciary obligation and responsibility to render decisions that are representative of the best interests of the organization (Figure 3.9). However, many times the sanctity of these decisions is compromised because of self-serving interests, and a variety of criminal activities become apparent. Examples include fraud, embezzlement,

Figure 3.9 Raising funds for the Fort Rucker Jail-a-Thon in conjunction with the AER Fund. This image is indicative of creative fund-raising. SSG Francis Ladson is led to a prison cell by SGT Phillip Avery. Ladson was "arrested" for "exceeding the age limit" and was sentenced to a half-hour in jail. (Photo by Russell Sellers. Courtesy of the U.S. Army, http://www.army.mil/media/125324.)

and money laundering. Therefore, controls must be established to influence the actors and characteristics of the decision domain. Such controls may be punitive or motivational.

The financing of organizations occurs primarily through a variety of methods. Although infrequent, organizational financing may also occur through the use of insurance policies during periods of duress or catastrophes. However, the leaders of organizations must be mindful that such funding is derived from sources that provide monies with good-faith expectations of satisfactory performance through time.

Regardless of the decision or method of financing, the leaders of an organization are responsible for creating and developing value. Such notions of value may produce tangible or intangible benefits for the organization. Two considerations of value are market value-added and economic value-added perspectives that influence organizations through time.

Although the creation of value may occur in a variety of methods, one method is through the use of prisoner labor. The use of work programs among prison settings provides a method through which revenue streams may be developed and used to offset the costs of incarceration. Further, work-release programs also provide similar financial benefits as well as provide opportunities to begin socialization and reintegration of offenders within society. Once released, despite a high rate of recidivism, some offenders become productive members of society, and contribute economically and financially within the financial and economic system.

3.11 Terminology

Agents
Agency
Best interests
Bond
Capital budgeting
Capital investment
Charity
Debt
Decision
Decision controls
Decision domain
Economic value-added
Equity
Fiduciary obligation
Goodwill
Grant
Insurance
Interest
Investment rating
Loan
Market value-added
Preventive
Principals
Principal–agency conundrum
Prison labor
Protective
Recidivism
Relationship
Society
Shareholder
Stakeholder
Value
Work release

3.12 Thought and Discussion Questions

1. Compare and contrast the terms *shareholder* and *stakeholder*. Within your discussion, cite and explain historical examples, using criminal justice perspectives, that delineate the salient characteristics of both entities.
2. The principal–agency conundrum was described within this chapter, and several control methods were identified as being factors through which the risks of unethical and illegal behavior may be reduced and diminished. Identify some historical examples, using a criminal justice perspective, of instances in which corruption impeded and influenced the leaders of criminal justice organizations. Within this discussion, provide a brief analysis of whether control mechanisms were effective or would have been effective methods of countering such unethical or illegal behavior.
3. What is the difference between prisoner labor and work-release concepts? Is there a difference between these two notions? Fully justify and substantiate your response.

4. Explain the differences between market value-added and economic value-added philosophies. Select a police department with which you are familiar, and discuss how its related programs and initiatives may be assessed with respect to each of these concepts. Fully justify and substantiate your response.

Bibliography

Aulds, T. J. "City Settles Lawsuit against Police." *Galveston County Daily News*, March 31, 2009. Accessed August 6, 2010: http://galvestondailynews.com/story.lasso?ewcd=a4127aa1272399c6.

Barnes, B. "2009 Drug Arrest/Drug Confiscation/Money Seizures." Guilford County Sheriff's Office. Accessed August 27, 2011: http://www.guilfordcountysheriff.com/index.php?option=com_content&view=article&id=390:2009-drug-arrestdrug-confiscationmoney-seizures&catid=91:2010-sheriffs-office-news&Itemid=293.

Botten, Neil. *Enterprise Strategy*. Oxford, UK: Elsevier, 2009.

Burnett, John. "Seized Drug Assets Pad Police Budgets." National Public Radio. Accessed August 17, 2010: http://www.npr.org/templates/story/story.php?storyId=91490480.

Caddo Parish Sheriff's Office. "Caddo Parish Work-Release Program." Accessed August 5, 2010: http://www.caddosheriff.org/workrelease.pdf.

Charles, Michelle. "Finance Authority Approves Justice, Police Loans." St. John Source, December 27, 2002. Accessed August 6, 2010: http://stjohnsource.com/content/news/local-news/2002/12/27/finance-authority-approves-justice-police-loans.

City of Memphis. "Police Services." Accessed August 6, 2010: http://www.cityofmemphis.org/pdf_forms/FY2011_AD_OP/POLICE_SERVICES.pdf.

City of Tupelo. "Tupelo Mississippi City Budget 2010." Accessed August 6, 2010: http://www.ci.tupelo.ms.us/bud-acc/budget_year.pdf.

City of Waco. "Bond Election Update." Accessed August 6, 2010: http://www.waco-texas.com/bond-police.asp.

"Corrections Corporation of America, Form 10-K." 2010. Accessed August 6, 2010: http://secfilings.nasdaq.com/edgar_conv_html%2f2010%2f02%2f24%2f0000950123-10-016309.html#G22193E10VK_HTM_125.

Davis, Gareth, David Muhlhausen, Dexter Ingram, and Ralph Rector. "The Facts about COPS: A Performance Overview of the Community Oriented Policing Services Program." The Heritage Foundation, September 25, 2000. Accessed August 6, 2010: http://www.heritage.org/Research/Reports/2000/09/The-Facts-about-COPS.

Derrick, Frederick, Charles Scott, and Thomas Hutson. "Prison Labor Effects on the Unskilled Labor Market." *American Economist*, 48 (2004): 74–81.

Durham County Government. "Sheriff's Community-Oriented Policing Effort." Accessed August 6, 2010: http://www.co.durham.nc.us/departments/shrf/Operations/Community_Oriented_P.html.

Evangelical Council for Financial Accountability. "Good News Jail & Prison Ministry." Accessed August 6, 2010: http://www.ecfa.org/MemberProfile.aspx?ID=5272.

Federal Trade Commission. "Facts for Consumers." Accessed August 6, 2010: http://www.ftc.gov/bcp/edu/pubs/consumer/telemarketing/tel01.shtm.

Florida Department of Corrections. "Frequently Asked Questions Regarding Work Release." Accessed August 5, 2010: http://www.dc.state.fl.us/oth/inmates/wr.html.

Good News Jail and Prison Ministry. "Fifty Years Providing Chaplains to the World's Jails and Prisons." Accessed August 6, 2010: http://www.goodnewsjail.org/.

GulfCoastNews.com. "Ex-Lumberton Police Chief Sentenced to Prison for Katrina Fraud." August 14, 2009. Accessed August 6, 2010: http://www.gulfcoastnews.com/GCNnewsLumbertonPoliceChiefKatrinaFraud081409.htm.

Hayes, Melissa. "City Council Adopts Jersey City Budget, Lessens Tax Hike." Accessed August 6, 2010: http://www.nj.com/hudson/index.ssf/2010/04/city_council_adopts_jersey_cit.html.

Johnson, Jason. (2010). "BP Uses Prison Labor and Tax Breaks to Clean Up Its Mess." *New Pittsburgh Courier*, July 30, 2010. Accessed August 5, 2010: http://www.newpittsburghcourieronline.com/index.php?option=com_content&view=article&id=2648:bp-uses-prison-labor-and-tax-breaks-to-clean-up-its-mess&catid=40:opinion&Itemid=54.

Kang, Susan. "Forcing Prison Labor: International Labor Standards, Human Rights and the Privatization of Prison Labor in the Contemporary United States." *New Political Science*, 31 (2009): 137–161.

National Rural Law Enforcement Association. "Grants-Funds." Accessed August 6, 2010: http://nrlea.org/grants/.

Office of the Mississippi Secretary of State Securities and Charities Division. "Summary Cease and Desist Order and Notice of Intent to Impose Administrative Penalty and Revoke Registration." Accessed August 6, 2010: http://www.sos.state.ms.us/SecCharities/Cease%20Order%20PDF/Document2.pdf.

Oklahoma Fraternal Order of the Police. "Oklahoma State Lodge." Accessed August 6, 2010: http://www.okfop.org/Citizens.htm.

Pirius, Rebecca. "Minnesota's Forfeiture Laws," *Information Brief—Research Department, Minnesota House of Representatives*, State of Minnesota, 2010.

Scott, Charles and Frederick Derrick. "Prison Labor: The Local Effects of Ohio Prison Industries." *International Advances in Economic Research*, 12 (2006): 540–550. Accessed September 17, 2010: http://findarticles.com/p/articles/mi_hb3090/is_4_12/ai_n29313893/.

Scott, Jeffry. "Atlanta Counties Look to Prison Labor to Relieve Budget Pressure." *Atlanta Journal-Constitution*, April 19, 2010. Accessed August 5, 2010: http://www.ajc.com/news/atlanta-counties-look-to-440430.html.

Standard & Poor's. "Credit Ratings Definitions and FAQs." Accessed August 6, 2010: http://www.standardandpoors.com/ratings/definitions-and-faqs/en/us.

Steurer, Stephen and Linda Smith. "Education Reduces Crime: Three-State Recidivism Study—Executive Summary." 2003. Accessed August 6, 2010: http://www.criminologycenter.fsu.edu/p/nationalDataClearinghouse/Publications%20Reports/3%20states%20executive%20summary.pdf.

Steurer, Stephen, Linda Smith, and Alice Tracy. "Three State Recidivism Study." Maryland Department of Public Safety and Correctional Services. Accessed August 6, 2010: http://dpscs.md.gov/publicinfo/publications/pdfs/three-state-recidivism-study-summary.pdf.

Strassman, Paul. *Information Productivity: Assessing the Information Management Costs of U.S. Industrial Corporations*. New Canaan, CT: Information Economic Press, 1999.

U.S. Department of Justice. "FY 2010 Budget Request." Accessed August 6, 2010: http://www.justice.gov/jmd/2010factsheets/pdf/state-local.pdf.

Valentine, Danny. "Two Accused of Using Police Charity to Scam Tampa Businesses." *St. Petersburg Times*, July 30, 2010. Accessed August 6, 2010: http://www.tampabay.com/news/publicsafety/crime/two-accused-of-using-police-charity-to-scam-tampa-businesses/1112082.

Witt, Howard. "Highway Robbery? Texas Police Seize Black Motorists' Cash, Cars." *The Chicago Tribune*, March 10, 2009. Accessed August 27, 2011: http://www.chicagotribune.com/news/nationworld/chi-texas-profiling_wittmar10,0,6051682.story.

WKBN News. "Police Station Ruined by Ohio Twister to Be Redone." Accessed August 6, 2010: http://www.wkbn.com/content/news/ohstate/story/Police-station-ruined-by-Ohio-twister-to-be-redone/AzcUKkGDV0SXvRa5GdfwXA.cspx?rss=1947.

Wurts, Bryan. "Lakewood Police Independent Guild." Accessed August 6, 2010: http://www.lpig.us/.

Tools of the Trade Making a Decision

4

> This is as true in everyday life as it is in battle: we are given one life and the decision is ours whether to wait for circumstances to make up our mind, or whether to act, and in acting, to live.*
>
> **General Omar Bradley**

4.1 Objectives

The objectives of this chapter are to:

- Understand the concept of the time value of money
- Understand the concept of capital budgeting
- Understand the primary methods of capital budgeting
- Understand the concept of risk

4.2 Introduction

The tools and techniques described and explained within this chapter approach financial decisions from a variety of perspectives and involve some element of risk. They also are representative of the economic concerns of resource allocation and the financial concerns of investing minimal capital in the hopes of gaining the best reward, through time, of investment decisions. The use of capital budgeting methods facilitates the rendering of decisions through time, strategically, by viewing the decision domain and the problem domain from the perspectives of rate, cash, profit, and time.

The basic concept of capital budgeting provides a mechanism through which organizational leaders and managers may approach financial decisions through a variety of perspectives involving rate, cash, profit, and time. Capital budgeting is the use of quantitative tools, through which financial decisions may be compared and contrasted, to yield potential courses of strategic action. Through the use of capital budgeting, within the context of the time value of money, financial leaders may evaluate the decision domain to

* Bradley, Omar, "Decision Quotations," Brainy Quote, http://www.brainyquote.com/quotes/keywords/larger_8.html (accessed July 11, 2011).

Figure 4.1 Money is expended among a variety of uses. Through the use of capital budgeting techniques, leaders improve their ability to invest financial resources through time. (Courtesy of the U.S. Army, http://www.monmouth.army.mil/monmouthmessage/stories111910/news_story_07.html.)

determine whether certain rates are justifiable regarding capital investment projects; to determine whether a sufficient period of time exists to complete a capital budgeting project with respect to any state financial goals and objectives (e.g., payback period analysis); and to compare and contrast various facets of profitability and monetary equivalencies to determine whether a capital project is acceptable, justifiable, and worthy of pursuit through time (Figure 4.1).

The mathematical basis of each of these perspectives is modeled mathematically through the use of a variety of capital budgeting formulas that might incorporate the time value of money as an underlying basis. Regardless of the time value of money considerations, each tool demonstrates a unique perspective of the decision domain and the problem domain. A sound understanding of the components of the time value of money is necessary before any undertaking of examining capital budgeting methods may occur.

This chapter introduces the notion that money has time value, that is, its value is influenced, through time, with respect to the effects of compounding and discounting rates. Both current monetary values and future monetary values may be contemplated regarding the influences of the characteristics of compounding and discounting rates. However, two additional time value of money concepts must be examined before one may consider capital budgeting formulas, methods, and decisions. These two remaining concepts involve the determinations of rates through time and the determination of periods through time.

An understanding of these two concepts is necessary for understanding the foundational characteristics of rendering financial management decisions. All decisions occur through time, and the effects of decisions may transcend generations. Therefore, an understanding of the time variable and its influences regarding monetary value are essential when considering financial management decisions. A consideration of time is incomplete without an examination of rates. Rates impact the discounting or the compounding of monetary values through time. Therefore, the concept of rate is a significant factor when examining equivalencies of monetary variables with respect to facets of time characteristics. Time and rates demonstrate an inseparable relationship and influence the perspectives of monetary value.

Therefore, given these notions, the concepts of time and rate are essential attributes of rendering financial decisions and provide the base components of generating mathematical models that facilitate the rendering of many financial investment decisions among organizations strategically. Hence, time and rate contribute toward the basic building blocks of quantitative analysis through which financial decisions may be contemplated, rendered, and pursued. Further, these two concepts provide a basis for understanding the intricacies of capital budgeting decisions.

4.3 The Time Value of Money

The relationship between money and time is simply expressed via the concept of the time value of money. No more, no less. The value of money fluctuates through time because of rate influences. With respect to financial and investment purposes, the time value of money is not synonymous with notions of economic purchasing capacity through time. The time value of money shows the relationship between time and money, with respect to an accepted, stated rate that impacts both discounting and compounding, that influences the changes of values of financial funds over short-term and long-term periods. Five basic variables govern the relationship between time and money. These variables consist of rate, future value, present value, payment instance, and time itself (Figure 4.2).

The notions of compounding and discounting also affect calculations involving the time value of money. The concept of compounding involves the calculation of an interest rate value and adding this value to the value of the principal amount periodically. Basically, compounding is the additional of an interest value to the current, existing value of a principal amount of money. This process may be repeated the considered period of time. The effects of compounding are manifested via the growth of monetary value

Figure 4.2 The value of money is related to time. Through manipulating the basic variables of money, any value may be calculated with respect to time. (Courtesy of the State of Oregon, http://sustainability.oregon.gov/DAS/PEBB/news/2007EEnewsletters/december07.shtml.)

through time. The emphasis of compounding demonstrates a forward approach to determining future monetary values.

The concept of discounting involves the calculation of a present monetary value given the specified value of money during a specific future period. Again, the use of a rate is necessary to determine the magnitude through which future monetary values are expressed in terms of current monetary values. The emphasis of discounting demonstrates a reverse approach, which conceptually begins in the future, to determine current, present-day monetary values.

The concept of the time value of money governs the basic principles of financial management. These five variables interact to provide outcomes to specific problems and may be used to provide conjecture regarding hypothetical situations. Through such considerations, humans may render stronger, more robust decisions that influence the investing of any available funds. Further, these five variables form the basis of capital budgeting functions. An understanding of their basic relationship and functioning is critical to understanding the capital budgeting formulas and examples presented within this text. The following examples demonstrate the simplest considerations of the interaction that occurs among these variables.

EXAMPLE 4.1

This year, the Sample Town Police Department borrows a total of $10,000.00 for infrastructure improvements that will pay the costs of painting the exterior of its building. It was agreed that this amount would be repaid over a period of five years. Annual payments, against the principal amount, are to be $2000.00

each year, and the rate of interest charged is 9.0%. An interest payment must also be made annually. Repayment begins next year. What is the total amount of money that will be repaid?

Solution for Example 4.1

This simple example provides sufficient data to solve the given problem. First, a consideration of the mathematical model that describes the relationships among the variables must be considered. An initial, borrowed value is expressed as $10,000.00. A period of five years will occur before the loan is fully repaid. Each year, at least $2000.00 must be repaid against the principal value. The established rate is 9.0%, and an interest payment is also due annually. When the overall period of five years is fulfilled, the loan and its interest will be completely repaid.

Conceptually, this situation may be expressed through the delineation of the considered period of time. Table 4.1 shows the salient characteristics of this time period. The data values show a decreasing principal amount through time, a static rate through time, the annual values of payments rendered each year, and the consideration of interest payment values that occur annually. The attributes of each individual year, comprising the overall period, are specified. The principal loan values are indicative of the values that occur at the beginning of each before a payment is made against them. A methodical consideration of this situation yields the calculated values that are presented within Table 4.1.

The consideration of interest must be calculated regarding the borrowed principal. The values of each of the annual interest amounts are calculated through the use of the following mathematical relationship:

$$\text{Annual Interest Payment} = (\text{Established Rate})(\text{Principal}) \tag{4.1}$$

No payments are required during the year in which borrowing occurred. Therefore, no considerations of either interest or principal payments are necessary during the current period that begins the overall time period. However, this condition is not applicable to the remaining years of the overall time

Table 4.1 Time Period Characteristics of Example 4.1

Period	Rate	Principal	Principal Payment	Interest Payment
0	9.0%	($10,000.00)	$0.00	$0.00
1	9.0%	($10,000.00)	$2000.00	$900.00
2	9.0%	($8000.00)	$2000.00	$720.00
3	9.0%	($6000.00)	$2000.00	$540.00
4	9.0%	($4000.00)	$2000.00	$360.00
5	9.0%	($2000.00)	$2000.00	$180.00

period. The following calculation shows the derivation of the annual amount of interest payment that is due during the first year.

$$\text{Year 1 Interest Payment} = (0.90)(\$10{,}000.00) = \$900.00$$

This calculated value, representing the amount of the annual interest payment of Year 1, is not the only payment that is due during the first year. The description of the example indicates that a $2000.00 principal payment is also due during the first year. Once this principal payment transaction is completed, the principal amount due is decreased by the amount of $2000.00. An updated principal due value of $8000.00 is generated.

The remaining years also are governed by these same processes of payment calculations and transactions. During the second year, the process is repeated, but incorporates the updated values of the decreased principal loan value and the annual interest payment. The following calculation shows the derivation of the annual amount of interest payment that is due during the second year.

$$\text{Year 2 Interest Payment} = (0.90)(\$8000.00) = \$720.00$$

Again, the amount of the principal loan value must be updated to reflect the mandatory, annual payment transaction of $2000.00. This annual principal payment decreases the current principal value by $2000.00. Therefore, a new principal value of $6000.00 is generated. These newly calculated values are again substituted into the mathematical construct for the succeeding year. The following substitutions show the next iteration of the process.

$$\text{Year 3 Interest Payment} = (0.90)(\$6000.00) = \$540.00$$

The mandatory principal payment amount of $2000.00 must again be transacted. This transaction again decreases the principal loan value by an amount of $2000.00. A new principal loan value of $4000.00 is calculated. Again, the process is iterated using the updated financial values. The following substitutions show the next iteration of the process.

$$\text{Year 4 Interest Payment} = (0.90)(\$4000.00) = \$360.00$$

The mandatory principal payment amount of $2000.00 must again be transacted. This transaction again decreases the principal loan value by an amount of $2000.00. A new principal loan value of $2000.00 is calculated. Again, the process is iterated using the updated financial values. The following substitutions show the next iteration of the process.

$$\text{Year 5 Interest Payment} = (0.90)(\$2000.00) = \$180.00$$

Table 4.2 Annual Payment Values of Example 4.1

Period	Principal Payment	Interest Payment	Annual Payment
0	\$0.00	\$0.00	\$0.00
1	\$2000.00	\$900.00	\$2900.00
2	\$2000.00	\$720.00	\$2720.00
3	\$2000.00	\$540.00	\$2540.00
4	\$2000.00	\$360.00	\$2360.00
5	\$2000.00	\$180.00	\$2180.00

This final year includes the remaining transaction of \$2000.00 against the principal loan value thereby reducing the value of the principal to \$0. The calculated interest payment value of \$180.00 represents the value of the final interest payment. The derivations of these final values represent the final calculations necessary for these two variables representing the principal value of the loan and the annual interest payment value.

Although these final values are indicative of the end states for the values of the variables associated with the principal loan amount and the consideration of annual interest, the problem remains unsolved. The problem description requires the calculation of the cumulative amount that is repaid to the lender. Therefore, further calculations are necessary to derive this overall value.

These additional calculations are used to derive the annual payment amounts, involving both the principal payment values and the annual interest payment values, for each individual year within the overall period of time. These annual payment values are calculated by adding the value of the principal payment amount with the value of the annual interest payment amount for each individual year within the affected period of time. After these values are calculated, they may be summed to determine the overall payment value that must be rendered to the lender. Table 4.2 shows the calculations of the annual payment amounts. The values within Table 4.2 are calculated via the following relationship:

$$(\text{Annual Payment})_{\text{year}} = (\text{Principal Payment})_{\text{year}} + (\text{Interest Payment})_{\text{year}} \quad (4.2)$$

When substituting the appropriate values, per annum, the following calculations are prescribed:

$$(\text{Annual Payment})_1 = (\$2000.00)_1 + (\$900.00)_1 = \$2900.00$$

$$(\text{Annual Payment})_2 = (\$2000.00)_2 + (\$720.00)_2 = \$2720.00$$

$$(\text{Annual Payment})_3 = (\$2000.00)_3 + (\$540.00)_3 = \$2540.00$$

$$(\text{Annual Payment})_4 = (\$2000.00)_4 + (\$360.00)_4 = \$2360.00$$

$$(\text{Annual Payment})_5 = (\$2000.00)_5 + (\$180.00)_5 = \$2180.00$$

These calculations derive the payments that must be rendered during each individual year of the overall period. However, the final outcome of the problem statement remains unknown. The final outcome requires another calculation to derive the overall value of the amount of money that is repaid to the lender. This cumulative value of the overall payment amount is determined through the summation of the derived individual, annual payments. The following calculations show this final process.

$$\$2900.00 + \$2720.00 + \$2540.00 + \$2360.00 + \$2180.00 = \$12{,}700.00$$

The outcome of these final calculations yields a value of $12,700.00 as the value that must be repaid. This value represents the total monetary value that will be returned to the lending entity. Its calculation involved nothing more than simple mathematics using addition and subtraction. However, these simple operations show the impact of rate impacting repayment over time. A total value of $10,000.00 was originally loaned, whereas a total value of $12,700.00 will be repaid in due time.

This example highlights the process of amortization. Basically, amortization is the repayment of a loan through time. Although this example demonstrates the concept of amortization, it also manifests the five basic variables that were identified as the base components affecting monetary values through time: rate, present value, future value, payments, and a period of time.

4.4 Concepts of Future Value and Present Value

Other queries may also be posed from the perspective of the time value of money. One of the simplest inquiries may be expressed through questioning how much an amount of money will be worth in the future, at some specified point in time, in conjunction with an accepted, stated rate. Another of the simplest inquiries may be expressed through questioning how much a future amount of money, specified at some point in the future, would be worth presently, in conjunction with an accepted, stated discount rate. Respectively, these notions are known as future value and present value.

The notions of compounding and discounting also affect calculations involving the time value of money. The concept of compounding involves the calculation of an interest rate value and adding this value to the value of the principal amount periodically. Basically, compounding is the addition of an interest value to the current, existing value of a principal amount of money. This process may be repeated the considered period of time. The effects of compounding are manifested via the growth of monetary value through time. The emphasis of compounding demonstrates a forward approach to determining future monetary values.

The concept of discounting involves the calculation of a present monetary value given the specified value of money during a specific future period. Again, the use of a rate is necessary to determine the magnitude through which future monetary values are expressed in terms of current monetary values. The emphasis of discounting demonstrates a reverse approach, which conceptually begins in the future, to determine current, present-day monetary values.

The concepts of present value and future value are important notions within the discipline of financial management. These two notions provide leaders with relevant perspectives of money that emphasize relationships between the past, present, and future values of money through time. Therefore, the use of such concepts provides a systematic framework from which financial decisions may be approached, understood, finalized, and implemented.

4.5 Future Value

The concept of future value is a primary consideration of finance. The notion of future value conceptually queries the value of an amount of money at some point in the future. Therefore, simply, examples of the basic question that underlies the notion of future value may be expressed through the following queries:

If I have $1.00 today, assuming annual compounding, how much will it be worth in five years using a 5.0% rate?
If I have $1.00 today, assuming annual compounding, how much will it be worth in seven years using a 7.0% rate?

These queries involve the concept of growth through time, and the magnitude of such growth is affected by the compounding effects of the specified rate and via time itself. When dealing with this notion of growth through time, a mathematical construct exists that expresses the relationships among the considered variables and their values. This construct is known as the future value of money formula. Mathematically, this formula involves the use of the following variables:

R_{per} Rate factor through time
P Period of time
V_{curr} Current monetary value
V_{futr} Future monetary value

With respect to the calculation of the future value of money, the relationship among these variable may be expressed through the use of a mathematical equation. This equation, representing the future value of money, is given as follows:

$$V_{futr} = (V_{curr})(R_{per} + 1.0)^{P} \tag{4.3}$$

The purpose of this equation is to mathematically express the concept of growth, over time, that affects monetary values. This relationship is expressed through observations regarding the value of current dollars being influenced through the mathematical growth of monetary value, exponentially, over time. This equation expresses the notion that the future value of a monetary amount is equivalent to the value of the current monetary value multiplied by the exponential calculation of a rate influence. This concept may be applied to the preceding sample questions.

EXAMPLE 4.2

A consideration of the application of this equation, with respect to the first question, may be delineated systematically. First, a statement of the problem may be given to show the supplied data and the queried data. This statement of the problem is given as follows:

> If I have \$1.00 today, assuming annual compounding, how much will it be worth in five years using a 5.0% rate?

Solution for Example 4.2

Next, one may specify the given and missing values that are commensurate with the mathematical construct of the necessary equation:

R_{per} = 5.0%
P = 5 years
V_{curr} = \$1.00
V_{futr} = This value is unknown.

The specification of the future monetary value equation is mandated. These identified monetary values may be substituted appropriately within the future value of money equation. Such substitutions are given as follows:

$$V_{futr} = (V_{curr})(R_{per} + 1.0)^{P}$$

$$V_{futr} = (\$1.00)(0.05 + 1.0)^{5}$$

After the substitutions are identified and appropriately assigned, the processing of mathematical functions occurs thereby yielding the value of the V_{futr} variable. This processing is demonstrated as follows:

$$V_{futr} = (\$1.00)(0.05 + 1.0)^5$$

$$V_{futr} = (\$1.00)(1.05)^5$$

$$V_{futr} = (\$1.00)(1.28)$$

$$V_{futr} = \$1.28$$

Based on these calculations, the value of V_{futr} is determined to be $1.28. Therefore, given the outcomes of the mathematical processing, $1.00 today, invested at a rate of 5.0%, assuming annual compounding effects, would be worth $1.28 in five years. Table 4.3 shows the annual compounding attributes that are innate to this determination of future value. Although this table shows the high-level perspective of growth, it may be helpful to view the specific processes, per annum, that contribute toward the compounded growth of monetary values through time. This approach also includes the specification of interest values per year and the addition of these values to the principal amount of investment. Table 4.4 shows these relationships. Although it is a very simple example, the solving of this problem delineates the basic principles of determining future value that govern the time value of money. From two perspectives, the contents of Table 4.3 and Table 4.4 show the compounded growth of money through time. An initial value of $1.00 increases, through time and the influences of the established rate, to a final value of $1.28.

Table 4.3 Example 4.2: Determination of Future Value

Period	Interest Factor	Calculation	Annual Investment Value
0	1.05	$(\$1.00)(1.05)^0$	$1.00
1	1.05	$(\$1.00)(1.05)^1$	$1.05
2	1.05	$(\$1.00)(1.05)^2$	$1.10
3	1.05	$(\$1.00)(1.05)^3$	$1.16
4	1.05	$(\$1.00)(1.05)^4$	$1.21
5	1.05	$(\$1.00)(1.05)^5$	$1.28

Table 4.4 Example 4.2: Annual Characteristics

Period	Rate	Investment Value	Interest Value	Updated Investment
0	5%	$1.00	$0.00	$1.00
1	5%	$1.00	$0.05	$1.05
2	5%	$1.05	$0.05	$1.10
3	5%	$1.10	$0.06	$1.16
4	5%	$1.16	$0.06	$1.22
5	5%	$1.22	$0.06	$1.28

EXAMPLE 4.3

The second question may also be examined through the use of this formula. Again, a statement of the problem may be given to show the supplied data and the queried data. This statement of the problem is given as follows:

> If I have \$70.00 today, assuming annual compounding, how much will it be worth in seven years using a 7.0% rate?

Solution for Example 4.3

Again, one may specify the given and missing values that are commensurate with the mathematical construct of the necessary equation:

R_{per} = 7.0%
P = 7 years
V_{curr} = \$70.00
V_{futr} = This value is unknown.

These values may be substituted appropriately within the future value of money equation. Such substitutions are given as follows:

$$V_{futr} = (V_{curr})(R_{per} + 1.0)^P$$

$$V_{futr} = (\$70.00)(0.07 + 1.0)^7$$

After the substitutions are identified and appropriately assigned, the processing of mathematical functions occurs thereby yielding the value of the V_{futr} variable. This processing is demonstrated as follows:

$$V_{futr} = (\$70.00)(0.07 + 1.0)^7$$

$$V_{futr} = (\$70.00)(1.07)^7$$

$$V_{futr} = (\$70.00)(1.61)$$

$$V_{futr} = \$112.40$$

Based on these calculations, the value of V_{futr} is determined to be \$112.40. Therefore, given the outcomes of the mathematical processing, \$70.00 today invested at a rate of 7.0%, assuming annual compounding effects, would be worth \$112.40 in seven years. Table 4.5 shows the annual compounding attributes that are innate to this determination of future value. Again, although this table shows the high-level perspective of growth, it may be helpful to view the specific processes, per annum, that contribute toward the compounded growth of monetary values through time. This approach also includes the specification of interest values per year and the addition of these values to the principal amount of investment. Table 4.6 shows these relationships.

Again, although it is a very simple example, the solving of this problem delineates the basic principles, from the perspective of determining future

Table 4.5 Example 4.3: Determination of Future Value

Period	Interest Factor	Calculation	Annual Investment Value
0	1.07	$(\$70.00)(1.07)^0$	$70.00
1	1.07	$(\$70.00)(1.07)^1$	$74.90
2	1.07	$(\$70.00)(1.07)^2$	$80.14
3	1.07	$(\$70.00)(1.07)^3$	$85.75
4	1.07	$(\$70.00)(1.07)^4$	$91.76
5	1.07	$(\$70.00)(1.07)^5$	$98.17
6	1.07	$(\$70.00)(1.07)^6$	$105.05
7	1.07	$(\$70.00)(1.07)^7$	$112.40

Table 4.6 Example 4.3: Annual Characteristics

Period	Rate	Investment Value	Interest Value	Updated Investment
0	7%	$70.00	$0.00	$70.00
1	7%	$70.00	$4.90	$74.90
2	7%	$74.90	$5.24	$80.14
3	7%	$80.14	$5.61	$85.75
4	7%	$85.75	$6.00	$91.75
5	7%	$91.75	$6.42	$98.17
6	7%	$98.17	$6.87	$105.05
7	7%	$105.05	$7.35	$112.40

value, that govern the time value of money. From two perspectives, the contents of Table 4.5 and Table 4.6 show the compounded growth of money through time. An initial value of $70.00 increases, through time and the influences of the established rate, to a final value of $112.40.

This consideration of future value provides a powerful tool that allows managers and leaders to project monetary values forward through time. The current year represents the immediate present period of time. The projected year of examination is determined and specified as some point in the future, and the necessary period of time exponentially affects the time value of money calculation. This notion allows leaders and managers to consider future values of money when contemplating decisions.

Although this perspective of examining and determining future value is a significant aspect of the time value of money, it is not the only method through which monetary values may be established. An additional consideration is the determination of a present value of money based upon future specifications of monetary value in conjunction with a specific period of time. This form of analysis is known as present value analysis.

4.6 Present Value

The concept of present value is another primary consideration of finance. The notion of present value conceptually queries the value of an amount of money, in terms of current monetary values, with respect to an established set of future monetary values and the specification of a period of time. Therefore, examples of the basic question that underlies the notion of present value may be expressed through the following queries:

After five years I anticipate having the amount of $1.28. Assuming a discount rate of 5.0%, what is the equivalent monetary amount in terms of current value?

After seven years I anticipate having the amount of $112.40. Assuming a discount rate of 7.0%, what is the equivalent monetary amount in terms of current value?

These two questions are similar to the questions posed within the discussions of future value concepts. These queries involve the concept of discounting through time, and the magnitude of such discounting is affected by the effects of the specified discount rate and via time itself. When dealing with this notion of discounting through time, a mathematical construct exists that expresses the relationships among the considered variables and their values. This construct is known as the current value of money formula. Mathematically, this formula involves the use of the following variables:

R_{per} Rate factor through time
P Period of time
V_{futr} Future monetary value
V_{curr} Current monetary value

With respect to the calculation of the current value of money, the relationship among these variable may be expressed through the use of a mathematical equation. The equation for the current value of money is given as follows:

$$V_{curr} = \frac{V_{futr}}{\left(R_{per} + 1.0\right)^{P}} \tag{4.4}$$

The purpose of this equation is to mathematically express the concept of discounting, through time, which affects monetary values. This relationship is expressed through observations regarding the value of money, being influenced through the mathematical discounting of monetary value, exponentially, over time. This equation is derived from the previously given future value monetary formula. This concept of present value may be applied to the preceding sample questions.

EXAMPLE 4.4

The considered problem statement is provided as follows:

> After five years I anticipate having the amount of $1.28. Assuming a discount rate of 5.0%, what is the equivalent monetary amount in terms of current value?

Solution for Example 4.4

Next, a determination of the provided variable values may be completed. Based on a reading of the problem statement, a future value may be identified as the amount of $1.28. A discount rate is identified as 5.0%, and the considered period of time involves the length of five years through which discounting must occur. Given these observations, the initial specifications of variables and their commensurate values may be expressed as follows:

R_{per} = 5%
P = 5 years
V_{futr} = $1.28
V_{curr} = This value is unknown.

Next, the specification of the current value equation occurs. The substituting of these values occurs within the current value equation appropriately. Substituting these values, into the current value equation, yields the following relationships:

$$V_{curr} = \frac{V_{futr}}{\left(R_{per} + 1.0\right)^P}$$

$$V_{curr} = \frac{\$1.28}{\left(0.05 + 1.0\right)^5}$$

Now that the substitutions are manifested, the performing of mathematical calculations occurs. The following calculations show the determining of the value of the current value variable.

$$V_{curr} = \frac{\$1.28}{\left(0.05 + 1.0\right)^5}$$

$$V_{curr} = \frac{\$1.28}{\left(1.05\right)^5}$$

$$V_{curr} = \frac{\$1.28}{1.28}$$

$$V_{curr} = \$1.00$$

Based on these calculations, the value of V_{curr} is determined to be $1.00. Therefore, given the outcomes of the mathematical processing, $1.28, at a point five years in the future, discounted at a rate of 5.0% assuming the effects of the discount rate, would be worth the amount of $1.00 in the terms

Table 4.7 Example 4.4: Determination of Current Value

Period	Discount Rate	Calculation	Annual Discounted Monetary Value
5	1.05	$\$1.28/(1.05)^0$	\$1.28
4	1.05	$\$1.28/(1.05)^1$	\$1.22
3	1.05	$\$1.28/(1.05)^2$	\$1.16
2	1.05	$\$1.28/(1.05)^3$	\$1.11
1	1.05	$\$1.28/(1.05)^4$	\$1.05
0	1.05	$\$1.28/(1.05)^5$	\$1.00

of current monetary value. Table 4.7 shows the annual discounting attributes that are innate to this determination of current monetary value.

Although it is a very simple example, the solving of this problem delineates the basic principles for determining current value that govern the time value of money. The ability to calculate backward, through time, is apparent among the calculations given within the preceding example. Based on these calculations, it is evident that a future monetary value of \$1.28 decreases, through time and the influences of the established discount rate, to manifest a current value of \$1.00.

EXAMPLE 4.5

Again, another example may be used to show the process of discounting future monetary value to reflect its current value equivalency. The problem statement is given as follows:

> After seven years I anticipate having the amount of \$112.40. Assuming a discount rate of 7.0%, what is the equivalent monetary amount in terms of current value?

Solution for Example 4.5

A determination of the provided variable values may be completed. Based on a reading of the problem statement, a future value may be identified as the amount of \$112.40. A discount rate is identified as 7.0%, and the considered period of time involves the length of seven years through which discounting must occur. Given these observations, the initial specifications of variables and their commensurate values may be expressed as follows:

R_{per} = 7%
P = 7 years
V_{futr} = \$112.40
V_{curr} = This value is unknown.

Next, the specification of the current value equation occurs. The substituting of these values occurs within the current value equation appropriately. Substituting these values into the current value equation yields the following relationships:

$$V_{curr} = \frac{V_{futr}}{(R_{per} + 1.0)^P}$$

$$V_{curr} = \frac{\$112.40}{(0.07 + 1.0)^7}$$

$$V_{curr} = \frac{\$112.40}{(1.07)^7}$$

$$V_{curr} = \frac{\$112.40}{1.61}$$

$$V_{curr} = \$69.81$$

Based on these calculations, the value of V_{curr} is determined to be \$69.81. Therefore, given the outcomes of the mathematical processing, \$112.40, at a point seven years in the future, discounted at a rate of 7.0% assuming the effects of the discount rate, would be worth the amount of \$69.81 in the terms of current monetary value. Although the manual calculations did not yield a full value of \$70.00, this difference arises because of numerical rounding that occurs within the mathematical calculations. The value of \$69.81 may be rounded upward to the value of \$70.00. Table 4.8 shows the annual discounting attributes that are innate to this determination of current monetary value.

Again, the solving of this problem delineates the basic principles for determining current value that govern the time value of money. The ability to calculate backward, through time, is again apparent among the calculations given within the preceding example. Based on these calculations, it is evident that a future monetary value of \$112.40 decreases, through time and the influences of the established discount rate, to manifest a current value of \$70.00.

Table 4.8 Example 4.5: Determination of Current Value

Period	Discount Rate	Calculation	Annual Discounted Monetary Value
7	1.07	$\$112.40/(1.07)^0$	\$112.40
6	1.07	$\$112.40/(1.07)^1$	\$105.05
5	1.07	$\$112.40/(1.07)^2$	\$98.17
4	1.07	$\$112.40/(1.07)^3$	\$91.75
3	1.07	$\$112.40/(1.07)^4$	\$85.75
2	1.07	$\$112.40/(1.07)^5$	\$80.14
1	1.07	$\$112.40/(1.07)^6$	\$74.90
0	1.07	$\$112.40/(1.07)^7$	\$70.00

4.7 Considerations of Rate

Modern connotations of rates incite mental images of interest rates. The concept of interest is quite old and involves a rather simple notion. During Biblical times, this concept was referred to as usury. With respect to modern considerations of financial management, this notion is expressed through the concept that one party receives some form of compensation from a second party in return for the use of its funds. Basically, interest is the return rate that one anticipates as a reward for the use of his or her funds by another party, through time. Another mental model for the term rate may involve the necessity of paying interest. For example, when one purchases a home or an automobile, the payments of interest must be paid regarding the principal of the obtained loan.

Examples of interest are prominent among modern society. Real estate mortgages involve some form of interest rate; building leases may involve some form of rate over long periods; vehicle purchases and leases require an interest rate; credit card payments involve the use of interest; and various and sundry business and personal loans require a consideration of interest. Interest rates may be either static or dynamic; that is, they may be unchanging or changing. In some cases, such rates may be negotiable. Regardless of the situation, they exist among a myriad of domains.

A consideration of the basic concept of rates was discussed within the preceding chapter. This discussion introduced the notions of rates for compounding and discounting with respect to the time value of money. The use of compounding rates provided the intermediary tool through which future monetary values were determined. In contrast, the use of the discounting rate provided the intermediary tool through which current monetary values were determined. Regardless of either the future or past perspective of monetary values, the notion of rates determined the magnitude of incremental compounding or discounting effects. Therefore, an understanding of the notion of rate is essential to fully understanding the premise of the time value of money.

The discussions of the preceding chapter provided known rates for compounding and discounting within the future monetary value and current monetary value situations. However, there are situations in which rates must be determined. For example, one may wish to compare various rates against varying investment principals, through time, to determine which combination of rate versus principal yields the highest and best benefit for the organization. The use of such examinations may also necessitate considerations of current monetary value and future monetary value formulas.

4.8 Determining the Rate Variable

An examination of either the future monetary value formula or the current monetary formula may yield the expression representing the value of the rate variable. This defining of the rate variable may be accomplished algebraically. Based on the discussions of the preceding chapters, the basic mathematical relationship among future monetary value, current monetary value, rate, and time is expressed as follows:

$$V_{futr} = (V_{curr})(R_{per} + 1.0)^P$$

Again, the variables within this equation are identified as follows:

R_{per} Rate factor through time
P Period of time
V_{curr} Current monetary value
V_{futr} Future monetary value

A determination of the expression representing the value of the R_{per} variable may be easily derived from the future monetary value formula. Such a determination may be accomplished through the algebraic manipulation of the established V_{futr} formula. The derivation is accomplished as follows:

$$V_{futr} = (V_{curr})(R_{per} + 1.0)^P$$

$$\frac{V_{futr}}{V_{curr}} = (R_{per} + 1.0)^P$$

$$\left(\sqrt[P]{V_{futr}/V_{curr}}\right) = R_{per} + 1.0 \qquad (4.5)$$

$$\left(\sqrt[P]{V_{futr}/V_{curr}}\right) - 1.0 = R_{per}$$

$$R_{per} = \left(\sqrt[P]{V_{futr}/V_{curr}}\right) - 1.0$$

This derivation yields the expression that represents the value of the R_{per} variable through time. The value of the R_{per} variable is indicative of the value of 1.0 being subtracted from the multiple root of the V_{futr} variable divided by the V_{curr} variable. This equation may be used to solve problems in which the values of V_{futr}, V_{curr}, and P are identified. Given this derivation, it is possible to determine the value of R_{per} with respect to the characteristics of the time value of money. The following example demonstrates the solution to such a problem.

EXAMPLE 4.6

An example problem may be stated as follows:

> If I have \$70.00 today, assuming annual compounding, and its value is worth \$112.40 in seven years, what is the appropriate rate that is commensurate with both the current monetary value and the future monetary value?

Solution for Example 4.6

The derived formula for determining the value of the rate variable is appropriate. Before the application of this formula occurs, specifications of the variables and their respective values must be established regarding the statement of the problem. These identifications are given as follows:

R_{per} = This value is unknown.
P = 7 years
V_{curr} = \$70.00
V_{futr} = \$112.40

This example involves a consideration of a period of seven years in which both the future monetary value and the current monetary value are established. In terms of current money value, the considered financial amount is \$70.00. In terms of the specified future amount, the future monetary value is \$112.40. The objective is to determine the rate that equates these two values with respect to the time value of money.

These values may be substituted within the derived R_{per} formula to manifest their mathematical relationship with respect to the characteristics of the time value of money. These substitutions of variable values are given as follows:

$$R_{per} = \left(\sqrt[P]{V_{futr}/V_{curr}}\right) - 1.0$$

$$R_{per} = \left(\sqrt[7]{\$112.40/\$70.00}\right) - 1.0$$

$$R_{per} = \left(\sqrt[7]{1.61}\right) - 1.0$$

$$R_{per} = 1.07 - 1.0$$

$$R_{per} = 0.07$$

This solution yields a value for the R_{per} variable. The value of the R_{per} variable is determined to be 0.07. When expressed as a percentage, the value of the R_{per} variable is determined to be 7.0%. Therefore, with respect to the characteristics of the time value of money, the rate at which a future monetary value of \$112.40 becomes equivalent to a current monetary value of \$70.00 is determined to be 7.00%. This calculated R_{per} value is commensurate with the stated R_{per} value that was provided within the sample problem sets regarding current monetary value and future monetary value.

4.9 Determining the Time Variable

The discussions of the preceding chapter identified methods through which the values of future monetary value and current monetary value may be calculated. This example of determining the R_{per} variable provided a consideration of determining the rate that affects the value of money through time. However, another consideration of the time value of money may be considered. This consideration is an examination of the time variable itself. In this case, one must determine the period of time that is contained within the mathematical relationships and formulas regarding the time value of money.

The time variable is indicative of either a single period or the use of multiple periods that facilitates the effects of the time value of money. It is through such considerations of time that the influences of compounding and discounting are manifested regarding monetary values. Similar to the derivation of the R_{per} variable, a determination of the time variable, P, may also be crafted through algebraic manipulations of the future monetary value formula. The basic formula expressing the variable relationships of future monetary value is again given as follows:

$$V_{futr} = (V_{curr})(R_{per} + 1.0)^P$$

Within this formula, the legend expressing the variable associations with the time value of money is given as follows:

R_{per} Rate factor through time
P Period of time
V_{curr} Current monetary value
V_{futr} Future monetary value

With a basic understanding of the mathematical relationships of these variables with respect to the tenets of the time value of money, one may derive an expression that yields the mathematical construct of the period variable. Again, an algebraic approach involving logarithms may be used to determine the characteristics of this relationship. The appropriate derivation is given as follows:

$$V_{futr} = (V_{curr})(R_{per} + 1.0)^P$$

$$\frac{V_{futr}}{V_{curr}} = (R_{per} + 1.0)^P \tag{4.6}$$

$$(R_{per} + 1.0)^P = \frac{V_{futr}}{V_{curr}}$$

$$\ln\left((R_{per}+1.0)^{P}\right)=\ln\left(\frac{V_{futr}}{V_{curr}}\right)$$

$$P\left(\ln(R_{per}+1.0)\right)=\ln\left(\frac{V_{futr}}{V_{curr}}\right)$$

$$P=\frac{\ln\left(\frac{V_{futr}}{V_{curr}}\right)}{\ln(R_{per}+1.0)}$$

This derivation yields the expression that represents the value of the period variable, P, through time. The value of the period variable, P, is indicative of the logarithmic relationship that exists within the concept of the time value of money. This equation may be used to solve problems in which the values of V_{futr}, V_{curr}, and R_{per} are identified. Given this derivation, it is possible to determine the value of the time variable, P, with respect to the characteristics of the time value of money. The following example demonstrates the solution to such a problem.

EXAMPLE 4.7

An example problem may be stated as follows:

> If I have \$70.00 today, assuming annual compounding, and its value is worth \$112.40 with respect to a 7.00% rate, what is the appropriate period of time that is commensurate with these specific characteristics of the time value of money?

Solution for Example 4.7

The derived formula for determining the value of the rate variable is appropriate. Before the application of this formula occurs, specifications of the variables and their respective values must be established regarding the statement of the problem. These identifications are given as follows:

R_{per} = 7.00%
P = This value is unknown.
V_{curr} = \$70.00
V_{futr} = \$112.40

This example involves a consideration of an unknown period of time in which both the future monetary value and the current monetary value are established, and a rate of 7.00% is mandated. In terms of current money value, the considered financial amount is \$70.00. In terms of the specified future amount, the future monetary value is \$112.40. The objective is to determine the period of time that equates these two values with respect to the time value of money.

These values may be substituted within the derived formula, regarding the mathematical expression of time period, *P*, to manifest their quantitative relationship with respect to the characteristics of the time value of money. These substitutions of variable values are given as follows:

$$P = \frac{\ln\left(\frac{V_{futr}}{V_{curr}}\right)}{\ln\left(R_{per} + 1.0\right)}$$

$$P = \frac{\ln\left(\frac{\$112.40}{\$70.00}\right)}{\ln\left(0.07 + 1.0\right)}$$

$$P = \frac{\ln(1.61)}{\ln(1.07)}$$

$$P = \frac{\ln(0.47)}{\ln(0.06)}$$

$$P = 7.03$$

This solution yields a value for the variable that represents the period of time, *P*, with respect to the time value of money. The value of the *P* variable is determined to be 7.03 periods. When rounded, the value of the *P* variable is determined to be 7.00 periods. Therefore, with respect to the characteristics of the time value of money, the period of time, with respect to a 7.00% rate, at which a future monetary value of $112.40 becomes equivalent to a current monetary value of $70.00 is determined to be 7.00 periods. This calculated *P* value is commensurate with the stated *P* value that was provided within the sample problem sets regarding current monetary value and future monetary value.

The natural logarithm was necessary to solve the stated problem of this example. The values of natural logarithms may be generated through the use of established tables that are commonly found within algebra texts, through the use of interpolative methods, through the use of financial or engineering calculators, or through the use of software spreadsheets that contain mathematical functions.

4.10 Comments Regarding the Time Value of Money

The examples of this chapter provided only instances of annual compounding effects. Further, the discounting examples of this chapter also considered annual periods. However, other periods of time regarding both compounding and discounting may be considered. Examples include monthly periods, quarterly periods, or any other set period that an analyst may desire to specify. Certainly, the basic formulas regarding current monetary value and future monetary value must be adjusted accordingly to incorporate the effects of such altered periods.

It is beyond the scope of this introductory chapter to delineate such additional considerations of compounding and discounting principles. However, the appendix materials of this text provide formulas and examples that accommodate such variations among compounding and discounting periods.

The aforementioned discussions and examples of compounding and discounting are demonstrative of two perspectives regarding monetary values: (1) the perspective of looking into the future given a specified period, rate, and current monetary value through the use of compounding; and (2) the perspective of looking backward into time to determine a previous monetary value given the specification of future value and an accepted, stated discount rate. These two perspectives form the basis of capital budgeting decision models. Therefore, it is imperative that an understanding of these basic concepts be established before any undertaking or examining of capital budgeting, scenario analysis, or sensitivity analysis commences.

The examples presented within this chapter were relatively simple to demonstrate, solve, and understand. However, they clearly show the basis of the time value of money. They also are indicative of the powerfulness, through time, of the interactions among the variables of time period, amount of payment, future value, present value, and rate. Again, a solid understanding of these interactions is necessary for understanding the basic concepts of capital budgeting, scenario analysis, and sensitivity analysis. (See Figure 4.3.)

Figure 4.3 Twentieth anniversary of Treasury's Office of Technical Assistance (OTA). Deputy Secretary of the Treasury Neal Wolin provided opening remarks on the work of the Office of Technical Assistance. In the last 20 years, OTA has helped finance ministries and central banks in nearly a hundred developing countries around the world strengthen their capacity to manage public finances, support their growing economies, and combat economic crimes, including corruption, which in turn helps governments provide more effective services to their citizens. (Courtesy of the U.S. Department of the Treasury, http://www.flickr.com/photos/ustreasury/5621906713/in/photostream.)

4.11 Foundational Understanding

The preceding discussions regarding the determinations of rates and time periods complement the earlier considerations of the determinations of both current monetary values and future monetary values. These four concepts provide the basis for solidly understanding the time value of money. A robust knowledge of the concepts that govern and influence the variables, among the relationships that pertain to the time value of money, is critical for understanding the basic concepts and methods of capital budgeting.

Considerations of the four time value of money formulas regarding discounting and compounding rates, current monetary values and future monetary values, and time periods provide the necessary constructs for establishing the time value of money relationships that are necessary to craft capital budgeting methods quantitatively. Through the use of such concepts and quantitative tools, four perspectives of rendering organizational, strategic decisions may be considered: (1) time periods regarding investments, (2) current monetary values and equivalencies, (3) future monetary values and equivalencies, and (4) rates that influence compounding and discounting. These four constructs provide the basis for delineating the perspectives that are necessary for rendering capital budgeting perspectives.

Given these notions, organizational leaders gain powerful tools through which their financial investment decisions may be contemplated and analyzed. Leaders may compare and contrast potential courses of actions and strategic investment initiatives to identify potential courses of actions that are acceptable and feasible with respect to their available resources, goals, and objectives. Such approaches are not solitary. Time value of money concepts and formulas provide a multifaceted perspective of the decision domain through which leaders and managers may gain additional perspectives for their decisions.

Such decisions may be multiple or they may be mutually exclusive. Multiple conditions occur when more than one course of action is considered through the use of analytical methods, and more than one course of action may be concurrently pursued. Mutually exclusive conditions are manifested when one, and only one, course of action may be pursued despite the existence of other, viable alternative courses of actions.

These notions are commensurate with the basic economic questions posed within the discussions of the preceding chapters. Organizational leaders must satisfy wants and needs, with respect to the limitations and availabilities of necessary resources, in conjunction with their organizational strategic interests. The use of such resources is the means through which such satisfaction may be accomplished. However, because of a variety of limitations (e.g., financial, political), not all identified courses of actions may be pursued strategically through time. Therefore, organizational leaders must render decisions that are indicative of courses of actions that are both feasible and achievable, and that provide the highest and best use of resources to benefit the organization through time.

Given this notion, it is imperative that organizational leaders examine the decision domain, and incorporate its attributes within the context of rendering decisions. From the perspective of financial management, such examinations may be accomplished through considerations of time, current monetary value, future monetary value, and both compounding and discounting rates. Therefore, the time value of money is a salient consideration of financial decisions that impact organizations strategically.

The opening paragraphs of this chapter indicated that a foundational understanding of the time value of money and its components was necessary before undertaking an examination of capital budgeting methods. The explanations associated with the discussions of rate and time provide delineations of the remaining concepts that are necessary for beginning an examination of capital budgeting methods. Given this observation, one may now begin an exploration of capital budgeting concepts. (See Figure 4.4.)

Figure 4.4 On August 20, 2009, Rosie Rios was sworn in as Treasurer of the United States. Her signature will be featured on all new bills printed by the Bureau of Engraving and Printing. Her position represents one of the highest positions of financial authority and responsibility within the United States. (Courtesy of the U.S. Department of the Treasury, http://www.flickr.com/photos/ustreasury/page26/.)

4.12 Capital Budgeting Methods

Capital budgeting provides a means through which organizational leaders may evaluate courses of actions involving capital projects and investments strategically. Regarding strategic decisions, the use of capital budgeting methods provides organizational leaders with perspectives of time, profitability, current and future monetary value, and discount and compounding rates. These perspectives are expressed quantitatively through mathematical formulas. These mathematical constructs are identified as the net present value method (NPV), the internal rate of return (IRR), the profitability index (PI), and the payback method. These methods may be applied separately or they may be applied through any appropriate combination of techniques that satisfies the requirements of the decision domain. The succeeding chapters of this text provide detailed discussions of these capital budgeting techniques.

4.12.1 Net Present Value

The NPV method provides perspectives regarding comparisons of the current monetary value of estimated capital project cash flows. The basic premise of the NPV method is to compare project valuations to determine which project yields the highest current monetary value in terms of present dollar values. Therefore, based on the outcome of an NPV analysis, organizational leaders can determine which projects are acceptable and which projects may be rejected. Hence, using NPV methods, organizational leaders may select from the projects that are deemed to be the most profitable as viable candidates for pursuit strategically through time. The NPV method may be used to evaluate cases of single projects, mutually exclusive projects, or multiple project acceptances.

4.12.2 Internal Rate of Return

The IRR method involves a determination of achieving a financial state of being that results in a null financial value being manifested for the NPV. Further, IRR incorporates a consideration of rate comparisons, between the outcome of the IRR analysis and a stated rate of acceptance, to determine which projects are deemed as acceptable versus those projects that should be rejected. Hence, using IRR methods, organizational leaders may select from the projects that are deemed to be the most profitable as viable candidates for pursuit strategically through time. The succeeding chapters present detailed discussions of such concepts. The IRR method may be used to evaluate cases of single projects, mutually exclusive projects, or multiple project acceptances.

4.12.3 Profitability Index

The PI method involves a determination of the potential profitability of an examined capital investment project. The PI method involves an examination of current monetary values versus the initial investment of a capital investment project, thereby generating a ratio that is indicative of payoff considerations. Such analysis also provides a means through which potential capital investment projects are classified as either acceptable or unacceptable. Through the use of the PI method, a ranking of capital investment projects may occur. Therefore, organizational leaders gain perspectives of potential profitability, payoff considerations, and comparisons among competing projects. Using the PI method, organizational leaders may select from the projects that are deemed to be the most profitable as viable candidates for pursuit strategically through time. The PI method may be used to evaluate cases of single projects, mutually exclusive projects, or multiple project acceptances. The succeeding chapters present detailed discussions of such concepts.

4.12.4 Payback Method

The payback method provides a perspective of time within the context of capital budgeting decisions. The basic premise of this method involves a determination of the amount of time that would be necessary to repay the costs of initial investment with respect to the eventual profitability of the proposed capital investment project. This situation involves a consideration of the amount of time that would be necessary for a project to pay for itself if it was implemented. Although a specific formula is not mandated for the payback period, its mathematical construct provides a systematic, methodical process through which a perspective of time is demonstrated within the context of capital budgeting. Again, based on the characteristics of time, potential projects may be classified as either acceptable or unacceptable, and comparisons of projects may occur to influence implementation decisions. The payback method may be used to evaluate cases of single projects, mutually exclusive projects, or multiple project acceptances.

4.13 Chapter Comments and Summary

This chapter emphasized the notion that money has time value. Basically, the value of money changes with respect to the influences of compounding and discount rates through periods of time. Such considerations of time pervade the concepts of rendering financial decisions. Two primary concepts form the basis for understanding the changes that occur among monetary values through time: (1) future money value and (2) current monetary value. The variables that influence the mathematical constructs through which these perspectives are examined include time periods, payment amounts, future monetary values, current monetary values, and rates. The notion of rates may be used within compounding activities or discounting activities. An understanding of these concepts is crucial before commencing any analysis of capital budgeting decisions.

Cumulatively, these notions are indicative of the characteristics of the time value of money. Through an understanding of the principles that influence time value of money calculations, organizational leaders gain perspectives of period, current monetary value and future monetary value, compounding and discounting rates, and the attributes of profitability. Examining these facets of the decision domain embellishes the rendering of strategic financial decisions.

Capital budgeting decisions may determine which vendor is the best option for providing food services within a correctional facility, may determine whether a police agency implements a long-term community-oriented policing initiative, or may determine whether to purchase a particular brand of automobile for patrol services. However, any such decisions must be rendered with respect to the best interests of the organization, its shareholders (if any), or its stakeholders. Further, those responsible for rendering such decisions must strive to maintain the integrity of their decisions and the decisions process. Through the use of mathematical tools, those responsible for rendering decisions may examine chronological attributes of the decision domain and yield decisions of greater robustness. (See Figure 4.5.)

Figure 4.5 Stacks of counterfeit money. Having the knowledge of financial concepts also assists during initiatives to deter counterfeiting operations. Although the U.S. Secret Service protects American dignitaries, it also pursues counterfeiting initiatives. (Courtesy of the U.S. Secret Service, http://www.secretservice.gov/photo_gallery_enlarge.shtml#Counterfeit_Investigations.)

4.14 Formulas

Interest Calculation

$$\text{Annual Interest Payment} = (\text{Established Rate})(\text{Principal})$$

Annual Payment

$$(\text{Annual Payment})_{\text{year}} = (\text{Principal Payment})_{\text{year}} + (\text{Interest Payment})_{\text{year}}$$

Future Monetary Value

$$V_{futr} = (V_{curr})(R_{per} + 1.0)^P$$

Current Monetary Value

$$V_{curr} = \frac{V_{futr}}{\left(R_{per} + 1.0\right)^P}$$

Rate Determination

$$R_{per} = \left(\sqrt[P]{V_{futr}/V_{curr}}\right) - 1.0$$

Time Period Determination

$$P = \frac{\ln\left(\dfrac{V_{futr}}{V_{curr}}\right)}{\ln\left(R_{per} + 1.0\right)}$$

4.15 Terminology

Capital budgeting
Capital investment
Compounding
Compounding rate
Current monetary value
Decision
Decision domain
Discounting
Discounting rate
Future monetary value
Interest
Interest rate
Internal rate of return
Net present value
Payback method
Profitability index
Rate
Rate determination
Relative value
Time value
Time period determination
Value

4.16 Thought and Discussion Questions

1. If I have $103.25 today, assuming annual compounding, how much will it be worth in three years using a 3.5% rate? Show the appropriate variable values, and then solve using the future monetary value formula.
2. After seven years I anticipate having the amount of $425.40. Assuming a discount rate of 7.0%, what is the equivalent monetary amount in terms of current value? Show the appropriate variable values, and then solve using the current monetary value formula.
3. I anticipate having the amount of $500.00 after an unknown period of time. The monetary current value is $257.35. The rate is 7.7%. What amount of time is necessary to realize this situation?
4. I anticipate having the amount of $378.22 after a period of seven years. The monetary current value is $357.35. However, the necessary rate is unidentified. What is the necessary rate to realize this situation?

It Is Time for Payback
The Payback Time Method

5

Time is money.*

Benjamin Franklin

5.1 Objectives

The objectives of this chapter are to:

- Understand the chronological perspective of capital budgeting
- Understand the concept of the payback time method
- Understand the mathematical formula necessary to use the payback time method
- Understand the rendering of decisions using the payback time method

5.2 Introduction

The methods of capital budgeting encompass perspectives of time, cash value, rate, and profitability potential. Examining projects from these perspectives involves the use of quantitative tools through which projects may be judged and selected as either acceptable or unacceptable for devoting the resources of the organization in the pursuit of such capital initiatives. The first capital budgeting method to be examined involves the time perspective of judging the acceptableness of potential capital investment projects. This method is known as the payback method.

Although the concepts of the time value of money were established among the previous chapters, the payback method ignores the basic premise of the time value of money. Time calculations using the payback method may involve the examination of long-term, strategic periods or they may involve much shorter periods. Regardless, the salient theme of the payback method provides organizational leaders with a perspective of time when judging the acceptableness of potential capital investment projects.

* Franklin, Benjamin, "Decision Quotations," Brainy Quote, http://www.brainyquote.com/quotes/quotes/b/benjaminfr101411.html (accessed July 11, 2011).

Having an understanding and knowledge of the perspective of time provides organizational leaders with information that may influence financial management decisions. Considerations of time are important for a variety of reasons. In some cases, both financial funding and other resources (e.g., personnel, vehicles) may be available to pursue capital investment projects, but an insufficient amount of time may exist in which the activities of the capital investment project are expected to be completed. In other cases, both time and financial funding may exist in sufficient quantities to facilitate the completion of a capital investment project, but other resources are insufficient to pursue a capital investment project. A third situation may arise in which all three considerations of financial funding, time, and additional resources may be insufficient to undertake and complete a capital initiative. Finally, another situation may be manifested in which all three considerations of financial funding, time, and additional resources are completely sufficient to undertake and complete a capital initiative.

A cursory consideration of the final situation may yield a belief that projects may be accepted and judged outright based solely on the perspective of time. In some cases, this notion may be correct. However, other attributes must be considered in addition to the perspective of time regarding the characteristics of capital investment projects, their acceptability, and their pursuit. A solitary consideration of time characteristics is insufficient to render a robust decision regarding the committing of organizational resources to the pursuing of potential capital initiatives.

Other considerations affect the pursuit of a capital project initiative. Factors of whether the project will create value for the organization through time and contribute toward the wealth maximization potential of shareholders must be considered. Other considerations may involve aspects of organizational politics, which may influence whether a capital project may be pursued, even if financial funding, time, and additional resources are completely sufficient to complete a capital initiative. Regardless, even though capital budgeting tools may be used to embellish the decisions of humans, other influences exist concerning the pursuance of capital initiatives. (See Figure 5.1.)

5.3 Payback Time Method

The payback time method is indicative of the perspective of time regarding capital initiatives. Essentially, the payback time method represents the amount of time that is necessary for compensating an organization for the cost amounts of financial funding that is necessary to instigate a capital initiative. However, the payback time method does not incorporate any considerations of the time value of money within its mathematical construct. The use of the payback time method neither necessitates the use of equivalencies

Figure 5.1 Capital budgeting influences investment decisions. Defense Secretary Robert M. Gates and Navy Admiral Mike Mullen, Chairman of the Joint Chiefs of Staff, conduct a press conference at the Pentagon, May 18, 2011, to discuss the actions that the DOD will take to ensure future budget cuts are targeted. (Photo by Cherie Cullen, DOD. Courtesy of the U.S. Army, http://www.army.mil/media/19630.)

regarding the current monetary value nor the future monetary value calculations within its processing of time calculations.

The payback time method represents the amount of monies that represent the initial costs of the capital investment versus the mathematical summation of each of the annual cash flows, which are anticipated during the duration of the lifetime of the capital investment, until a payback time threshold is manifested. Therefore, the payback time method represents a ratio between initial costs of the capital investment and the summation of necessary cash flows, annually, until the payback period is demonstrated.

The payback time method is expressed as the summation of the costs of investment divided by these annual amounts. Because time values cannot be expressed as a negative number, the absolute value of the outcome of the payback time method represents the amount of time that is required to compensate financially for the expended costs of investment regarding a capital initiative.

The following variables are used to represent the entities that exist within the mathematical relationships of the payback time method:

- T Time required for payback to occur
- P Period currently examined within the current payback time method iteration
- A_P Annual cash flow value

V_I Value amount of the initial funding
E_R Financial effect of a partial year (if any)
T_P Partial year period (if any)

With respect to an overall period of years, the following expression represents the mathematical relationships among the variables that comprise the payback time method:

$$T = \left| \frac{V_I}{\sum A_P} \right| \tag{5.1}$$

Note: The value of the variable *P* does not exceed the time required for the threshold value to occur.

Further, with respect to a partial period, which is indicative of a period that represents a partial year, the following expression represents the mathematical relationships among the variables that comprise the payback time method:

$$T_P = \left| \frac{E_R}{\sum A_P} \right| \tag{5.2}$$

Note: The value of the variable *P* does not exceed the time required for the threshold value to occur.

The concept of the payback time method is fairly straightforward because it is merely the consideration of a ratio between the amounts of financial funds invested versus the amounts of annual cash flows that are necessary to surpass a threshold of compensation regarding the investment costs of the capital initiative. The following section considers the basic premise of the payback time method.

5.4 Application of the Payback Time Method

The application of the payback time method may be viewed from multiple perspectives. The first perspective involves a consideration of only one project that is being contemplated. Another perspective involves the concept of mutual exclusion—the selection of one, and only one initiative, from multiple capital initiatives. An additional perspective involves the selection of two (or more) projects from many projects. The example problems of this chapter demonstrate payback time method calculations that are applicable among each of these situations.

Although the payback time method may be used as a solitary capital budgeting tool, its usefulness is limited as a sole method of capital investment analysis. The most obvious limitation is that the payback time method ignores the concept of the time value of money because it does not necessitate any future monetary value or current monetary value equivalencies. Only the cash flow amounts, as derived, are used within the mathematical constructs of the payback time method. Therefore, if a project is deemed as acceptable via the outcomes of the payback time method, then it is appropriate to examine the characteristics of the proposed initiative from the perspectives of additional capital budgeting methods. Such methods include the net present value, internal rate of return, and profitability analysis. Although it may be used as a solitary method, it is recommended that the payback time method be used as a complement to other capital budgeting methods.

The payback time method may be a repetitive, cyclical process, in which its iterations are repeated until an established payback threshold is identified. Once this threshold is identified, the payback time method is terminated. Such termination ignores any cash flows that may exist beyond the established point of termination. Therefore, regardless of their values, any such cash flow values are immaterial within the context of the iterative processes of the payback time method.

Because the theme of the method is relevant only to a chronological perspective, the scope and magnitude of the potential capital investment initiative is also immaterial. Therefore, the payback time method concept may be applicable among projects of varying scope and magnitude. Hence, it may find application among the financial environments of small businesses as well as among the financial settings of conglomerate corporations.

Although the payback time method may have drawbacks, its application is characteristic of some advantages. The method itself is simple and straightforward, thereby demonstrating its relative ease of understanding and implementation. Because contemporary organizations are concerned with facets of time, the chronological basis of this method provides a tool through which capital initiatives may be evaluated as a prerequisite to stronger methods of analysis. Simply, if an organization does not have time to pursue a capital initiative, then it may be discarded before any further analysis occurs involving its cash flows, rates, or profitability.

Overall, the payback time method provides a unique perspective of capital investment initiatives: chronological. It is a time-sensitive method in which a determination may be made regarding the amount of time that is necessary for a capital initiative to return the affiliated costs of investment. Through such analysis, organizational leaders may quickly gain a perspective of whether the considered initiative is feasible based solely on the time it takes to return the costs of investment versus any organizational restrictions regarding time constraints.

This chapter contains solved examples of problems that are indicative of the payback time method. Each of the examples is given from the perspective of law enforcement and criminal justice entities. These problems consider the application of the payback time method regarding single investment situations, mutually exclusive situations, and multiple capital initiative situations.

5.5 Single Investment Initiative

Single investment initiatives occur only when one capital investment initiative is considered and examined for acceptance as a viable pursuit of organizational resources. The following example demonstrates this concept.

EXAMPLE 5.1

A hypothetical problem example, necessitating a solution involving the payback time method, is given as follows.

Last year, a tornado destroyed the police training facility of an urban area. The damages were sufficient enough to warrant the total loss of the building and its supporting infrastructure. After the devastating event occurred, the city council approved a measure to erect a new police training facility. The destroyed facility served as a training institute for regional first responders, among the four bordering states, whose functions included the provision of emergency services during both natural and man-made disasters. Therefore, it is imperative that this facility be restored.

The training tuition dollars of local personnel were provided by the devastated city. However, any nonlocal personnel were responsible for providing their own tuitions (e.g., self-pay, sponsor pay, grants). Because it was a regional training facility, the majority of the trainees were not local personnel. Therefore, this training facility provided a source of revenue for the city and its police department.

A combination of monies—to be obtained via taxation, city bond investments, a limited insurance policy, loans, and goodwill and charitable donations—is proposed to fund the initial costs of the capital investment. The cost of the new building is estimated to be $291,000.00. However, because of existing debt obligations, the city must begin paying its debt within the next two years.

Based on the following listing of anticipated cash flow values, what is the amount of time necessary before the payback time threshold occurs? Based on the calculated payback time required, is it feasible and advisable for the city to pursue this proposed course of action?

The cash flows describing the financial values of this problem are given in Table 5.1.

Solution Overview of Example 5.1

A systematic, methodical process is required to solve this problem. The payback time method is an appropriate solution to this problem because it involves viewing the capital initiative from the perspective of time, and because it facilitates the determination of the payback threshold period.

The first observation concerns the amount of investment necessary for the instigation of the capital project. Based on the problem statement and the

Table 5.1 Cash Flows of Example 5.1

Period	Anticipated Cash Flows
0	($291,000.00)
1	$109,527.00
2	$129,034.00
3	$135,068.00
4	$148,927.00
5	$159,000.00
6	$168,000.00
7	$174,980.00

contents of Table 5.1, this amount is determined to be $291,000.00. Therefore, the value of the variable representing the initial capital investment cost, V_I, is determined to be $291,000.00. The remainder of the values, representing the additional entities within the payback time value relationship, must be determined.

Although the initial cost of investment and the anticipated, annual cash flows are given within the problem statement, the remainder of the variable values must be calculated from these given observations. The payback time method is a systematic, methodical process through which such values may be derived. The basic process of the payback time method may be repeated, as necessary, until the value of the payback threshold period is determined.

Solution for Example 5.1: First Iteration

Initially, a comparison of the initial investment cost value may be compared to the value of the cash flow of the first year. A specification of this comparison is given as follows:

$$V_I = \$291,000.00$$

$$\sum_{1}^{2} A_P = \$109,527.00 + \$129,034.00$$

$$\sum_{1}^{2} A_P = \$238,561.00$$

Evaluation: $V_I > \Sigma A_P$
Recommendation: Continue iterations

This evaluation of the initial cost of the capital investment initiative versus the anticipated cash flow values of the first year of operating the new facility show a difference between the two dollar amounts. The cost of the initial investment is greater than the revenues associated with the cash flows of the first year. The cost of the initial capital investment project, $291,000.00, is greater than the revenue cash flows, totaling $109,527.00, that are anticipated during the first year. With respect this comparison, an insufficient amount of money is generated to compensate for the initial costs of the facility during the first year. Therefore, a threshold point, indicative of achieving a payback period, is not demonstrated. Hence, the process of the payback time method is repeated with respect to the succeeding, anticipated cash flow values.

The initial repetition of the payback time method compares the initial investment cost value with the value of the cash flows anticipated during the operational stages of the facility. Within this iteration of the payback time method, a summation of the cash flow revenues of the first and second years occurs. This comparison is given as follows:

Initial investment of capital project: \$291,000.00
Year one anticipated cash flows: \$109,527.00
Evaluation: $V_I > \Sigma A_P$
Recommendation: Continue iterations

This evaluation of the initial cost of the capital investment initiative versus the anticipated cash flow values of the combined first year and second year of operating the new facility show a difference between the two dollar amounts. The cost of the initial investment is greater than the revenues associated with the cash flows of the first year. The cost of the initial capital investment project, \$291,000.00, remains greater than the summation of the revenue cash flows totaling \$238,561.00. With respect to this comparison, an insufficient amount of money is generated to compensate for the initial costs of the facility during these years. Therefore, a threshold point, indicative of achieving a payback period, is not demonstrated. Hence, the process of the payback time method is repeated with respect to the incorporation of the succeeding, anticipated cash flow value.

Solution for Example 5.1: Second Iteration

The next repetition of the payback time method compares the initial investment cost value with the value of the cash flows anticipated during the succeeding year. Within this iteration of the payback time method, a summation of the cash flow revenues of the first, second, and third years occurs. This comparison is given as follows:

$$V_I = \$291{,}000.00$$

$$\sum_{1}^{3} A_P = \$238{,}561.00 + \$135{,}068.00$$

$$\sum_{1}^{3} A_P = \$373{,}629.00$$

Evaluation: $V_I < \Sigma A_P$
Recommendation: Continue iterations

This iteration of the payback time method differs from its predecessors. For the first time in the process, the value of the summation of the anticipated cash flows (A_P), \$373,629.00, surpasses the value of the initial capital investment monies (V_I), \$291,000.00. Because this situation is manifested, it is evident that the payback time threshold is surpassed during this iteration. Therefore, somewhere between the second and third year, there exists a threshold point denoting the payback period.

These calculations have determined that the payback period exists between the second and the third year of the anticipated cash flow revenue values. Therefore, at least two years are required for the payback period to occur, but no more than three years are necessary. However, the exact value of the payback period remains unknown. Therefore, additional calculations are necessary to definitively indicate the specific amount of time that is required for the compensation of the initial capital investment, via payback, to occur in due time.

These additional calculations again consider the mathematical ratio between the initial investment value of the capital initiative, V_I, and the anticipated cash flow revenue value, A_P. However, this portion of the payback time method involves a consideration of the period of time that represents the period between the second year and the third year.

Solution for Example 5.1: Partial Year Calculation

This point in the payback method calculations does not yield a specific period in which the payback time threshold is satisfied. Instead, it only provides a general perspective of time regarding the period in which this threshold is surpassed. Additional calculations are necessary to determine the specific amount of time that represents the remainder of the annual period in which the payback time threshold is manifested.

The payback time method outcome indicated that the period in which the payback time threshold occurs is somewhere between the second and the third year. It is necessary to determine the remainder time effects of the anticipated cash flows with respect to the value of the initial investment required of the capital initiative. The value of these effects may be expressed mathematically via the following expression:

$$E_R = \Sigma A_P - V_I$$

Within this expression, the variable V_I represents the cost of the initial capital investment, \$291,000.00. The variable ΣA_P represents only the summed value of cash flow revenues that were calculated during the iterations of the payback time method, \$373,629.00. Substituting these values into the expression yields the following outcome:

$$ER = \Sigma A_P - V_I$$

$$ER = \$373{,}629.00 - \$291{,}000.00$$

$$ER = \$82{,}629.00$$

The outcome of the remainder effect calculation, E_R, yields a value of \$82,629.00. Based on the payback time method calculations, it is evident that the limitations of the range of the remainder period do not surpass the third year. Therefore, with respect to the considerations of anticipated cash flow revenues, a cash flow value limitation may be established as the value of the variable ΣA_P because it represents only the summed cash flows that were included within the payback time calculations. The value of the variable ΣA_P is \$373,629.00. This determination of the remainder effect value, E_R, and the calculated ΣA_P value provide the data that is necessary to calculate the value of the unknown period threshold that is commensurate with the partial year.

The previously defined expression, denoted through the variable *T*, may be used to determine the value of the partial year. The calculated values of

ΣA_P and E_R may be substituted into the expression appropriately to determine the value of the unknown partial year. These substitutions are given as follows:

$$T_P = \left| \frac{E_R}{\sum A_P} \right|$$

$$T_P = \left| \frac{\$82{,}629.00}{\$373{,}629.00} \right|$$

$$T_P = 0.22$$

The partial year calculation yields a T_P value of 0.22. This T_P value represents 22% of a one-year period that is required for the manifestation of the payback time threshold to occur. Therefore, based on this outcome, 22% of the second year must occur before the payback threshold time is manifested.

Solution for Example 5.1: Calculation of the Payback Time Period

The preceding discussions necessitated the use of the payback time method as a means of calculating a general value regarding the occurrence of a payback time threshold. This value was determined to be somewhere between two and three years. However, although a general value was derived, it is insufficient to exactly specify the value of the payback time. An additional calculation, based on a partial year, was necessary to determine the value of the unknown period between the second and the third year.

These two values may be combined to identify the payback threshold period. Adding these values yields the following determination of the payback threshold period:

$$2 \text{ years} + 0.22 \text{ years} = 2.22 \text{ years}.$$

Based on the outcome of this calculation, the payback time threshold occurs in 2.22 years. Therefore, it will require a period of 2.22 years before the capital investment project returns enough monies to pay for its costs of investment.

Solution for Example 5.1: Capital Budgeting Decision

The determination of the specific payback time threshold provides sufficient information for rendering a capital budgeting decision. According to the problem statement, the cost of the new building is estimated to be $291,000.00. However, because of existing debt obligations, the city must begin paying its debt within the next two years. Two questions were posed within the original problem statement:

1. Based on the following listing of anticipated cash flow values, what is the amount of time necessary before the payback time threshold occurs?
2. Based on the calculated payback time required, is it feasible and advisable for the city to pursue this proposed course of action?

The answer to the first question was determined to be a payback time value of 2.22 years. However, the answer for the second question requires a consideration of the determined payback period value versus the constraints of the problem statement. The problem statement indicates that the city has debt obligations, and it must begin repaying its existing debt within two years. The calculated payback period requires at least 2.22 years before the capital investment initiative would, potentially, be profitable. However, the city must begin disbursements within the next two years.

Therefore, it is unfeasible and inadvisable for the city to pursue this capital investment initiative. It is recommended that the city investigate other methods of financing, attempt to increase the monetary amount of the initial investment required for the capital initiative, or attempt to revise the terms of its anticipated disbursements.

5.6 Mutually Exclusive Investment Initiatives

The notion of mutual exclusion encompasses the notion that one, and only one, course of action may be selected and pursued from among multiple courses of actions. Although many or all of the evaluated courses of actions may be viable, mutual exclusion implies that only one course of action shall be pursued. Within the context of mutual exclusion, the following example demonstrates the application of the payback time method. Because a detailed description of mathematical operations was provided in Example 5.1, a higher level of description of the payback time method is provided within Example 5.2.

EXAMPLE 5.2

Another hypothetical problem statement involving the use of the payback time method within the context of mutual exclusion is given as follows:

The ABD Criminal Corrections Corporation, a for-profit entity, is evaluating four potential capital initiatives. Because of funding shortcomings, the organization is unable to pursue all of its possible initiatives. The board of directors indicated that one, and only one, initiative may be pursued during the coming year. Therefore, the organization must select only one project from among many to pursue as its choice of capital initiatives.

The first project, Initiative A, involves the purchasing and installation of new telephone equipment. This project would update and improve the telephone system of the correctional facility. Through the use of this system, inmates would be charged to make telephone calls (when permitted to do so).

The second project, Initiative B, involves the implementation of laundry services for the correctional facility. A private vendor is now used as an outsourced method of providing cleaning services for linens and clothing. However, laundry facilities exist within the correctional infrastructure, and such duties could be performed by inmates. If this project is selected, then the correctional facility would annually save money via the use of prisoner labor.

The third project, Initiative C, involves the potential replacement of food services from a private contractor. The current food service provides prepacked meals that are sufficient for breakfast, dinner, and supper meals within the facility. However, the correctional facility is considering the development and implementation of its own agricultural program, and inmates could grow their own food and prepare their meals. If this option is selected, then cost saving could be manifested through the use of prisoner labor.

Table 5.2 Values for Example 5.2

Period	Initiative A (Telephones)	Initiative B (Laundry)	Initiative C (Food)	Initiative D (Printing)
0	($1000.00)	($13,200.00)	($3000.00)	($12,000.00)
1	$500.00	$1272.00	$800.00	$1700.00
2	$200.00	$2122.00	$900.00	$2400.00
3	$300.00	$2534.00	$1300.00	$3100.00
4	$600.00	$2900.00	$1700.00	$3300.00
5	$700.00	$3400.00	$1900.00	$3700.00
6	$800.00	$3770.00	$2500.00	$4600.00
7	$900.00	$3400.00	$2900.00	$5300.00

The fourth project, Initiative D, involves the development and implementation of newspaper services. The corrections facility would serve as an outsourcing agent for the newspapers of the surrounding townships. The correctional facility houses a printing area, and the use of prisoner labor could be leveraged to provide writing and printing services. These services would have a subscription fee and would provide a source of revenue for the corporation. The anticipated, annual cash flows and the investment costs of each project are given in Table 5.2.

These four initiatives are all acceptable ideas. However, because of security, financial, and control concerns, the board of directors agreed only to approve only one pursuit of a capital initiative for the coming fiscal year. The board of directors also stipulated that the selected project must pay itself off within four years of its inception. Based on the use of the payback time method, which projects are recommended for acceptance? Based on this outcome, which project should be pursued?

Solution Overview of Example 5.2

This problem involves the consideration of multiple capital initiatives within a for-profit, prison environment. Each of these potential projects either provides cost savings or additional revenues through time. However, only one initiative may be pursued during the upcoming year, and the selected initiative must compensate for its investment costs within four years. This situation represents mutual exclusion.

Solution for Example 5.2: Payback Time Method

The payback time method may be used to facilitate the provision of a recommended course of action. Again, this method involves a consideration of the chronological aspects of these potential capital initiatives. It also incorporates the limitations of the host environment regarding any specifications of mandatory payback compensation periods. These notions may be applied to the data sets associated with Example 5.2. An initial examination of the cash flows may be performed regarding their overall time to repay the costs of investment. These considerations are given as follows:

Initiative A—The investment costs of the telephone system are anticipated to be $1000.00. A cursory examination of the anticipated cash flows shows that the first three years of operation are required before the anticipated cash flows

Table 5.3 Initiative A Cash Flow Running Totals

Period	Initiative A (Telephones)	Running Totals: A
0	($1000.00)	N/A
1	$500.00	$500.00
2	$200.00	$700.00
3	$300.00	$1000.00
4	$600.00	$1600.00
5	$700.00	$2300.00
6	$800.00	$3100.00
7	$900.00	$4000.00

will total at least $1000.00. Table 5.3 shows the running totals of the cash flows over time.

The observation of the payback time threshold is manifested through the addition of the values associated with the first three years of operation. The values of $500.00, $200.00, and $300.00, respectively representing the first, second, and third years, are added to yield a value of $1000.00. This calculated value of $1000.00 is equivalent to the investment cost of $1000.00. Therefore, the payback time threshold occurs during the third year. Because the board of directors mandated that any initiative must generate enough cash flow to compensate for its investment costs within four years, this initiative is determined to be acceptable.

Initiative B—The investment costs of the laundry service are $13,200.00. A cursory examination of the anticipated cash flows shows that the first six years of operation are required before the anticipated cash flows will total at least $13,200.00. Again, running totals of the anticipated cash flows may be used to determine the occurrence of the payback threshold period. Table 5.4 shows the running totals of the cash flows over time.

The observation of the payback time threshold is manifested through the addition of the values associated with the first six years of operation. The values of $1272.00, $2122.00, $2354.00, $2900.00, $3400.00, and $3770.00, respectively representing the first through the sixth years, are added to yield a value of $15,998.00. This calculated value of $15,998.00 surpasses the investment cost of $13,200.00. Therefore, the payback time threshold occurs around the sixth year. Because the board of directors mandated that any initiative must

Table 5.4 Initiative B Cash Flow Running Totals

Period	Initiative B (Laundry)	Running Totals: B
0	($13,200.00)	N/A
1	$1272.00	$1272.00
2	$2122.00	$3394.00
3	$2534.00	$5928.00
4	$2900.00	$8828.00
5	$3400.00	$12,228.00
6	$3770.00	$15,998.00
7	$3400.00	$19,398.00

Table 5.5 Initiative C Cash Flow Running Totals

Period	Initiative C (Food)	Running Totals: C
0	($3000.00)	N/A
1	$800.00	$800.00
2	$950.00	$1750.00
3	$1300.00	$3050.00
4	$1700.00	$4750.00
5	$1900.00	$6650.00
6	$2500.00	$9150.00
7	$2900.00	$12,050.00

generate enough cash flow to compensate for its investment costs within four years, this initiative is determined to be unacceptable.

Initiative C—The investment costs of the food services initiative are anticipated to be $3000.00. A cursory examination of the anticipated cash flows shows that the first three years of operation are required before the anticipated cash flows will total at least $3000.00. Table 5.5 shows the running totals of the cash flows over time.

The observation of the payback time threshold is manifested through the addition of the values associated with the first three years of operation. The values of $800.00, $950.00, and $1300.00, respectively representing the first, second, and third years, are added to yield a value of $3050.00. This calculated value of $3050.00 exceeds the investment cost of $3000.00. Therefore, the payback time threshold occurs around the third year. Because the board of directors mandated that any initiative must generate enough cash flow to compensate for its investment costs within four years, this initiative is determined to be acceptable.

Initiative D—The investment costs of the printing service are $12,000.00. A cursory examination of the anticipated cash flows shows that the first five years of operation are required before the anticipated cash flows will total at least $12,000.00. Again, running totals of the anticipated cash flows may be used to determine the occurrence of the payback threshold period. Table 5.6 shows the running totals of the cash flows over time.

The observation of the payback time threshold is manifested through the addition of the values associated with the first five years of operation. The values of $1700.00, $2400.00, $3100.00, $3300.00, and $3700.00, respectively

Table 5.6 Initiative D Cash Flow Running Totals

Period	Initiative D (Printing)	Running Totals: D
0	($12,000.00)	N/A
1	$1700.00	$1700.00
2	$2400.00	$4100.00
3	$3100.00	$7200.00
4	$3300.00	$10,500.00
5	$3700.00	$14,200.00
6	$4600.00	$18,800.00
7	$5300.00	$24,100.00

representing the first through the fifth years, are added to yield a value of \$14,200.00. This calculated value of \$14,200.00 surpasses the investment cost of \$12,000.00. Therefore, the payback time threshold occurs around the fifth year. Because the board of directors mandated that any initiative must generate enough cash flow to compensate for its investment costs within four years, this initiative is determined to be unacceptable.

Solution for Example 5.2: Partial Year Analysis

The payback time method was applied to the situations regarding all four of the proposed capital initiatives. The judgment decisions regarding whether to accept or to reject the considered initiative were also considered. Based on the outcomes of the payback time method, two of the projects were accepted, whereas two of the projects were rejected. The two initiatives that qualified for acceptance were Initiative A and Initiative C. The two disqualified initiatives were Initiative B and Initiative D. Therefore, the telephone initiative and the food service initiative qualified as acceptable, whereas the laundry initiative and the printing services initiative were disqualified. Hence, additional consideration must be given to selecting the final outcome regarding which initiative should be pursued.

The payback time method calculations demonstrated that Initiative A and Initiative C both qualified as acceptable candidates. Both Initiative A and Initiative C demonstrated a payback time threshold that did not surpass four years. Both Initiative A and Initiative C demonstrated a payback time threshold of approximately three years. However, the high-level application of the payback time method only provided a general period in which the payback threshold occurs. Therefore, additional analysis is required to further separate these potential initiatives as candidates for pursuance. Although a general period of time was established through the use of the payback time method, a further examination of partial year periods is necessary to determine the exact points at which the payback time threshold occurs during Initiative A and Initiative C.

This point in the payback method calculations does not yield a specific period in which the payback time threshold is satisfied. Instead, it only provides a general perspective of time regarding the period in which this threshold is surpassed. Additional calculations are necessary to determine the specific amount of time that represents the remainder of the annual period in which the payback time threshold is manifested.

The payback time method outcome indicated that the period in which the payback time threshold occurs is somewhere around the third year. The partial year formula, given in Example 5.1, may be used to examine the partial year effects, E_R, of Initiative A and Initiative C. The value of these effects may be expressed mathematically via the following expression:

$$E_R = \Sigma A_P - V_I$$

This equation may be used to examine the characteristics of Initiative A and Initiative C. Within this expression, the variable V_I represents the cost of the initial capital investments. For Initiative A, the corresponding value is \$1000.00. For Initiative C, the corresponding value is \$3000.00.

The variable ΣA_P represents only the summed value of cash flow revenues that were calculated during the iterations of the payback time method. For Initiative A, the corresponding value is \$1000.00. For Initiative C, the corresponding value is \$3050.00. Substituting these values into the partial year effect expression, E_R, yields the following outcomes.

Initiative A: Telephones

$$E_R = \Sigma A_P - V_I$$

$$E_R = \$1000.00 - \$1000.00$$

$$E_R = \$0.00$$

Initiative C: Food Services

$$E_R = \Sigma A_P - V_I$$

$$E_R = \$3050.00 - \$3000.00$$

$$E_R = \$50.00$$

For these initiatives, the outcomes of the remainder effect calculation, E_R, regarding Initiative A and Initiative C, respectively yields a value of \$0.00 and \$50.00. These calculated E_R values may be substituted into the partial year equation to determine the payback threshold partial periods for both Initiative A and Initiative C.

The previously defined expression given within Example 5.1, denoted through the variable T, may be used to determine the value of the partial years for both Initiative A and Initiative C. The calculated values of ΣA_P and E_R may be substituted into the expression appropriately to determine the value of the unknown partial years. These substitutions are given as follows.

Initiative A: Telephones

$$T_P = \left| \frac{E_R}{\sum A_P} \right|$$

$$T_P = \left| \frac{\$0.00}{\$1000.00} \right|$$

$$T_P = 0.00$$

Initiative C: Food Services

$$T_P = \left| \frac{E_R}{\sum A_P} \right|$$

$$T_P = \left| \frac{\$50.00}{\$3050.00} \right|$$

$$T_P = 0.00$$

For Initiative A, the partial year calculation yields a T_P value of 0.00. For Initiative C, the partial year calculation yields a T_P value of 0.01. These T_P values represent 0% and 1% of a one-year period for each capital initiative, which is required for the manifestation of the payback time threshold to occur within each initiative. Therefore, for Initiative A, based on this outcome, 0% of the third year must occur before the payback threshold time is manifested. For Initiative C, based on this outcome, 1% of the third year must occur before the payback threshold time is manifested.

Solution for Example 5.2: Calculation of the Payback Time Period

The partial year determinations may be used to calculate the exact point when the payback time thresholds are anticipated for both Initiative A and Initiative C. For Initiative A, the partial year period, T_P, was determined to be 0.00. For Initiative C, the partial year period, T_P, was determined to be 0.01. The payback time method indicated that the payback threshold was anticipated around the third year for both initiatives. Therefore, the calculated T_P values may be added to their respective outcomes of the high-level payback time method analyses. Adding these values yields the following determination of the payback threshold period for both Initiative A and Initiative C. These calculations are given as follows.

Initiative A: Telephones

$$3 \text{ years} + 0.00 \text{ years} = 3.00 \text{ years}$$

Initiative C: Food Services

$$3 \text{ years} + 0.01 \text{ years} = 3.01 \text{ years}$$

Based on the outcome of these calculations, the payback time threshold for Initiative A occurs in 3.00 years, whereas the payback time threshold for Initiative C occurs in 3.01 years. Therefore, it will require a period of 3.00 years before the telephone capital initiative returns enough monies to pay for its costs of investment, whereas it will require a period of 3.01 years before the food services capital investment returns enough monies to pay for its costs of investment.

Solution for Example 5.2: Capital Budgeting Decision

The stated problem described four capital investment projects that were considered by the organization. The problem statement also involved a time restriction: any capital initiative must demonstrate sufficient cash flows to compensate for its investment costs within a four-year period. The concepts of mutual exclusion influence the rendering of the acceptance decision of capital budgeting.

With respect to these restrictions, a high-level implementation of the payback time method yielded that two projects were qualified as contenders, whereas two projects were disqualified. Initiative A, the telephone initiative, and Initiative C, the food services initiative, were qualified because their respective, high-level payback time outcomes were approximately three years. Initiative B, the laundry initiative, and Initiative D, the printing services initiative, were disqualified because their respective, high-level payback time outcomes surpassed the stated four-year limitation regarding the expected time of investment returns.

Given these observations, it is evident that two initiatives remain as contenders: Initiative A and Initiative C. Therefore, the leaders of the organization must decide between the selection of either the telephone initiative or the food services initiative. This final selection is accomplished through a consideration of the outcomes of the complete payback time outcomes for both initiatives. These periods are given as follows:

Initiative A (Telephone): 3.00 years
Initiative B (Food services): 3.01 years

Based solely on the mathematical outcomes, in conjunction with the stated requirements of the problem, and the tenets governing acceptance of the payback time method, the selected initiative is the telephone initiative. Although both projects demonstrate a potential of repaying their investment costs within four years, a comparison of their identified, complete payback time thresholds indicates that the telephone initiative, Initiative A, yields the quickest time to maturation with respect to the generation of cash flows that compensate for the costs of investment. Therefore, Initiative A, the telephone initiative, is the accepted and recommended choice for pursuance.

5.7 Multiple Capital Investment Initiatives

The conditions governing Example 5.2 were indicative of mutual exclusion. Mutual exclusion necessitates the selection of one, and only one, initiative from multiple capital initiatives. However, an additional capital budgeting perspective involves the selection of two (or more) projects from many projects. Again, the payback time method may be used to render such decisions. If the rules governing the scenario of Example 5.2 did not involve mutual exclusion, other outcomes may be possible regarding capital budgeting decisions. The following example changes the rules of Example 5.2 to demonstrate a situation in which multiple projects may be deemed as acceptable.

EXAMPLE 5.3: ACCEPTING MULTIPLE INITIATIVES

If all of the data sets remain unchanged within Example 5.2, no additional mathematical calculations are necessary regarding any determinations of high-level or discrete time perspectives. If the rules of Example 5.2 are altered to eliminate the condition of mutual exclusion, then a different problem statement may be given as follows:

The ABD Criminal Corrections Corporation, a for-profit entity, is evaluating four potential capital initiatives. Because of funding shortcomings, the organization is unable to pursue all of its possible initiatives. However, the board of directors indicates that the organization can possibly pursue more than one initiative provided that such pursuance will generate sufficient cash flow to compensate for the investment costs within a period of four years. Therefore, the organization must select only acceptable projects from among many to pursue as its choice(s) of capital initiatives.

The descriptions of the potential capital investment initiatives are given in Example 5.2 and are unchanged. These same initiatives are considered within this problem. Further, the anticipated cash flows of each project, given in Table 5.2, may be used again. It may be helpful to refer to this table. Using this data, the following queries are posed: Based on the use of the payback time method, which projects are recommended for acceptance? Based on this outcome, which project should be pursued?

Solution Overview of Example 5.3

This problem involves the consideration of multiple capital initiatives within a for-profit prison environment. Each of these potential projects either provides cost savings or additional revenues through time. However, only initiatives that compensate for their investment costs within four years can be pursued. This situation represents the possible acceptance of multiple investment initiatives.

Solution for Example 5.3: Payback Time Method

The payback time method may be used to facilitate the provision of a recommended course of action. Again, this method involves a consideration of the chronological aspects of these potential capital initiatives. It also incorporates the limitations of the host environment regarding any specifications of mandatory payback compensation periods. These notions may be applied to the data sets associated with Example 5.3. The results of the payback time method may be used again within the solution of this problem. Therefore, any curiosities regarding the quantitative application of the payback time method, regarding the mathematical derivation of threshold periods, may be viewed within Example 5.2.

The updated problem considers four capital investment projects that are considered by the organization. The problem statement also involved a time restriction: any capital initiative must demonstrate sufficient cash flows to compensate for its investment costs within a four-year period. The concepts of mutual exclusion are no longer invoked within the context of Example 5.3 and do not influence the rendering of the acceptance decision of capital budgeting.

Solution for Example 5.3: Capital Budgeting Decision

Regarding Example 5.2, a high-level implementation of the payback time method yielded that two projects were qualified as contenders and two projects were disqualified. Initiative A, the telephone initiative, and Initiative C, the food services initiative, were qualified because their respective, high-level payback time outcomes were approximately three years. Initiative B, the laundry initiative, and Initiative D, the printing services initiative, were disqualified because their respective, high-level payback time outcomes surpassed the stated four-year limitation regarding the expected time of investment returns.

It is evident that two initiatives remain as contenders: Initiative A and Initiative C. Therefore, the leaders of the organization must decide between the selection of either the telephone initiative or the food services initiative. This final selection is accomplished through a consideration of the outcomes of the complete payback time outcomes for both initiatives. Based on the outcomes of Example 5.2, these periods are given as follows:

Initiative A (Telephone): 3.00 years
Initiative B (Food services): 3.01 years

Based solely on the mathematical outcomes, in conjunction with the newly stated requirements of the problem, and the tenets governing acceptance of the payback time method, both the telephone initiative and the food services initiative may be recommended for pursuance during the upcoming fiscal year. This recommendation is made because the payback time method outcomes of both Initiative A and Initiative C each conform to the specifications given within the updated problem statement.

The updated problem statement eliminated the condition of mutual exclusion thereby making it possible to pursue the implementation of multiple initiatives during the upcoming fiscal year. However, the condition regarding the necessities of cash flows remained static. This condition indicated that projects must demonstrate a sufficient set of cash flows to compensate for the costs of investment within a period of four years. The problem statement also indicated that the selection of multiple projects was allowed, but only with respect to the stated limitations of time.

Because Initiative A demonstrated an overall payback time outcome of 3.00 years, it is qualified as acceptable. Because Initiative C demonstrated an overall payback time outcome of 3.01 years, it is also qualified as acceptable. Therefore, both initiatives demonstrate the potential to return their respective costs of investments within the limitations of the specified four-year period. Therefore, the organization may choose to pursue both initiatives.

5.8 Discounted Payback Method

Although the basic payback time method ignores the time value of money, a variation of the basic payback time concept may be considered that does incorporate the time value of money. This variation may use the discounted values of the anticipated, future cash flows within the basic model of the payback time method to determine whether a potential capital initiative should be accepted or rejected.

The formula for discounting future cash values was presented in Chapter 4. This formula may be used to equate the anticipated, future values of cash flows with their current monetary values. Once this equivalency is accomplished, the payback time method may be applied to these discounted cash flows. However, despite the manifestation of equivalent cash values between future monetary value and current monetary value, no difference is observed regarding the outcome of the payback time method calculations. Therefore, any impacts of the time value of money equivalencies are immaterial when a period of time is derived. The following example provides a consideration of the discounted payback time method of analysis.

EXAMPLE 5.4

A basic example of the integrated capital budgeting analysis concept may be used to show how data is processed within its mathematical construct. A single capital initiative may be considered. The following capital initiative data may be used to demonstrate the primary concept of the integrated capital budgeting analysis method:

Anticipated initiative period: 4 years
Specified financial rate: 4.7%
Initial cost of the initiative: $100,000.00
First year cash flow: $84,000.00
Second year cash flow: $93,000.00
Third year cash flow: $101,000.00
Fourth year cash flow: $110,000.00

Given this data, the following questions may be posed.

Question 1: What is the discounted payback period for this situation?
Question 2: Based on the outcome of the discounted payback period method, should this initiative be accepted if it is stipulated that the capital investment must recover its cost of investment within a period of three years?

Solution Overview of Example 5.4

The examples of the preceding chapter provided a demonstration of solving time value of money equivalencies manually. Because of the tediousness and impracticality of solving again this problem manually, the time value of money equivalencies and the payback method calculations are completed using software spreadsheets. The reader may verify the accuracy of these outcomes manually through the use of spreadsheets or through the use of a financial calculator. If solved manually, this problem involves the same method of systematically and methodically deriving capital budgeting analysis outcome values that were presented in the preceding examples after the current monetary value function is exercised regarding each of the annual cash flows. Table 5.7 shows the initial investment cost, the anticipated cash flows, and the converted cash flow values representing their equivalencies in the terms of current monetary values.

Solution for Example 5.4: Discounted Payback Time Method Calculation

When solved using an electronic spreadsheet, the discounted payback time method outcome is determined to be the value of 1.33 years. Therefore, a period of at least 1.33 years is required before the capital initiative may recover its cost of investment.

Table 5.7 Converted Cash Flow Specifications

Period	Cash Flow	Current Cash Flow Value
0	($100,000.00)	($100,000.00)
1	$84,000.00	$80,229.23
2	$93,000.00	$84,837.84
3	$101,000.00	$87,999.73
4	$110,000.00	$91,538.96

Solution for Example 5.4: Capital Budgeting Decision

When solved using an electronic spreadsheet, the discounted payback time method outcome is 1.33. Therefore, a period of at least 1.33 years is required before the capital initiative may recover its cost of investment. The first question of the statement of the problem queried the amount of time that was necessary to recover the cost of investment. The statement of the problem mandated the use of the discounted payback method. It was determined that the period of 1.33 years was necessary for the capital initiative to recover its cost of investment.

The second question of the statement of the problem queried whether the initiative should be accepted with respect to the value of its calculated discount payback method outcome. Within the problem statement, it was specified that the investment must recover its cost within a period of four years. The calculated discounted payback method outcome indicates that a period of 1.33 years is necessary for the capital investment to recover its cost. This period of 1.33 years is sufficiently less than the mandated four-year limitation specified within the statement of the problem. Therefore, this initiative may be recommended for acceptance.

5.9 Chapter Comments and Summary

This chapter introduced the payback time method of capital budgeting. The methods of capital budgeting encompass perspectives of time, cash value, rate, and profitability potential. The payback time method is representative of the time characteristics of capital budgeting decisions. Therefore, it is expressed using a time-sensitive model regarding periods that are necessary to recover the amounts of investment regarding capital initiatives. The use of the payback time method may influence both strategic and tactical organizational decisions. Because it is a time-sensitive approach to capital budgeting, the use of the payback time method may be appropriate for both large and small organizations.

Within the organizational context, any anticipated initiative must contribute toward the value goals and objectives of the organization. This notion is commensurate with the contents of the previous discussions regarding the payback time method. The use of the payback time method provides a tool through which the chronological aspects of such potential value may be investigated. Through the use of the payback time model, organizations may determine whether they have sufficient time to pursue a project or whether the costs of the project are justified given the attributes of time.

Each work environment is highly unique, and demonstrates a variety of influences that impact the rendering of capital budgeting decisions through time. Although the payback time method may contribute toward such decisions, other factors exist that also may overshadow any outcomes of the payback time method calculations. Organizational politics may favor one initiative over another despite the quantitative outcomes of the payback time method. Budgetary constraints may eliminate the acceptance of projects. Many other factors may be identified.

Further, the payback time method is demonstrative of a solitary perspective of the decision domain. It is applicable regarding facets of time and ignores any attributes of the time value of money. Therefore, its outcomes are not the only factors that should be considered when rendering capital budgeting decisions. Instead, organizational leaders may use the payback time method as a supplement and complement to other capital budgeting tools (i.e., net present value, internal rate of return, and profitability).

5.10 Formulas

Payback Time Concept

$$T = \left| \frac{V_I}{\sum A_P} \right|$$

Note: The value of the variable P does not exceed the time required for the threshold value to occur.

Partial Year Effects

$$E_R = V_I - \Sigma A_P$$

Partial Year Concept

$$T_P = \left| \frac{E_R}{\sum A_P} \right|$$

Note: The value of the variable P does not exceed the time required for the threshold value to occur.

5.11 Terminology

Acceptance
Annual cash flow
Capital budgeting
Capital budgeting decision
Capital investment
Decision influences
Initial investment
Multiple initiatives
Mutual exclusion
Partial year

Payback time method
Payback time threshold
Rejection
Single initiatives
Time limitation
Time sensitive
Value

5.12 Thought and Discussion Questions

Based on the examples given within this chapter, the following situation provides a description for consideration:

The hypothetical Country Law Enforcement Training School (CLETS) is a for-profit training organization that supplies a variety of training materials and courses among law enforcement environments and their served communities. Their services include the provision of combatives and weapons safety courses among both urban and rural communities. The CLETS operations were successful during the last few years, and now the firm seeks to grow its operations.

The CLETS organization is considering expanding its operations into three new locations. However, it has a restriction in that it may pursue no more than three investments during the upcoming years. Table 5.8 shows the anticipated costs of investments and the anticipated cash flows that are affiliated with each of the potential capital investment initiatives. Regardless of the initiative(s) selected, the capital investment must recover its investment costs within a period of four years. Further, the rates of each capital investment differ. The following rates are applicable to the considered capital investments:

Initiative A: 4.36%
Initiative B: 4.25%
Initiative C: 4.23%
Initiative D: 4.41%
Initiative E: 4.12%

Table 5.8 presents the annual periods and cash flows of the CLETS organization.

1. Using both the payback time method and the discounted payback time method, calculate the appropriate payback period thresholds for each of the above initiatives. Both of these methods should yield the same value regarding the necessary period of time.
2. Based on Table 5.8 and descriptions, if the concept of mutual exclusion is applicable, which of the initiatives may be recommended for pursuance during the upcoming year? Use the payback time method to determine the appropriate outcome.
3. Based on Table 5.8 and descriptions, if mutual exclusion is not applicable and no more than three initiatives may be simultaneously

Table 5.8 CLETS Expansion Options

Period	Initiative A	Initiative B	Initiative C	Initiative D	Initiative E
0	($21,000.00)	($16,200.00)	($3000.00)	($12,000.00)	($12,000.00)
1	$3000.00	$2534.00	$800.00	$1700.00	$2000.00
2	$3700.00	$2900.00	$950.00	$2400.00	$2150.00
3	$3925.00	$3400.00	$1300.00	$3100.00	$2750.00
4	$4125.00	$3770.00	$1700.00	$3300.00	$3000.00
5	$4400.00	$3400.00	$1900.00	$3700.00	$3500.00
6	$4675.00	$3925.00	$2500.00	$4600.00	$4000.00
7	$4825.00	$4750.00	$2900.00	$5300.00	$4700.00
8	$4850.00	$5150.00	$2975.00	$5400.00	$4775.00
9	$4875.00	$5200.00	$2900.00	$5500.00	$4800.00
10	$4900.00	$5300.00	$2955.00	$5600.00	$5000.00

pursued during the upcoming year, which of the initiatives may be recommended for pursuance during the upcoming year? Use the payback time method to determine the appropriate outcome.

4. Using only the discounted payback time method, determine the payback time method outcome for Initiative A and Initiative B. Compare the outcomes of the discounted method with the outcomes of the basic payback time method. Discuss and explain the reason why the value of time remains unchanged when the monetary values of the considered cash flows are changed.

6 A Present for the Present: The Net Present Value Method

Never spend your money before you have earned it.*

Thomas Jefferson

6.1 Objectives

The objectives of this chapter are to:

- Understand the concept of net present value
- Understand the concept of discounting
- Understand decision rules of net present value

6.2 Introduction

The methods of capital budgeting encompass perspectives of time, cash value, rate, and profitability potential. Examining projects from these perspectives involves the use of quantitative tools through which projects may be judged and selected as either acceptable or unacceptable for devoting the resources of the organization in the pursuit of such capital initiatives. The second capital budgeting method to be examined involves a time value of money perspective of judging the acceptableness of potential capital investment projects. This method is known as the net present value (NPV) method. This method is also synonymous with the concept of net present worth analysis.

The NPV is used among a variety of settings and environments. It is a cornerstone of corporate finance theory and is a popular analytical tool among applied settings. Its use is varied within both for-profit and nonprofit environments. Both corporate and government entities find the NPV method a valuable tool through which capital budgeting activities are completed. Numerous capital initiatives are examined through the use of the NPV method. (See Figure 6.1.)

* Jefferson, Thomas, "Decision Quotations," Brainy Quote, http://www.brainyquote.com/quotes/keywords/money.html (accessed July 11, 2011).

Figure 6.1 Rendering financial decisions and explaining the associated reasoning is difficult. Defense Secretary Robert M. Gates and Navy Admiral Mike Mullen, Chairman of the Joint Chiefs of Staff, brief the press regarding the 2011 budget request at the Pentagon, February 1, 2010. (Photo by Navy Petty Officer 1st Class Chad J. McNeeley, http://www.army.mil/media/106166.)

The use of NPV was used to explore the potential of implementing wireless Internet connectivity in Pittsburgh, Pennsylvania.* The City of Beaufort, South Carolina, indicates that the use of NPV contributes toward profitability and integrates profitability to creditworthiness.† During 2005, the City of Salem, Oregon, facilitated a bond transaction involving an "overall true interest cost of 5.004%, resulting in a net present value savings of $18,873,735 and reducing PERS costs starting in fiscal year 2007–2008 by over $1.0 million per year."‡ Such uses of the NPV concept are not uncommon among a variety of city administrations. Although these examples are representative of administrative functions, the use of the NPV method is also applicable within law enforcement environments.

From the perspective of law enforcement entities, the use of the NPV is beneficial when examining potential monetary savings through time. During 2010, this economic analysis was conducted by the City of Tacoma, Washington, with respect to its assigning of law enforcement vehicles among patrol officers. The use of NPV was conducted during this economic examination. According to the City of Tacoma, the interpreted outcomes of the

* Carnegie Mellon University, "Wireless Metropolitan Area Network (WIMAN) to Pittsburgh."
† Dadson, "Getting Our Heads Out of the Sand."
‡ City of Salem, Oregon, "Comprehensive Annual Financial Report."

NPV analysis suggested that it is beneficial to "assign vehicles to officers than to have them share vehicles from a pool" because increases of officer productivity occur through time. This increase of personnel productivity occurs because of "of not having to check out a pool vehicle and transfer equipment in and out of them each day." The outcome of this analysis showed that annual savings of approximately "$1.5 million per year for assigned vs. pool vehicles" could be generated.*

This example shows the use of the NPV concept to examine cost savings within an organizational setting. The use of the NPV method demonstrates the relevancy of its construct because it provides a means through which cash flows may be examined and compared in terms of current dollars. It involves the discounting of future monetary values into the terms of present monetary values for a monetary comparison of values. Therefore, organizational leaders gain a perspective of value regarding the pursuit of a potential capital investment project.

6.3 Net Present Value (NPV) Method

The NPV method involves a consideration of the anticipated cash flows of a capital investment through time. These anticipated future values are discounted to determine their current monetary equivalencies. Conceptually, the NPV is the sum of the present monetary value of the anticipated future cash flows of a potential capital investment excluding the costs of investment. Therefore, the NPV method provides a cash-based perspective regarding capital budgeting initiatives. The NPV may be used as a solitary method of capital budgeting or may be used in conjunction with any (or all) of the capital budgeting methods described in this text. The NPV method may be used to examine single capital initiatives or multiple capital initiatives. Further, this method may be used with or without the constraints imposed by mutual exclusion conditions.

The following variables are used to represent the entities that exist within the mathematical relationships of the net present value method:

- NPV Net present value
- P Period currently examined within the net present value method iteration
- R_{per} Rate factor through time
- A_P Annual cash flow value
- V_I Value amount of the initial funding

* City of Tacoma, "Executive Summary Cost-Benefit Analysis."

With respect to an overall period of years, the following expression represents the mathematical relationships among the variables that comprise the net present value method:

$$NPV = \left(\sum_{P=1}^{P} \frac{A_P}{\left(R_{per} + 1.0\right)^P} \right) - V_I$$

The basic concept of the NPV function is both straightforward and simple to conceptualize. The NPV formula is indicative of the summation of the discounted, future values of anticipated cash flows excluding the costs of investment. Because it incorporates the time value of money, the value of period, *P*, representing time, will never be a negative value. The following section considers circumstances that govern the application of the NPV method.

6.4 Application of the NPV Method

From the perspective of rendering a capital budgeting decision, the NPV method demonstrates a superior approach that the processes necessitated within the payback time method. The NPV does not ignore the time value of money but incorporates the time value of money in its mathematical construct. Through the use of the NPV, organizational leaders gain a perspective of cash monetary value regarding potential investment initiatives. Unlike the payback time method, which ignores any cash flows that exist after a payback time threshold is established, the NPV examines all anticipated future cash flows that are specified through time.

Although the NPV method incorporates the time value of money in its mathematical construct, it only presents a perspective regarding the equivalency of future cash flows in terms of current dollar values. Therefore, it does not directly consider the characteristics of time that might impact the rendering of a capital budgeting decision. Hence, it is recommended that the NPV method be applied, in conjunction with the payback time method, the internal rate of return, and the profitability index, as a complementary and supplementary analysis of capital budgeting initiatives.

The application of the NPV method may be viewed from multiple perspectives. The first perspective involves a consideration of only one project that is being contemplated. Another perspective involves the concept of mutual exclusion—the selection of one, and only one initiative, from multiple capital initiatives. An additional perspective involves the selection of two (or more) projects from many projects. The example problems of this chapter demonstrate the NPV method calculations that are applicable among each of these situations.

Although the outcomes of the NPV method present quantitative findings, the outcomes must be interpreted. The rules governing the interpretation of the NPV outcomes are quite basic:

1. Discard the potential initiative(s) that demonstrate NPV outcomes that are less than the value of 0.00.
2. Retain potential initiatives that have an NPV outcome that is greater than the value of 0.00.
3. Select the initiative that demonstrates the highest NPV outcome when mutual exclusion or other limitations are applicable.

These rules provide the basis for judging a project as either acceptable or unacceptable with respect to an analysis of cash flows through time. However, other factors exist that may influence the rendering of a capital budgeting decision. Even though the NPV outcome may be positive and may indicate that a project should be accepted, the ultimate decision to accept or reject a project is rendered by humans. Humans must also incorporate the characteristics of the domain environment that influence the decision process. Factors such as time, organizational politics, contribution to organizational value, and the availability of necessary resources also contribute toward the rendering of capital budgeting decisions. Therefore, regardless of any NPV outcome, the decisions to accept and to pursue capital initiatives are subject to a variety of influences.

EXAMPLE 6.1

A basic example of the NPV concept may be used to show how data is processed in its mathematical construct. A single capital initiative may be considered. The following capital initiative data may be used to demonstrate the primary concept of the NPV method:

Anticipated initiative period: 4 years
Specified financial rate: 4.7%
Initial cost of the initiative: $100,000.00
First year cash flow: $84,000.00
Second year cash flow: $93,000.00
Third year cash flow: $101,000.00
Fourth year cash flow: $110,000.00

Given this data, the following questions may be posed.

Question 1: What is the NPV?
Question 2: Based on the NPV outcome, should this initiative be accepted or rejected?

An initial observation of this data set yields immediate values that may be identified. The values of the following variables are provided in the given data set:

$P = 4$
$R_{per} = 4.7\%$
$V_I = \$100,000.00$
$A_1 = \$84,000.00$
$A_2 = \$93,000.00$
$A_3 = \$101,000.00$
$A_4 = \$110,000.00$

First, each of the annual values, A_P, must be discounted to represent their valuations in the terms of current monetary dollars using the current monetary value formula, which was demonstrated in the preceding chapters. This formula is expressed as follows:

$$V_{curr} = \frac{V_{futr}}{(R_{per} + 1.0)^P} \quad (6.1)$$

The data values may be substituted appropriately for each year to render equivalent monetary values that are representative of current monetary amounts. These substitutions and calculations are given as follows:

$$V_1 = \frac{\$84,000.00}{(0.047 + 1.0)^1} = \$80,229.23$$

$$V_2 = \frac{\$93,000.00}{(0.047 + 1.0)^2} = \$84,837.84$$

$$V_3 = \frac{\$101,000.00}{(0.047 + 1.0)^3} = \$87,999.73$$

$$V_4 = \frac{\$110,000.00}{(0.047 + 1.0)^4} = \$91,538.96$$

Now that these equivalences are established, a sufficient amount of data exists to implement the NPV formula. With respect to the specified period of years, the appropriate substitutions and NPV values are given as follows:

$$NPV = \left(\sum_{P=1}^{P} \frac{A_P}{(R_{per} + 1.0)^P} \right) - V_I$$

$$NPV = \$80,229.23 + \$84,837.84 + \$87,999.73 + \$94,538.96 - \$100,000.00$$

$$NPV = \$344,605.75 - \$100,000.00$$

$$NPV = \$244,605.75$$

The first question of the problem statement queried the value of the NPV outcome. The outcome of the NPV calculations demonstrates a value of \$244,605.75. This value is indicative of the sum of the present monetary value of the anticipated future cash flows of a potential capital investment excluding the costs of investment. Discounting occurred using the specified rate of

4.7%. The second question of the problem statement queried whether the initiative should be accepted or rejected. Based on the calculated NPV outcome, this initiative should be recommended for acceptance because the calculated NPV outcome exceeds the value of 0.00. Further considerations of the NPV method are given in the succeeding examples.

EXAMPLE 6.2: NPV AND MUTUAL EXCLUSION

The following example again examines the cash flows of the hypothetical example introduced in Chapter 5. The problem domain of this example is representative of the mutual exclusion condition. The problem statement is given as follows:

Last year, a tornado destroyed the police training facility of an urban area. The damages were sufficient enough to warrant the total loss of the building and its supporting infrastructure. After the devastating event occurred, the city council approved a measure to erect a new police training facility. The destroyed facility served as a training institute for regional first responders, among the four bordering states, whose functions included the provision of emergency services during both natural and man-made disasters. Therefore, it is imperative that this facility be restored.

The training tuition dollars of local personnel were provided by the devastated city. However, any nonlocal personnel were responsible for providing their own tuitions (e.g., self-pay, sponsor pay, grants). Because it was a regional training facility, the majority of the trainees were not local personnel. Therefore, this training facility provided a source of revenue for the city and its police department.

A combination of monies—to be obtained via taxation, city bond investments, a limited insurance policy, loans, and goodwill and charitable donations—are proposed to fund the initial costs of the capital investment. Through time, additional debt payments are to be made from the revenue stream of the restored facility.

Three contractors submitted bids for the rebuilding project. The bids of the contractors were \$291,000.00, \$293,000.00, and \$295,000.00. The rates associated with these values, respectively, are 4.30%, 4.57%, and 5.00%. Regardless of which contractor is selected, the pursued course of rebuilding must return an amount of at least \$500,000.00.

Because of other obligations, these contractors are unable specify identical dates to begin the construction of the new facility. Therefore, these time differences may offset the estimated cash flows of the facility. Further, because of existing debt obligations, the city must begin paying its debt within the next two years.

Based on the listing of anticipated cash flow values in Table 6.1, what are the NPV outcomes of each of the proposals? Based on the NPV outcomes, which contractor is the recommended entity? Based on the calculated NPV values, is it feasible and advisable for the city to pursue this proposed course of action?

Solution Overview of Example 6.2

This problem considers capital budgeting decisions from the perspective of mutual exclusion. Within the context of mutual exclusion, one, and only one, capital initiative may be recommended for pursuance through time. Although multiple NPV outcomes may qualify as acceptable because they surpass the

Table 6.1 Cash Flows of Example 6.2

Period	Contractor A	Contractor B	Contractor C
0	($291,000.00)	($293,000.00)	($295,000.00)
1	$109,527.00	$110,527.00	$108,000.00
2	$129,034.00	$125,034.00	$127,000.00
3	$135,068.00	$133,368.00	$129,068.00
4	$148,927.00	$148,927.00	$135,000.00
5	$159,000.00	$159,000.00	$147,000.00
6	$168,000.00	$168,000.00	$155,000.00
7	$174,980.00	$174,980.00	$159,980.00

value of 0.00, only one initiative is recommended for acceptance and pursuance through time. This example demonstrates the use of the NPV method with respect to this constraint.

The proposed cash flows of Contractor A are examined first. The application of the present monetary value formula is applied to determine the values, in the terms of present monetary amounts, of the cash flows associated with Contractor A. The current monetary formula incorporates a period of seven years involving a rate of 4.3% and is used to determine the current monetary equivalencies of the values listed within its anticipated cash flow. Table 6.2 shows the calculations that are necessary to evaluate the cash flow equivalencies of Contractor A. Further, Table 6.2 shows the summation of these current monetary equivalencies. This summation is used within the calculation of the NPV outcome. The values in Table 6.2, when coupled with the data given within the statement of the problem, provide sufficient data to implement the NPV formula. The following calculations demonstrate the appropriate use of the NPV formula to derive an outcome regarding the cash flows of Contractor A.

$$NPV = \left(\sum_{P=1}^{P} \frac{A_P}{\left(R_{per} + 1.0\right)^P} \right) - V_I$$

$$NPV_A = (\$858{,}144.02) - \$291{,}100.00$$

$$NPV_A = \$567{,}144.45$$

Table 6.2 Cash Flow Equivalencies of Contractor A

Period	Contractor A	Calculation	Current Values
0	($291,000.00)	N/A	N/A
1	$109,527.00	$\$109{,}527.00/(0.043 + 1)^1$	$105,011.51
2	$129,034.00	$\$129{,}034.00/(0.043 + 1)^2$	$118,613.89
3	$135,068.00	$\$135{,}068.00/(0.043 + 1)^3$	$119,041.82
4	$148,927.00	$\$148{,}927.00/(0.043 + 1)^4$	$125,845.07
5	$159,000.00	$\$159{,}000.00/(0.043 + 1)^5$	$128,817.71
6	$168,000.00	$\$168{,}000.00/(0.043 + 1)^6$	$130,497.87
7	$174,980.00	$\$174{,}980.00/(0.043 + 1)^7$	$130,316.15
		Summation:	$858,144.02

Table 6.3 Cash Flow Equivalencies of Contractor B

Period	Contractor B	Calculation	Current Monetary Values
0	($293,000.00)	N/A	N/A
1	$110,527.00	$\$110,527.00/(0.0457 + 1)^1$	$105,696.66
2	$125,034.00	$\$125,034.00/(0.0457 + 1)^2$	$114,344.14
3	$133,368.00	$\$133,368.00/(0.0457 + 1)^3$	$116,635.38
4	$148,927.00	$\$148,927.00/(0.0457 + 1)^4$	$124,550.37
5	$159,000.00	$\$159,000.00/(0.0457 + 1)^5$	$127,163.24
6	$168,000.00	$\$168,000.00/(0.0457 + 1)^6$	$128,489.20
7	$174,980.00	$\$174,980.00/(0.0457 + 1)^7$	$127,978.98
		Summation:	$844,857.98

The outcome of this calculation demonstrates that an NPV of $567,144.02 results for the anticipated cash flows of Contractor A.

The second proposal is examined using an identical NPV method. Again, the current monetary formula is applied to determine equivalencies between future anticipated cash flows and their respective values in terms of current monetary dollars. In this case, a rate of 4.57% is mandated during the period of seven years. The calculations necessary for deriving the current monetary equivalencies of the cash flows of Contractor B are given in Table 6.3. Further, Table 6.3 shows the summation of these current monetary equivalencies. This summation is used in the calculation of the NPV outcome. The values contained within Table 6.3, when coupled with the data given within the statement of the problem, provide sufficient data to implement the NPV formula. The following calculations demonstrate the appropriate use of the NPV formula to derive an outcome regarding the cash flows of Contractor B.

$$NPV = \left(\sum_{P=1}^{P} \frac{A_P}{(R_{per} + 1.0)^P} \right) - V_I$$

$$NPV_B = (\$844,857.98) - \$293,000.00$$

$$NPV_B = \$551,857.98$$

The outcome of this calculation demonstrates that a NPV of $551,857.98 results regarding the evaluation of the anticipated cash flows of Contractor B. This NPV outcome of $551,857.98 demonstrates a value, in terms of current dollars, that does not exceed the NPV of the cash flow of Contractor A, $567,144.02. Given this observation of the two calculated NPV outcomes, Contractor A is now the primary contender for consideration. This observation may be used during any considerations of ranking the potential capital initiatives.

The third proposal is examined using an identical NPV method. Again, the current monetary formula is applied to determine equivalencies between future, anticipated cash flows and their respective values in terms of current monetary dollars. In this case a rate of 5.00% is mandated during the period of seven years. The calculations necessary for deriving the current monetary equivalencies of the cash flows of Contractor C are given in Table 6.4. Further, Table 6.4 shows the summation of these current monetary equivalencies. This

Table 6.4 Cash Flow Equivalencies of Contractor C

Period	Contractor C	Calculation	Current Monetary Values
0	($295,000.00)	N/A	N/A
1	$108,000.00	$\$108,000.00/(0.0457 + 1)^1$	$102,857.14
2	$127,000.00	$\$127,000.00/(0.0457 + 1)^2$	$115,192.74
3	$129,068.00	$\$129,068.00/(0.0457 + 1)^3$	$111,493.79
4	$135,000.00	$\$135,000.00/(0.0457 + 1)^4$	$111,064.83
5	$147,000.00	$\$147,000.00/(0.0457 + 1)^5$	$115,178.35
6	$155,000.00	$\$155,000.00/(0.0457 + 1)^6$	$115,663.39
7	$159,980.00	$\$159,980.00/(0.0457 + 1)^7$	$113,694.80
		Summation:	$785,145.04

summation is used within the calculation of the NPV outcome. The values contained within Table 6.4, when coupled with the data given within the statement of the problem, provide sufficient data to implement the NPV formula. The following calculations demonstrate the appropriate use of the NPV formula to derive an outcome regarding the cash flows of Contractor C.

$$NPV = \left(\sum_{P=1}^{P} \frac{A_P}{\left(R_{per} + 1.0\right)^P} \right) - V_I$$

$$NPV_C = (\$785{,}145.04) - \$295{,}000.00$$

$$NPV_C = \$490{,}145.04$$

The outcome of this calculation demonstrates that a NPV of $498,145.04 results for the anticipated cash flows of Contractor C. This NPV outcome of $498,145.04 demonstrates a value, in terms of current dollars, that does not exceed the NPV of the cash flow of Contractor A, $567,144.02. Given this observation of the two calculated NPV outcomes, Contractor A remains as the primary contender for consideration. This observation may also be used during any considerations of ranking these potential capital initiatives.

Solution for Example 6.2: Capital Budgeting Decision

A determination of the NPV outcomes of Contractor A, Contractor B, and Contractor C provides a sufficient amount of information to facilitate the rendering of a capital budgeting decision. Within the problem statement, the following questions were posed:

> Based on the following listing of anticipated cash flow values, what are the NPV outcomes of each of the proposals?
> Based on the NPV outcomes, which contractor is the recommended entity?
> Based on the calculated NPV values, is it feasible and advisable for the city to pursue this proposed course of action?

With respect to the first question, the NPV outcomes are now calculated for Contractor A, Contractor B, and Contractor C. Respectively, these NPV outcomes are as follows:

NPV of Contractor A: $567,144.02
NPV of Contractor B: $551,857.98
NPV of Contractor C: $498,145.04

The second question queries the identity of the recommended contractor. In order to determine which contractor is the primary choice, a ranking of these potential initiatives may occur based on their NPV outcomes. This ranking may occur from the highest value to the lowest value. When ranked, these NPV are listed as follows:

NPV of Contractor A: $567,144.02
NPV of Contractor B: $551,857.98
NPV of Contractor C: $498,145.04

Now that these NPV outcomes are determined, enough data exists to facilitate the rendering of a human decision regarding potential, strategic courses of actions. Given the content of the problem statement, the condition of mutual exclusion is applicable. Therefore, one, and only one, contractor may be selected as the entity that shall facilitate the rebuilding effort. The ranked NPV outcomes may be examined to determine which contractor is the primary choice for the rebuilding efforts. Contractor A manifested an NPV outcome of $567,144.02, Contractor B manifested an NPV outcome of $551,857.98, and Contractor C manifested an NPV outcome of $498,145.04.

These NPV outcomes may be evaluated with respect to the established rules of acceptance. The first NPV tenet indicates that any initiative that manifests an NPV outcome that is less than the value of 0.00 should be discarded. None of the calculated NPV values were less than the value of 0.00. Therefore, all of the potential initiatives remain as contenders. The second NPV tenet necessitates the selection of initiatives that demonstrate NPV outcomes that are greater than the value of 0.00. All three NPV outcomes satisfy this requirement and are retained for evaluation. All three potential initiatives have the capacity to contribute some value for the organization through time. The third NPV tenet necessitates the selection of the highest NPV outcomes when mutual exclusion or other limitations are applicable. Based on this requirement, the choice NPV is represented by Contractor A whose NPV outcome is $567,144.02. Therefore, Contractor A is the recommended contracting entity.

The third question queries whether it is feasible and advisable for the city to pursue the recommended course of action. Based on the outcome of the NPV analysis, the recommended contractor is Contractor A. However, a recommendation regarding the actual pursuit, based solely on NPV considerations, may be appropriate but is certainly not the only consideration that affects the decision to pursue the recommended course of action. Other factors also affect this decision.

The problem statement does indicate that any certain minimum financial return is required regarding the selected capital initiative. The problem statement indicates that any pursued initiative must return a current monetary value of $500,000.00. The recommended contractor, Contractor A, demonstrated an NPV outcome of $567,144.02. This calculated NPV value surpasses the stated minimum return amount of $500,000.00. Therefore, given the description provided within the problem statement, it is possibly feasible and advisable for Contractor A to be selected for the rebuilding initiative. Again, this recommendation is based primarily from the considerations of the NPV outcomes.

However, other factors also influence the considerations of the problem statement. The NPV analysis does not consider the two-year limitation that was imposed within the payback time method. The decision has not yet considered the outcomes of the remaining methods of capital budgeting consisting of the internal rate of return and the profitability index. Also, although such items are not mentioned within the problem state, organizational politics, the securing of building permits, the availability of labor, and an array of other factors also affect the decision of rebuilding.

The use of the NPV method provides a solitary perspective of the decision domain through an evaluation of the cash flows that occur through time. Obviously, the NPV evaluation is conducted through examining comparisons of the potential cash flows, through time, in terms of current monetary values. Because the NPV method represents only a solitary perspective, it is recommended that it be used in conjunction with the other methods of capital budgeting.

6.5 Multiple Capital Investment Initiatives

The conditions governing Example 6.2 were indicative of mutual exclusion. Mutual exclusion necessitates the selection of one, and only one initiative, from multiple capital initiatives. However, an additional capital budgeting perspective involves the selection of two (or more) projects from many projects. Again, the NPV method may be used to render such decisions. If the rules governing the scenario of Example 6.2 did not involve mutual exclusion, other outcomes may be possible regarding capital budgeting decisions. The following example changes the rules of Example 6.2 to demonstrate a situation in which multiple projects may be deemed as acceptable.

6.6 Accepting Multiple Initiatives

The example of the ABD Criminal Corrections Corporation given in Chapter 5 may again be examined from the perspective of capital budgeting. However, the next examination may be completed through the use of the NPV method, and the condition of mutual exclusion may be removed. Therefore, it becomes possible for multiple initiatives to be considered as potential courses of actions. The updated problem statement reflecting the removal of mutual exclusion is given next.

EXAMPLE 6.3: ACCEPTING MULTIPLE NPV OUTCOMES

The following problem statement is adapted from Chapter 5. It demonstrates alterations of the decision domain that allow the acceptance of multiple initiatives during the upcoming fiscal year. Therefore, the conditions of mutual exclusion are not applicable.

The ABD Criminal Corrections Corporation, a for-profit entity, is evaluating four potential capital initiatives. Because of funding shortcomings, the organization is unable to pursue all of its possible initiatives. The board of directors indicated that only two initiatives may be pursued during the coming year. Therefore, the organization must select only two projects from among many to pursue as its choice of capital initiatives.

The first project, Initiative A, involves the purchasing and installation of new telephone equipment. This project would update and improve the telephone system of the correctional facility. Through the use of this system, inmates would be charged to make telephone calls (when permitted to do so). The rate associated with this initiative is 4.86%.

The second project, Initiative B, involves the implementation of laundry services for the correctional facility. A private vendor is now used as an outsourced method of providing cleaning services for linens and clothing. However, laundry facilities exist within the correctional infrastructure, and inmates could perform such duties. If this project is selected, then the correctional facility would annually save money via the use of prisoner labor. The rate associated with this initiative is 4.25%.

The third project, Initiative C, involves the potential replacement of food services from a private contractor. The current food service provides prepacked meals that are sufficient for breakfast, dinner, and supper meals within the facility. However, the correctional facility currently is considering the development and implementation of its own agricultural program, and inmates could grow their own food and prepare their meals. If this option is selected, then cost saving could be manifested through the use of prisoner labor. The rate associated with this initiative is 4.62%.

The fourth project, Initiative D, involves the development and implementation of newspaper services. The corrections facility would serve as an outsourcing agent for the newspapers of the surrounding townships. The correctional facility houses a printing area, and the use of prisoner labor could be leveraged to provide writing and printing services. These services would have a subscription fee, and would provide a source of revenue for the corporation. The rate associated with this initiative is 3.99%.

The anticipated, annual cash flows and the investment costs of each project are given in Table 6.5.

These four initiatives are all acceptable ideas. However, because of security, financial, and control concerns, the board of directors agreed that only two capital initiatives may be considered for the coming fiscal year. Based on the use

Table 6.5 Values for Example 6.3

Period	Initiative A (Telephones)	Initiative B (Laundry)	Initiative C (Food)	Initiative D (Printing)
0	($1000.00)	($13,200.00)	($3000.00)	($12,000.00)
1	$500.00	$1272.00	$800.00	$1700.00
2	$200.00	$2122.00	$950.00	$2400.00
3	$300.00	$2534.00	$1300.00	$3100.00
4	$600.00	$2900.00	$1700.00	$3300.00
5	$700.00	$3400.00	$1900.00	$3700.00
6	$800.00	$3770.00	$2500.00	$4600.00
7	$900.00	$3400.00	$2900.00	$5300.00

of the NPV method, which projects are recommended for acceptance? Based on these NPV outcomes, which project should be pursued?

Solution Overview of Example 6.3

This problem considers capital budgeting decisions from the perspective of accepting multiple initiatives. Therefore, more than one capital initiative may be recommended for pursuance through time. This example demonstrates the use of the NPV method with respect to such conditions.

The use of the current monetary value formula is applied to equate the future cash flow values into the terms of contemporary financial values. Because the current monetary value formula was demonstrated in both Chapter 4 and in the preceding example, the mathematical processing of equivalences is not delineated within the solution to this example. Only the outcomes of the current monetary value calculations are shown in the solution to Example 6.4.

The cash flow values of initiative A, the telephone system, are examined first. Equivalencies between the future cash flow values and the current monetary values must be established through the application of the current monetary value formula. Table 6.6 shows these established equivalencies.

When summed, the cumulative value of the current monetary value amounts is \$3214.70. Within the NPV method formula, this amount is commensurate with the ΣA_P variable. When substituted into the NPV method formula, the following expression represents the mathematical basis of determining the NPV outcome of Initiative A.

$$NPV_A = \Sigma A_P - V_I$$

$$NPV_A = \$3214.70 - \$1000.00$$

$$NPV_A = \$2214.70$$

The cash flow values of Initiative B, the laundry services, are examined next. Equivalencies between the future cash flow values and the current monetary values must be established through the application of the current monetary value formula. Table 6.7 shows these established equivalencies.

When summed, the cumulative value of the current monetary value amounts is \$3214.70. Within the NPV method formula, this amount is commensurate with the ΣA_P variable. When substituted into the NPV method formula, the following expression represents the mathematical basis of determining the NPV outcome of Initiative B.

Table 6.6 Initiative A Monetary Equivalencies

Period	Future Monetary Value	Current Monetary Value
0	(\$1000.00)	(\$1000.00)
1	\$500.00	\$476.83
2	\$200.00	\$181.89
3	\$300.00	\$260.19
4	\$600.00	\$496.26
5	\$700.00	\$552.14
6	\$800.00	\$601.77
7	\$900.00	\$645.61

Table 6.7 Initiative B Monetary Equivalencies

Period	Future Monetary Value	Current Monetary Value
0	($13,200.00)	($13,200.00)
1	$1272.00	$1220.14
2	$2122.00	$1952.51
3	$2534.00	$2236.55
4	$2900.00	$2455.24
5	$3400.00	$2761.20
6	$3770.00	$2936.87
7	$3400.00	$2540.66

Table 6.8 Initiative C Monetary Equivalencies

Period	Future Monetary Value	Current Monetary Value
0	($3000.00)	($3000.00)
1	$800.00	$764.67
2	$950.00	$867.95
3	$1300.00	$1135.27
4	$1700.00	$1419.03
5	$1900.00	$1515.93
6	$2500.00	$1906.57
7	$2900.00	$2113.95

$$NPV_B = \Sigma A_P - V_I$$

$$NPV_B = \$16{,}103.18 - \$13{,}200.00$$

$$NPV_B = \$2903.18$$

The cash flow values of Initiative C, the food services, may be examined next. Equivalencies between the future cash flow values and the current monetary values must be established through the application of the current monetary value formula. Table 6.8 shows these established equivalencies.

When summed, the cumulative value of the current monetary value amounts is $9723.37. Within the NPV method formula, this amount is commensurate with the ΣA_P variable. When substituted into the NPV method formula, the following expression represents the mathematical basis of determining the NPV outcome of Initiative C.

$$NPV_C = \Sigma A_P - V_I$$

$$NPV_C = \$9723.37 - \$3000.00$$

$$NPV_C = \$6723.37$$

The cash flow values of Initiative D, the printing services, may be examined next. Equivalencies between the future cash flow values and the current monetary

Table 6.9 Initiative D Monetary Equivalencies

Period	Future Monetary Value	Current Monetary Value
0	($12,000.00)	($12,000.00)
1	$1700.00	$1634.77
2	$2400.00	$2219.36
3	$3100.00	$2756.68
4	$3300.00	$2821.94
5	$3700.00	$3042.59
6	$4600.00	$3637.54
7	$5300.00	$4030.28

values must be established through the application of the current monetary value formula. Table 6.9 shows these established equivalencies.

When summed, the cumulative value of the current monetary value amounts is $20,143.17. Within the NPV method formula, this amount is commensurate with the ΣA_P variable. When substituted into the NPV method formula, the following expression represents the mathematical basis of determining the NPV outcome of Initiative D.

$$NPV_D = \Sigma A_P - V_I$$

$$NPV_D = \$20{,}143.17 - \$12{,}000.00$$

$$NPV_D = \$8143.17$$

This determination of the NPV outcome of Initiative D completes the calculations necessary for specifying each of the NPV outcomes for all of the considered initiatives. Each of the NPV values is listed as follows:

$NPV_A = \$2214.7$
$NPV_B = \$2903.18$
$NPV_C = \$6723.37$
$NPV_D = \$8143.17$

These NPV outcome values may be ranked from the highest to the lowest value. This ranking is listed as follows:

$NPV_D = \$8143.17$
$NPV_C = \$6723.37$
$NPV_B = \$2903.18$
$NPV_A = \$2214.70$

Solution for Example 6.3: Capital Budgeting Decision

Now that these NPV outcomes are determined, enough data exists to facilitate the rendering of a human decision regarding potential strategic courses of actions. Given the content of the problem statement, the condition of mutual exclusion is applicable. Therefore, one, and only one, contractor may be selected as the entity that shall facilitate the rebuilding effort. The ranked NPV outcomes may be examined to determine which contractor is the primary choice for the rebuilding efforts. Initiative A manifested an NPV outcome of

$2214.70, Initiative B manifested an NPV outcome of $2903.18, Initiative C manifested an NPV outcome of $6723.37, and Initiative D manifested an NPV outcome of $8143.17.

These NPV outcomes may be evaluated with respect to the established rules of acceptance. The first NPV tenet indicates that any initiative that manifests an NPV outcome less than the value of 0.00 should be discarded. None of the calculated NPV values were less than the value of 0.00. Therefore, all of the potential initiatives remain as contenders. The second NPV tenet necessitates the selection of initiatives that demonstrate NPV outcomes that are greater than the value of 0.00. All of the NPV outcomes satisfy this requirement and are retained for evaluation. All of these potential initiatives have the capacity to contribute some value for the organization through time. The third NPV tenet necessitates the selection of the highest NPV outcomes with respect to conditions associated with the decision domain. The condition of mutual exclusion no longer exists, and no more than two initiatives may be pursued during the upcoming fiscal year.

Based on these requirements governing NPV outcome selection, only two initiatives may be recommended for acceptance. With respect to the tenets of NPV and the characteristics of the problem domain, both Initiative C and Initiative D qualify as acceptable capital investments.

6.7 Advanced NPV Considerations

The discussions and examples in this text serve as an introduction to the NPV concept. This introduction considers examples that are relatively understandable and that require only the implementation of the basic NPV construct for their solution. Regardless of the period of time considered, the basic NPV concept may be applied to any specific, anticipated cash flows to examine their relevancy within the context of capital budgeting decisions.

Some initiatives may require periods that are longer than those that are considered within this text. When these situations occur, it is recommended that NPV calculations be performed through the use of software spreadsheets, proprietary software, or financial calculators. Also, within the context of collegiate finance courses, a tabular solution is also available to solve NPV problems involving a variety of periods. However, for the purposes of this text, the use of the basic formula is appropriate to demonstrate the basic concept of net present value and to delineate the calculations through which NPV problems are solved. Future editions of this text, if any, are anticipated to contain the tabular solution methods of NPV problems.

6.8 Chapter Comments and Summary

This chapter introduced the net present value (NPV) method of capital budgeting. The methods of capital budgeting encompass perspectives of time, cash value, rate, and profitability potential. The NPV is indicative of a cash perspective regarding the rendering of capital budgeting decisions. Further, the NPV method incorporates the time value of money within its primary construct. Derivation of the NPV method can occur through algebraic manipulation of the current monetary value formula given in Chapter 4.

The NPV method involves a consideration of the anticipated cash flows of a capital investment through time. These anticipated future values are discounted to determine their current monetary equivalencies. Conceptually, the NPV is the sum of the present monetary value of the anticipated future cash flows of a potential capital investment excluding the costs of investment. Therefore, the NPV method provides a cash-based perspective regarding capital budgeting initiatives. The NPV may be used as a solitary method of capital budgeting or may be used in conjunction with any (or all) of the capital budgeting methods described within this text. The NPV method may be used to examine single capital initiatives or multiple capital initiatives. Further, this method may be used with or without the constraints imposed by mutual exclusion conditions.

The rules governing the interpretation of the NPV outcomes are quite basic:

1. Discard the potential initiative(s) that demonstrate NPV outcomes that are less than the value of 0.00.
2. Retain potential initiatives that have an NPV outcome that is greater than the value of 0.00.
3. Select the initiative that demonstrates the highest NPV outcome when mutual exclusion or other limitations are applicable.

These rules provide the basis for judging a project as either acceptable or unacceptable with respect to an analysis of cash flows through time. However, other factors exist that may influence the rendering of a capital budgeting decision. Even though the NPV outcome may be positive and may indicate that a project should be accepted, the ultimate decision to accept or reject a project is rendered by humans. Humans must also incorporate the characteristics of the domain environment that influence the decision process. Factors such as time, organizational politics, contribution to organizational value, and the availability of necessary resources also contribute to the rendering of capital budgeting decisions. Therefore, regardless of any NPV outcome, the decisions to accept and to pursue capital initiatives are subject to a variety of influences.

The use of the NPV is varied. Its application occurs among the environments of global corporations and small businesses. Within the context of criminal justice and law enforcement entities, its use is appropriate. Such entities may use the NPV to examine cost savings through time regarding operational aspects of departments, to examine the erection of new buildings, to examine the purchasing of vehicles and other equipment, and to examine the effects of retirement contributions through time. Regardless of the type of capital initiative explored via the use of the NPV method, its implementation provides organizational leaders with an additional, cash-based perspective of the decision domain.

6.9 Formulas

Net Present Value Concept

$$NPV = \left(\sum_{P=1}^{P} \frac{A_P}{\left(R_{per} + 1.0\right)^P} \right) - V_I$$

6.10 Terminology

Acceptance	Interest
Capital budgeting	Limitations
Capital budgeting decision	Monetary equivalency
Cash flow	Monetary value
Constraints	Net present value
Current monetary value	Present monetary value
Discount rate	Priority
Discounting	Ranking
Equivalency	Rate
Future monetary value	Rejection
Initial investment cost	Time value of money

6.11 Thought and Discussion Questions

Based on the examples given in this chapter, the following situation provides a description for consideration:

The Country Law Enforcement Training School (CLETS) is a for-profit training organization that supplies a variety of training materials and courses among law enforcement environments and their served communities. Its services include the provision of combatives and weapons safety courses among both urban and rural communities. The CLETS operations were successful during the last few years, and now the firm seeks to grow its operations.

The CLETS organization is considering expanding its operations into three new locations. However, it has a restriction in that it may pursue no

Table 6.10 CLETS Expansion Options

Period	Initiative A	Initiative B	Initiative C	Initiative D	Initiative E
0	($21,000.00)	($16,200.00)	($3000.00)	($12,000.00)	($12,000.00)
1	$3000.00	$2534.00	$800.00	$1700.00	$2000.00
2	$3700.00	$2900.00	$950.00	$2400.00	$2150.00
3	$3925.00	$3400.00	$1300.00	$3100.00	$2750.00
4	$4125.00	$3770.00	$1700.00	$3300.00	$3000.00
5	$4400.00	$3400.00	$1900.00	$3700.00	$3500.00
6	$4675.00	$3925.00	$2500.00	$4600.00	$4000.00
7	$4825.00	$4750.00	$2900.00	$5300.00	$4700.00
8	$4850.00	$5150.00	$2975.00	$5400.00	$4775.00
9	$4875.00	$5200.00	$2900.00	$5500.00	$4800.00
10	$4900.00	$5300.00	$2955.00	$5600.00	$5000.00

more than three investments during the upcoming years. Table 6.10 shows the anticipated costs of investments and the anticipated cash flows that are affiliated with each of the potential capital investment initiatives. Regardless of the initiative(s) selected, the capital investment must recover its investment costs within a period of four years. Further, the rates of each capital investment differ. The following rates are applicable to the considered capital investments:

Initiative A: 4.36%
Initiative B: 4.25%
Initiative C: 4.23%
Initiative D: 4.41%
Initiative E: 4.12%

Table 6.10 presents the annual periods and cash flows of the CLETS organization:

1. Using the NPV method, calculate the appropriate NPV outcomes for each of the initiatives.
2. Based on Table 6.10 and descriptions, if the concept of mutual exclusion is not applicable, which of the initiatives may be recommended for pursuance during the upcoming year? Use the NPV method to determine the appropriate outcome.
3. Based on Table 6.10 and descriptions, if mutual exclusion is applicable, which of the initiatives may be recommended for pursuance during the upcoming year? Use the NPV method to determine the appropriate outcome.

Bibliography

Carnegie Mellon University, Department of Engineering and Public Policy. "Bringing a Wireless Metropolitan Area Network (WIMAN) to Pittsburgh." Presentation to Pittsburgh City Council. Accessed August 8, 2010: http://www.city.pittsburgh.pa.us/district8/assets/07_CMU_wifi_presentation_City_Council.pdf.

City of Salem, Oregon. "Comprehensive Annual Financial Report for the Year Ended June 30, 2005." Accessed August 8, 2010: http://www.cityofsalem.net/Departments/AdministrativeServices/Finance/Documents/CAFRJune2005.pdf.

City of Tacoma. "Executive Summary Cost-Benefit Analysis of the Tacoma Police Department's Assigned Vehicle Program." Accessed August 8, 2010: http://www.cityoftacoma.org/Page.aspx?hid=2052.

Dadson, Scott. "Getting Our Heads Out of the Sand." City of Beaufort, 2009. Accessed August 8, 2010: http://www.cityofbeaufort.org/client_resources/city%20manager/getting%20our%20heads%20out%20of%20the%20sand%20rev%20cwm.pdf.

7 How Do We Rate? With the Internal Rate of Return

Government always finds a need for whatever money it gets.*

President Ronald Reagan

7.1 Objectives

The objectives of this chapter are to:

- Understand the concept of rate
- Understand the concept of internal rate of return
- Understand how to make an internal rate of return financial decision

7.2 Introduction

The methods of capital budgeting encompass perspectives of time, cash value, rate, and profitability potential. Examining projects from these perspectives involves the use of quantitative tools through which projects may be judged and selected as either acceptable or unacceptable. The preceding chapters introduced two capital budgeting methods, the payback time method and the net present value method, through which such decisions may be explored. Respectively, these methods involved perspectives of time and cash flow analysis.

This chapter introduces another perspective of capital budgeting referred to as the internal rate of return (IRR). This perspective involves a consideration of rate involving the anticipated cash flows of potential capital investment initiatives. The basic concepts of rates were defined and explained in the preceding chapters. This chapter expands the conceptual discussions of the IRR and demonstrates the usefulness of rate comparisons among potential capital investments. (See Figure 7.1.)

The IRR is used among a variety of environments to evaluate potential capital investment initiatives. According to the City of Las Vegas, the use

* Reagan, Ronald, "Decision Quotations," Brainy Quote, http://www.brainyquote.com/quotes/keywords/money_2.html (accessed July 11, 2011).

Figure 7.1 A goal of capital budgeting is to determine the highest and best use of organizational funding. Army Chief of Staff General George W. Casey, Jr., foreground, explains his four imperatives for getting the force back into "balance," as Secretary of the Army John McHugh listens on Tuesday to the Senate Armed Services Committee about the Army's budget for Fiscal Year 2011. (Photo by Alexandra Hemmerly-Brown. Courtesy of the U.S. Army, http://www.army.mil/media/109899.)

of the IRR method may be used to demonstrate the validity of requests for redevelopment funding.[*] From the perspective of building infrastructures, a 20% rate of return is expected regarding building strategies.[†]

Regarding a similar rate of return for retirement investments, the City of Pontiac, Michigan, during 2006, considered investment services firms that implemented the IRR method as a form of investment analysis. The architecture of the investment structures mandated that valuations demonstrate a "20% or greater internal rate of return with expected returns of structured equity at a rate of 8%" involving multiple strategies of investment.[‡]

Other building applications are common. The City of Newton, Kansas, considered the securing of existing infrastructures for redevelopment purposes. This capital initiative involved the acquisition of aging housing complexes for the purposes of redevelopment, with respect to a 15% to 20% rate of return. Because this rate is a relatively high yield, the investments retain

[*] City of Las Vegas, "City of Las Vegas Downtown Redevelopment Agency."
[†] Environmental Protection Agency, "What Is Your Share of $130 Billion?"
[‡] City of Pontiac, Michigan, "General Employees Retirement System."

their value.[*] This type of investment, coupled with its potential return rates, instigates cost savings because of the differences between the costs of new construction versus the costs of renovating existing buildings.

Other numerical rates of return are not uncommon when considering capital initiatives. In Missoula, Montana, the consideration of a 20% to 25% rate of return was considered regarding public capital initiatives. Only projects that demonstrated a potential rate of return of at least 20% were categorized as acceptable. This rate of return would only be applicable to initiatives that demonstrated "very little risk and uncertainty," and contracting firms would also "seek a return closer to 40 percent for projects with moderate risk."[†]

From the perspective of law enforcement use, the IRR is a tool through which potential capital investments may be examined. Such capital investments often are associated with the planning, structuring, and implementation of retirement systems. The use of the IRR may be applied to considerations of retirement systems and retirement planning among agencies and personnel. During 2009, the Fort Lauderdale Police and Fire Pension Board considered the use of such returns within the context of retirement projections among city personnel.[‡] Similarly, the cities of Richmond Heights, Missouri,[§] and Lakeland, Florida,[¶] also considered the rate of return as a method through which its retirement valuations occurred.

These examples show the potency of the IRR method as a tool through which capital budgeting decisions may be embellished. The use of the IRR method provides a tool through which an additional examination of capital initiatives may occur through considerations of whether potential capital initiatives are worthwhile investment pursuits through time. Regardless, the IRR is a tool through which organizational leaders may examine a rate with respect to the characteristics of the considered problem domain.

7.3 Internal Rate of Return (IRR) Method

The IRR is a capital budgeting tool that is used primarily to determine the potential profitability of capital investments through time. The period of time may be either strategic or tactical. Regardless, the basic concepts of the IRR are applicable within both situations. The IRR method incorporates the time value of money within its basic, mathematical construct. Therefore, it is indicative of monetary value equivalencies through time.

[*] City of Newton, "City of Newton Comprehensive Plan."

[†] City of Missoula, "Economic Analysis."

[‡] Fort Lauderdale Police and Firefighters' Retirement System, "Investment Workshop 2009."

[§] City of Richmond Heights, "Policemens' and Firemens' Retirement Fund."

[¶] City of Lakeland, Florida, "Police Officers' Retirement System Board of Trustees."

Conceptually, the IRR is the "annualized, effective compounded return rate that can be earned on the invested capital," and is the "interest rate at which the costs of the investment lead to the benefits of the investment." Further, the IRR is demonstrative of the concept that "all gains from the investment are inherent to the time value of money and that the investment has a zero net present value at this interest rate."* Therefore, there is a relationship between the IRR method and the net present value (NPV) method both quantitatively and mathematically.

Given these notions, the IRR is representative of a point in which the value of the NPV outcome of a project is zero. Through equating the NPV outcomes of potential capital investments to a common value of zero, comparisons may be made among multiple projects to determine which initiatives are suitable for pursuance. Further, with respect to the considerations of a single initiative, the use of the IRR provides a mechanism through which the calculated IRR value of the examined capital initiative may also be compared with an established benchmark to determine is suitability for pursuance.

The basic IRR concept involves a variety of variables within its mathematical relationship. These variables are given as follows:

IRR Internal rate of return
P Period of time considered
A_P Annual cash flow value
V_I Cost of initial investment value

With respect to a period of time, the basic mathematical relationship of the IRR method is expressed through the following formula:

$$NPV = 0.00 = \left(\sum_{P=1}^{P} \frac{A_P}{(IRR + 1.0)^P} \right) \tag{7.1}$$

The basic concept of the IRR function is both straightforward and simple to conceptualize. The IRR formula is indicative of the summation of the rate value regarding the annual cash flows through time, A_P, which equates the NPV outcome to a value of 0.00. Because it incorporates the time value of money, the value of period, P, representing time, will never be a negative value. The following section considers circumstances that govern the application of the IRR method.

* Waukesha, "IRR."

7.4 Application of the IRR Method

From the perspective of rendering a capital budgeting decision, the IRR method demonstrates a superior approach than is shown through the processes necessitated within the payback time method. The IRR does not ignore the time value of money but incorporates the time value of money within its mathematical construct. Through the use of the IRR, organizational leaders gain a perspective of rate influences that impact decisions concerning potential investment initiatives. Unlike the payback time method, which ignores any cash flows that exist after a payback time threshold is established, the IRR examines all anticipated future cash flows that are specified through time.

Although the IRR method incorporates the time value of money within its mathematical construct, it only presents a perspective regarding the rate characteristics of future cash flows. Therefore, it does not directly consider the characteristics of time limitations that may impact the rendering of a capital budgeting decision. Hence, it is recommended that the IRR method be applied, in conjunction with the payback time method, the net present value method, and the profitability index method, as a complementary and supplementary analysis of capital budgeting initiatives.

The application of the IRR method may be viewed from multiple perspectives. The first perspective involves a consideration of only one project that is being contemplated. Another perspective involves the concept of mutual exclusion—the selection of one, and only one initiative, from multiple capital initiatives. An additional perspective involves the selection of two (or more) projects from many projects. The example problems of this chapter demonstrate the IRR method calculations that are applicable among each of these situations.

Although the outcomes of the IRR method present quantitative findings, the outcomes must be interpreted. The rules governing the interpretation of the IRR outcome are quite basic:

1. Accept the capital initiative if the value of the calculated IRR outcome is higher than the specified discount rate.
2. Reject the capital initiative if the value of the calculated IRR outcome is lower than the discount rate.
3. When the conditions of mutual exclusion govern the problem domain, select the capital initiative that demonstrates the highest IRR outcome.

These rules provide the basis for judging a project as either acceptable or unacceptable with respect to an analysis of cash flows, through time. However, other factors exist that may influence the rendering of a capital budgeting decision. Even though the IRR outcome may be positive and may indicate that a project should be accepted, the ultimate decision to accept or reject a project is rendered by humans. Humans must also incorporate the characteristics of the domain environment that influence the decision process. Factors such as time, organizational politics, contribution to organizational value, and the availability of necessary resources also contribute toward the rendering of capital budgeting decisions. Therefore, regardless of any IRR outcome, the decisions to accept and to pursue capital initiatives are subject to a variety of influences.

The solution of problems involving the IRR method may occur through the use of spreadsheet software, financial calculators, trial-and-error approaches necessitating the use of mathematical interpolation, or through the use of the secant method. However, the use of the IRR method may manifest varying levels of difficulty because it necessitates the solution of polynomials of varying degrees. For larger data sets, it is highly recommended that solutions involve the use of financial calculators or software spreadsheets.

EXAMPLE 7.1: SOLITARY PROJECT

A basic example of the IRR concept may be used to show how data is processed within its mathematical construct. A single capital initiative may be considered. The following capital initiative data may be used to demonstrate the primary concept of the IRR method:

Anticipated initiative period: 4 years
Specified financial rate: 4.7%
Initial cost of the initiative: \$100,000.00
First year cash flow: \$84,000.00
Second year cash flow: \$93,000.00
Third year cash flow: \$101,000.00
Fourth year cash flow: \$110,000.00

Given this data, the following questions may be posed.

Question 1: What is the IRR?
Question 2: Based on the calculated IRR value, should this initiative be accepted?

An initial observation of this data set yields immediate values that may be identified. The values of the following variables are provided within the given data set:

$P = 4$
$R_{per} = 4.7\%$
$V_I = \$100{,}000.00$
$A_1 = \$84{,}000.00$
$A_2 = \$93{,}000.00$
$A_3 = \$101{,}000.00$
$A_4 = \$110{,}000.00$

The trial-and-error approach can be used to solve this problem. First, initial guesses must be made about the possible IRR solution. Because the exact IRR value is unknown, initial guesses must have a wide variety of values. For the first, initial approximation, the values of 0.9 and 0.1 are selected. These values may be substituted appropriately into the IRR formula. The first approximation may be substituted as follows:

$$NPV = 0.00 = \left(\sum_{P=1}^{P} \frac{A_P}{(IRR+1.0)^P} \right)$$

$$NPV_{0.90} = \frac{\$84,000.00}{(0.90+1.0)^1} + \frac{\$93,000.00}{(0.90+1.0)^2} + \frac{\$101,000.00}{(0.90+1.0)^3} + \frac{\$110,000.00}{(0.90+1.0)^4}$$

$$NPV_{0.90} = \$44,210.53 + \$35,761.77 + \$14,725.18 + \$8440.70$$

$$NPV_{0.90} = \$93,138.17$$

These calculations show the methods that are necessary for manually calculating potential values using guesses. When substituted appropriately, the outcomes associated with value substitutions of 0.1, 0.2, 0.3, 0.4, 0.5, 0.6, 0.7, and 0.8 may also be calculated using the same method. Because of space limitations, these manual iterations are not demonstrated within this text. However, when the appropriate substitutions are made within the IRR formula, the outcomes in Table 7.1 are derived from these IRR guesses. Examining the contents of Table 7.1 provides a synopsis of outcome ranges, between the values of 0.1 through 0.9, which were used as guesses within the IRR calculations. Within the problem statement, a value of $100,000.00 was identified as the cost of investment regarding the potential capital initiative. Comparing the investment cost to the cost outcomes of Table 7.1 yields an interesting observation. Eight of the nine calculated outcomes, ranging between 0.1 and 0.8, exceeded the investment cost that was specified within the problem statement. Therefore, the possible IRR values associated with these outcomes are unacceptable as problem solutions because the calculated NPV values exceed the investment cost. Hence, they may be discarded as possible solutions to the problem. The

Table 7.1 Example 7.1: IRR Guess Outcomes

IRR Guess	Outcome
0.1	$304,237.42
0.2	$246,080.25
0.3	$204,130.81
0.4	$172,890.46
0.5	$148,987.65
0.6	$130,271.00
0.7	$115,319.74
0.8	$103,167.20
0.9	$93,138.17

value of 0.9 is retained because its associated NPV outcome did not exceed the specified cost of investment.

However, this value of 0.90 is not the solution to the problem. Because the basic premise of the IRR concept indicates that the NPV of the anticipated cash flows must be equivalent to a value of zero, it is obvious that 0.90 is not the solution. Therefore, given that an exact IRR outcome was not manifested, the use of mathematical interpolation is necessitated as the method through which the appropriate IRR value may be calculated.

Because its calculated NPV value did not exceed the \$100,000.00 cost of investment, the value of 0.90 may be used as a mathematical constraint that will facilitate the derivation of the specified IRR value. The next highest, potential IRR value that is less than the value of 0.90 and whose calculated NPV outcome is the closest to the specified cost of investment is also retained as a constraint of interpolation. Given these three observations, three categories of observations are present: (1) an upper limitation consisting of NPV and IRR values that do not exceed the cost of investment; (2) a lower limitation consisting of NPV and IRR values that approach and slightly exceed the cost of investment; and (3) the specification of the actual cost of investment.

These three observations provide enough data to perform the function of mathematical interpolation to determine the unknown IRR value. The basic interpolative relationships may be identified thusly:

$0.8 = \$103{,}167.20$
$IRR = \$100{,}000.00$
$0.9 = \$93{,}138.17$

Sufficient data now exists to perform the function of interpolation. Using simple, algebraic concepts, the following processes show the interpolative process that determines the value of the unknown IRR variable. First, the interpolative relationship is demonstrated as follows:

$0.8 = \$103{,}167.20$
$IRR = \$100{,}000.00$
$0.9 = \$93{,}138.17$

Second, subtractions occur between the third and the second rows to yield the following relationships:

$0.9 - IRR$
$\$93{,}138.17 - \$100{,}000.00 = \$6861.83$

Third, subtractions occur between the third and the first rows to yield the following relationships:

$0.9 - 0.8 = 0.1$
$\$93{,}138.17 - \$103{,}167.20 = -\$10{,}029.03$

A ratio relationship may now be established using these values. This ratio basis is given as follows:

$$\frac{0.9 - IRR}{0.1} = \frac{\$6861.83}{-\$10{,}029.03}$$

This relationship now allows for the algebraic solution of the IRR variable. This solution is accomplished via the following process:

$$(0.9 - IRR)(-\$10{,}029.03) = (0.1)(\$6861.83)$$

$$(0.9 - IRR) = \frac{(0.1)(\$6861.83)}{(-\$10{,}029.03)}$$

$$(0.9 - IRR) = (-\$0.07)$$

$$-IRR = -0.83$$

$$IRR = 0.83$$

Based on the calculated outcome, the IRR value is 0.83. The first question of the problem statement queries the value of the IRR outcome. The IRR outcome that is commensurate with the given data set is 0.83 or 83%. The second question of the problem statement queries whether this initiative should either be accepted or rejected. Based on the IRR selection rule, this initiative should be recommended for acceptance because the calculated IRR outcome surpasses the established discount rate of 4.70%.

EXAMPLE 7.2: IRR AND MUTUAL EXCLUSION

The following example again examines the cash flows of the hypothetical example introduced in Chapter 5. The problem domain of this example is representative of the mutual exclusion condition. The problem statement is given as follows:

Last year, a tornado destroyed the police training facility of an urban area. The damages were sufficient enough to warrant the total loss of the building and its supporting infrastructure. After the devastating event occurred, the city council approved a measure to erect a new police training facility. The destroyed facility served as a training institute for regional first responders, among the four bordering states, whose functions included the provision of emergency services during both natural and man-made disasters. Therefore, it is imperative that this facility be restored.

The training tuition dollars of local personnel were provided by the devastated city. However, any nonlocal personnel were responsible for providing their own tuitions (e.g., self-pay, sponsor pay, grants). Because it was a regional training facility, the majority of the trainees were not local personnel. Therefore, this training facility provided a source of revenue for the city and its police department.

A combination of monies—to be obtained via taxation, city bond investments, a limited insurance policy, loans, and goodwill and charitable donations—are proposed to fund the initial costs of the capital investment. Through time, additional debt payments are to be made from the revenue stream of the restored facility.

Three contractors submitted bids for the rebuilding project. The bids of the contractors were \$291,000.00, \$293,000.00, and \$295,000.00. The rates associated with these values, respectively, are 4.30%, 4.57%, and 5.00%. Regardless of which contractor is selected, the pursued course of rebuilding must return an amount of at least \$500,000.00.

Because of other obligations, these contractors are unable specify identical dates to begin the construction of the new facility. Therefore, these time

Table 7.2 Cash Flows of Example 7.2

Period	Contractor A	Contractor B	Contractor C
0	($291,000.00)	($293,000.00)	($295,000.00)
1	$109,527.00	$110,527.00	$108,000.00
2	$129,034.00	$125,034.00	$127,000.00
3	$135,068.00	$133,368.00	$129,068.00
4	$148,927.00	$148,927.00	$135,000.00
5	$159,000.00	$159,000.00	$147,000.00
6	$168,000.00	$168,000.00	$155,000.00
7	$174,980.00	$174,980.00	$159,980.00

differences may offset the estimated cash flows of the facility. Further, because of existing debt obligations, the city must begin paying its debt within the next two years.

Based on the following listing of anticipated cash flow values (Table 7.2), what are the IRR outcomes of each of the proposals? Based on the IRR outcomes, which contractor is the recommended entity? Based on the calculated IRR values, is it feasible and advisable for the city to pursue this proposed course of action?

Solution Overview of Example 7.2

This problem considers capital budgeting decisions from the perspective of mutual exclusion. Within the context of mutual exclusion, one, and only one, capital initiative may be recommended for pursuance through time. Although multiple IRR outcomes may qualify as acceptable because they surpass the stated discount rates, only one initiative is recommended for acceptance and pursuance through time. This example demonstrates the use of the IRR method with respect to this constraint.

Example 7.1 provided a demonstration of solving IRR problems manually. Because of the tediousness and impracticality of solving IRR situations manually, the IRR values demonstrated in this example are solved using software spreadsheets. The reader may verify the accuracy of these IRR outcomes manually through the use of spreadsheets or a financial calculator. If solved manually, this problem involves the same method of systematically and methodically deriving IRR values for each of the stated contractor entities, comparing them with respect to the appropriate discount rates, and then providing a recommendation of acceptance or rejection.

When calculated through the use of a software spreadsheet, the IRR values shown in Table 7.3 are manifested. The contents of Table 7.3 show the three potential capital project cash flows, the three commensurate rates, and the three appropriate IRR values. Contractor A demonstrates an IRR value of 41.51% with respect to a 4.30% rate. Contractor B demonstrates an IRR value of 40.88% with respect to a 4.57% rate. Contractor C demonstrates an IRR value of 38.75% with respect to a 5.00% rate.

Regarding Contractor A, the manifested IRR outcome value of 41.51% surpasses the discount rate of 4.30%. The initiative proposed by Contractor A is valid, and may be retained for consideration. Regarding Contractor B, the manifested IRR outcome value of 40.88% surpasses the discount rate of 4.57%.

Table 7.3 Calculation of IRR Outcomes

Period	Contractor A	Contractor B	Contractor C
0	($291,000.00)	($293,000.00)	($295,000.00)
1	$109,527.00	$110,527.00	$108,000.00
2	$129,034.00	$125,034.00	$127,000.00
3	$135,068.00	$133,368.00	$129,068.00
4	$148,927.00	$148,927.00	$135,000.00
5	$159,000.00	$159,000.00	$147,000.00
6	$168,000.00	$168,000.00	$155,000.00
7	$174,980.00	$174,980.00	$159,980.00
Rate	4.30%	4.57%	5.00%
IRR	41.51%	40.88%	38.75%

The initiative proposed by Contractor B is valid and may be retained for consideration. Regarding Contractor C, the manifested IRR outcome value of 38.75% surpasses the discount rate of 5.00%. The initiative proposed by Contractor C is valid and may be retained for consideration.

Solution for Example 7.2: Capital Budgeting Decision

None of the potential initiatives were discarded during the initial, cursory examinations of their respective IRR values. A determination of the IRR outcomes of Contractor A, Contractor B, and Contractor C provides a sufficient amount of information to facilitate the rendering of a capital budgeting decision. Within the problem statement, the following questions were posed:

Based on the following listing of anticipated cash flow values, what are the IRR outcomes of each of the proposals?
Based on the IRR outcomes, which contractor is the recommended entity?
Based on the calculated IRR values, is it feasible and advisable for the city to pursue this proposed course of action?

With respect to the first question, the three IRR outcomes are now calculated for Contractor A, Contractor B, and Contractor C. Respectively, these NPV outcomes are as follows:

IRR of Contractor A: 41.51%
IRR of Contractor B: 40.88%
IRR of Contractor C: 38.75%

The second question queries the identity of the recommended contractor. In order to determine which contractor is the primary choice, a ranking of these potential initiatives may occur based on their IRR outcomes. This ranking may occur from the highest value to the lowest value. When ranked, these IRR values are listed as follows:

IRR of Contractor A: 41.51%
IRR of Contractor B: 40.88%
IRR of Contractor C: 38.75%

Now that these IRR outcomes and rankings are determined, enough data exists to facilitate the rendering of a human decision regarding potential, strategic courses of actions. Given the content of the problem statement, the condition of mutual exclusion is applicable. Therefore one, but only one, contractor may be selected as the entity that shall facilitate the rebuilding effort. The ranked NPV outcomes may be examined to determine which contractor is the primary choice for the rebuilding efforts. Contractor A manifested an IRR outcome of 41.51%, Contractor B manifested an IRR outcome of 40.88%, and Contractor C manifested an NPV outcome of 38.75%.

These IRR outcomes may be evaluated with respect to the established rules of acceptance. The IRR acceptance judgment is commensurate with the notion that an initiative is acceptable if the calculated IRR value exceeds the established, stated discount rate. Further, when comparing multiple initiatives, the initiative demonstrating the highest IRR outcome should be selected when the conditions of mutual exclusion are applicable. The problem statement indicated that the conditions of mutual exclusion governed the problem domain. Therefore, only one contracting agency may be recommended for acceptance. Based on these requirements, the choice IRR is represented by Contractor A whose IRR outcome is 41.51%. Therefore, Contractor A is the recommended contracting entity.

The third question queries whether it is feasible and advisable for the city to pursue the recommended course of action. Based on the outcome of the IRR analysis, the recommended contractor is Contractor A. However, a recommendation regarding the actual pursuit based solely on IRR considerations may be appropriate but is certainly not the only consideration that affects the decision to pursue the recommended course of action. Other factors also affect this decision.

However, other factors also influence the considerations of the problem statement. The IRR analysis does not directly consider the NPV outcomes. The IRR analysis does not directly consider the two-year limitation that was imposed within the payback time method. The IRR decision does not directly consider the outcomes of the remaining methods of capital budgeting consisting of the profitability index. Also, although such items are not mentioned in the problem statement, organizational politics, the securing of building permits, the availability of labor, and an array of other factors also affect the decision of rebuilding.

The use of the IRR method provides a solitary perspective of the decision domain through an evaluation of the rates in which NPV values are equivalent to the value of zero. Through such equivalencies of values among multiple projects, a common basis for evaluation capital initiatives is established. Because the IRR method represents only a solitary perspective, it is recommended that it be used in conjunction with the other methods of capital budgeting.

7.5 Accepting Multiple Initiatives

The example of the ABD Criminal Corrections Corporation in Chapter 5 may again be examined from the perspective of capital budgeting. However, the next examination may be completed through the use of the NPV method, and the condition of mutual exclusion may be removed. Therefore, it becomes possible for multiple initiatives to be considered as potential courses of actions. The updated problem statement reflecting the removal of mutual exclusion is given next.

EXAMPLE 7.3: ACCEPTING MULTIPLE IRR OUTCOMES

The following problem statement is adapted from Chapter 5. It demonstrates alterations of the decision domain that allow the acceptance of multiple initiatives during the upcoming fiscal year. Within this example, the conditions of mutual exclusion are not applicable.

The ABD Criminal Corrections Corporation, a for-profit entity, is evaluating four potential capital initiatives. Because of funding shortcomings, the organization is unable to pursue all of its possible initiatives. The board of directors indicated that only two initiatives can be pursued during the coming year. Therefore, the organization must select only two projects from among many to pursue as its choice of capital initiatives.

The first project, Initiative A, involves the purchasing and installation of new telephone equipment. This project would update and improve the telephone system of the correctional facility. Through the use of this system, inmates would be charged to make telephone calls (when permitted to do so). The rate associated with this initiative is 4.86%.

The second project, Initiative B, involves the implementation of laundry services for the correctional facility. A private vendor is now used as an outsourced method of providing cleaning services for linens and clothing. However, laundry facilities exist within the correctional infrastructure, and inmates could perform such duties. If this project is selected, then the correctional facility would annually save money via the use of prisoner labor. The rate associated with this initiative is 4.25%.

The third project, Initiative C, involves the potential replacement of food services from a private contractor. The current food service provides prepacked meals that are sufficient for breakfast, dinner, and supper meals within the facility. However, the correctional facility is considering the development and implementation of its own agricultural program, and inmates could grow their own food and prepare their meals. If this option is selected, then cost saving could be manifested through the use of prisoner labor. The rate associated with this initiative is 4.62%.

The fourth project, Initiative D, involves the development and implementation of newspaper services. The corrections facility would serve as an outsourcing agent for the newspapers of the surrounding townships. The correctional facility houses a printing area, and the use of prisoner labor could be leveraged to provide writing and printing services. These services would have a subscription fee and would provide a source of revenue for the corporation. The rate associated with this initiative is 3.99%.

The anticipated annual cash flows and the investment costs of each project are given in Table 7.4. These four initiatives are all acceptable ideas. However, because of security, financial, and control concerns, the board of directors agreed that only two capital initiatives may be considered for the coming fiscal year. Based on the use of the IRR method, which projects are recommended for acceptance? Based on these IRR outcomes, which projects should be pursued?

Table 7.4 Values for Example 7.3

Period	Initiative A (Telephones)	Initiative B (Laundry)	Initiative C (Food)	Initiative D (Printing)
0	($1000.00)	($13,200.00)	($3000.00)	($12,000.00)
1	$500.00	$1272.00	$800.00	$1700.00
2	$200.00	$2122.00	$950.00	$2400.00
3	$300.00	$2534.00	$1300.00	$3100.00
4	$600.00	$2900.00	$1700.00	$3300.00
5	$700.00	$3400.00	$1900.00	$3700.00
6	$800.00	$3770.00	$2500.00	$4600.00
7	$900.00	$3400.00	$2900.00	$5300.00

Solution Overview of Example 7.3

This problem considers capital budgeting decisions from the perspective of accepting multiple initiatives. Therefore, more than one capital initiative may be recommended for pursuance through time. This example demonstrates the use of the IRR method with respect to such conditions.

Example 7.1 provided a demonstration of solving IRR problems manually. Because of the tediousness and impracticality of solving IRR situations manually, the IRR values demonstrated within this example are solved using software spreadsheets. The reader may verify the accuracy of these IRR outcomes manually through the use of spreadsheets or a financial calculator. If solved manually, this problem involves the same method of systematically and methodically deriving IRR values for each of the stated contractor entities, comparing them with respect to the appropriate discount rates, and then providing a recommendation of acceptance or rejection.

When calculated through the use of a software spreadsheet, the IRR values in Table 7.5 are manifested. The contents of Table 7.5 show the four potential capital project cash flows, the four commensurate discount rates, and the four appropriate IRR values. Based on the outcomes of Table 7.5, the following IRR outcomes are demonstrated:

Table 7.5 Multiple Initiative IRR Outcomes

Period	Initiative A (Telephones)	Initiative B (Laundry)	Initiative C (Food)	Initiative D (Printing)
0	($1000.00)	($13,200.00)	($3000.00)	($12,000.00)
1	$500.00	$1272.00	$800.00	$1700.00
2	$200.00	$2122.00	$950.00	$2400.00
3	$300.00	$2534.00	$1300.00	$3100.00
4	$600.00	$2900.00	$1700.00	$3300.00
5	$700.00	$3400.00	$1900.00	$3700.00
6	$800.00	$3770.00	$2500.00	$4600.00
7	$900.00	$3400.00	$2900.00	$5300.00
Rate	4.86%	4.25%	4.62%	3.99%
IRR	41.99%	9.16%	39.11%	17.36%

Initiative A: 41.99%
Initiative B: 9.16%
Initiative C: 39.11%
Initiative D: 17.36%

Initiative A demonstrates an IRR value of 41.99% with respect to a 4.86% rate. Initiative B demonstrates an IRR value of 9.16% with respect to a 4.25% rate. Initiative C demonstrates an IRR value of 39.11% with respect to a 4.62% rate. Initiative D demonstrates an IRR value of 17.36% with respect to a 3.99% rate. Each of the IRR outcomes of these potential initiatives surpasses its respective discount rate. Therefore, each of these initiatives may be retained for consideration as acceptable capital initiatives.

The IRR outcomes may be ranked according to their order of precedence. From highest to lowest, the following ranking of these IRR outcomes is demonstrated:

Initiative A: 41.99%
Initiative C: 39.11%
Initiative D: 17.36%
Initiative B: 9.16%

Solution for Example 7.3: Capital Budgeting Decision

Now that these IRR outcomes are determined, enough data exists to facilitate the rendering of a human decision regarding potential, strategic courses of actions. Given the content of the problem statement, the condition of mutual exclusion is not applicable. Therefore, more than one contractor may be selected as the entity that shall facilitate the rebuilding effort. The ranked IRR outcomes may be examined to determine which contractor is the primary choice for the rebuilding efforts. The two highest IRR outcomes were manifested by Initiative A, telephone services, and Initiative C, food services. Respectively, these IRR outcome values are 41.99% and 39.11%.

The first question of the problem statement is concerned with the recommendation of potential initiatives. Each of the IRR outcomes of these potential initiatives surpasses its respective discount rate. Therefore, each of these initiatives may be retained for consideration as acceptable capital initiatives. The second question is concerned with which initiatives should be pursued. Based on the requirements governing IRR outcome selection and the restrictions of the problem domain, only two initiatives may be recommended for acceptance. With respect to the tenets of IRR and the characteristics of the problem domain, both Initiative A and Initiative C qualify as acceptable capital investments.

7.6 Advanced IRR Considerations

The discussions and examples in this text serve as an introduction to the IRR concept. This introduction considers examples that are relatively understandable and that require only the implementation of the basic IRR construct for their solution. Regardless of the period of time considered, the basic IRR concept may be applied to any specific, anticipated cash flows to examine their relevancy within the context of capital budgeting decisions.

Other considerations of the IRR involve the existence of multiple instances of IRR values spawned from irregularities within cash flows through time. It is beyond the scope and magnitude of this introductory text to address such issues. However, extended discussions may be found among the writings of contemporary financial management texts.

Some initiatives may require periods that are longer than those that are considered in this text. When these situations occur, it is recommended that IRR calculations be performed through the use of software spreadsheets, proprietary software, or financial calculators. Also, within the context of collegiate finance courses, a tabular solution is also available to solve IRR problems involving a variety of periods. However, for the purposes of this text, the use of the basic formula is appropriate to demonstrate the basic concept of the internal rate of return, and to delineate the calculations through which IRR problems are solved. Future editions of this text, if any, are anticipated to contain the tabular solution methods of IRR problems.

7.7 Chapter Comments and Summary

This chapter introduced the internal rate of return (IRR) method of capital budgeting. The methods of capital budgeting encompass perspectives of time, cash value, rate, and profitability potential. The IRR is indicative of a rate-based perspective regarding the rendering of capital budgeting decisions. Further, the IRR method incorporates the time value of money within its primary construct. Derivation of the IRR method may occur through algebraic manipulation of the net present value formula that is given in Chapter 6.

Although the outcomes of the IRR method present quantitative findings, the outcomes must be interpreted. The rules governing the interpretation of the IRR outcome are quite basic:

1. Accept the capital initiative if the value of the calculated IRR outcome is higher than the specified discount rate.
2. Reject the capital initiative if the value of the calculated IRR outcome is lower than the discount rate.
3. When the conditions of mutual exclusion govern the problem domain, select the capital initiative that demonstrates the highest IRR outcome.

These rules provide the basis for judging a project as either acceptable or unacceptable with respect to an analysis of cash flows, through time. However, other factors exist that may influence the rendering of a capital budgeting decision. Even though the IRR outcome might be positive and indicate that a project should be accepted, the ultimate decision to accept or reject a project is rendered by humans. Humans must also incorporate the characteristics of the domain environment that influence the decision process. Factors such as time, organizational politics, contribution to organizational value, and the availability of necessary resources also contribute toward the rendering of capital budgeting decisions. Therefore, regardless of any IRR outcome, the decisions to accept and to pursue capital initiatives are subject to a variety of influences.

The solution of problems involving the IRR method may occur through the use of spreadsheet software, financial calculators, trial-and-error approaches necessitating the use of mathematical interpolation, or through the use of the secant method. However, the use of the IRR method may manifest varying levels of difficulty because it necessitates the solution of polynomials of varying degrees. For larger data sets, it is highly recommended that solutions involve the use of financial calculators or software spreadsheets.

The use of the IRR method provides a solitary perspective of the decision domain through an evaluation of the rates in which NPV values are equivalent to the value of zero. Through such equivalencies of values among multiple projects, a common basis for evaluation capital initiatives is established. Because the IRR method represents only a solitary perspective, it is recommended that it be used in conjunction with the other methods of capital budgeting.

The use of the IRR is varied. Its application occurs among the environments of global corporations and small businesses. Within the context of criminal justice and law enforcement entities, its use is appropriate. Such entities may use the IRR to examine cost savings through time regarding operational aspects of departments, to examine the erection of new buildings, to examine the purchasing of vehicles and other equipment, and to examine the effects of retirement contributions through time. Regardless of the type of capital initiative explored via the use of the IRR method, its implementation provides organizational leaders with an additional rate-based perspective of the decision domain.

7.8 Formulas

Internal Rate of Return Concept

$$NPV = 0.00 = \left(\sum_{P=1}^{P} \frac{A_P}{(IRR + 1.0)^P} \right)$$

7.9 Terminology

Acceptance
Capital budgeting
Capital budgeting decision
Capital investment
Cash flow
Constraints
Current monetary value
Discount rate
Equivalency
Future monetary value
Initial investment cost
Internal rate of return
Limitations
Monetary equivalency
Monetary value
Rate
Required rate
Rejection

7.10 Thought and Discussion Questions

Based on the examples given in this chapter, the following situation provides a description for consideration:

The hypothetical Country Law Enforcement Training School (CLETS) is a for-profit training organization that supplies a variety of training materials and courses among law enforcement environments and their served communities. Its services include the provision of combatives and weapons safety courses among both urban and rural communities. The CLETS operations were successful during the last few years, and now the firm seeks to grow its operations.

The CLETS organization is considering expanding its operations into three new locations. However, it has a restriction in that it may pursue no more than three investments during the upcoming years. Table 7.6 shows the anticipated costs of investments and the anticipated cash flows that are affiliated with each of the potential capital investment initiatives. Regardless

Table 7.6 CLETS Expansion Options

Period	Initiative A	Initiative B	Initiative C	Initiative D	Initiative E
0	($21,000.00)	($16,200.00)	($3000.00)	($12,000.00)	($12,000.00)
1	$3000.00	$2534.00	$800.00	$1700.00	$2000.00
2	$3700.00	$2900.00	$950.00	$2400.00	$2150.00
3	$3925.00	$3400.00	$1300.00	$3100.00	$2750.00
4	$4125.00	$3770.00	$1700.00	$3300.00	$3000.00
5	$4400.00	$3400.00	$1900.00	$3700.00	$3500.00
6	$4675.00	$3925.00	$2500.00	$4600.00	$4000.00
7	$4825.00	$4750.00	$2900.00	$5300.00	$4700.00
8	$4850.00	$5150.00	$2975.00	$5400.00	$4775.00
9	$4875.00	$5200.00	$2900.00	$5500.00	$4800.00
10	$4900.00	$5300.00	$2955.00	$5600.00	$5000.00

of the initiative(s) selected, the capital investment must recover its investment costs within a period of four years. Further, the rates of each capital investment differ. The following rates are applicable to the considered capital investments:

Initiative A: 4.36%
Initiative B: 4.25%
Initiative C: 4.23%
Initiative D: 4.41%
Initiative E: 4.12%

Table 7.6 presents the annual periods and cash flows of the CLETS organization.

1. Using the IRR method, calculate the appropriate IRR outcomes for each of the initiatives.
2. Based on Table 7.6 and descriptions, if the concept of mutual exclusion is not applicable, which of the initiatives may be recommended for pursuance during the upcoming year? Use the IRR method to determine the appropriate outcome.
3. Based on Table 7.6 and descriptions, if mutual exclusion is applicable, which of the initiatives may be recommended for pursuance during the upcoming year? Use the IRR method to determine the appropriate outcome.

Bibliography

City of Lakeland, Florida. "City of Lakeland Police Officers' Retirement System Board of Trustees." Accessed August 10, 2010: http://www.lakelandgov.net/civilservice/retirement/police/files/15D54A43B5E14123B5F6944D397709A6.pdf.

City of Las Vegas. "City of Las Vegas Downtown Redevelopment Agency Project Information Checklist." Accessed August 10, 2010: http://www.lasvegasnevada.gov/files/redevechklist.pdf.

City of Missoula. "Economic Analysis." Accessed August 9, 2010: http://www.ci.missoula.mt.us/DocumentView.aspx?DID=665.

City of Newton. "City of Newton Comprehensive Plan." Accessed August 10, 2010: http://www.newtonkansas.com/Modules/ShowDocument.aspx?documentid=114.

City of Pontiac, Michigan. "City of Pontiac, Michigan General Employees' Retirement System Board of Trustees November 29, 2006." Accessed August 10, 2010: http://www.pontiac.mi.us/pdf/gers112906.pdf.

City of Richmond Heights. "City of Richmond Heights Policemens' and Firemens' Retirement Fund: Actuarial Valuation Report as of July 1, 2007." Accessed August 10, 2010: http://www.richmondheights.org/DocumentView.aspx?DID=1612.

Environmental Protection Agency. "What Is Your Share of $130 Billion?" Accessed August 10, 2010: http://www.epa.gov/enviroed/pdf/share130b.pdf.

Fort Lauderdale Police & Firefighters' Retirement System. "Fort Lauderdale Police and Fire Pension Board Investment Workshop 2009." December 3–4, 2009. Accessed August 10, 2010: http://www.scribd.com/doc/23528492/Fort-Lauderdale-Police-and-Fire-Pension-Board-Investment-Workshop-2009.

Waukesha. "IRR." Accessed August 11, 2010: http://www.ci.waukesha.wi.us/web/guest/processautomationglossary.

Red or Black? The Profitability Index Method

8

A rich man is nothing but a poor man with money.*

W. C. Fields

8.1 Objectives

The objectives of this chapter are to:

- Understand the concept of the profitability ratio/index method
- Understand the mathematical formula of the profitability method
- Understand how to make a financial decision via the profitability method

8.2 Introduction

The methods of capital budgeting encompass perspectives of time, cash value, rate, and profitability potential. Examining projects from these perspectives involves the use of quantitative tools through which projects may be judged and selected as either acceptable or unacceptable. The preceding chapters introduced three capital budgeting methods, the payback time method, the net present value method, and the internal rate of return method, through which such decisions may be explored. Respectively, these methods involved perspectives of time, cash-flow analysis, and rate analysis.

This chapter introduces another perspective of capital budgeting referred to as the profitability index method (PIM) or profitability index (PI). This perspective involves a consideration of the potential profitability of considered capital initiatives. This perspective of profitability is applicable among a variety of domains. Through using the PIM, financial managers gain an understanding of the potential profitability of considered projects. (See Figure 8.1.)

According to the State of Alaska, the use of the profitability index method serves as a tool through which energy initiative decisions may be evaluated.† Similar observations are provided by the U.S. Department of the

* Fields, W. C., "Money Quotes," Brainy Quote, http://www.brainyquote.com/quotes/keywords/money_5.html (accessed July 11, 2011).
† Alaska State Legislature, "Action Narrative."

Figure 8.1 Conducting a budget analysis. Deana Haikes (left) and Annette Wassell discuss Budget Execution Reviews, which focus on the reasons for deviations between planned expenses and actual execution. Haikes and Wassell are budget analysts. (Photo by Tony Medici. Courtesy of the U.S. Army, http://www.army.mil/media/112191.)

Interior regarding the initiatives of its Bureau of Ocean Energy Management, Regulation and Enforcement (BOEMRE). According to the BOEMRE, the use of the profitability index contributes toward the "physical and economic performance measures to characterize lease sales and development in the U.S. Gulf of Mexico" through quantitative lease analysis.* Other energy uses of the PI method are not uncommon. The PI method also is applicable among the capital initiatives of green energy. Chabot, Kellet, and Saulnier use the PI method as a tool through which evaluations of the French wind system occur.†

The PI method also is useful within the domains of banking and finance. Knight examines financial comparisons among loans, and considers the rate effects regarding changes in profitability indices. According to Knight, such profitability indices would rise accordingly in conjunction with increases among interest rates.‡ This observation is associated with perceptions of trade-off characteristics among different loans.

Within the context of the legal system, the profitability method is applicable. During 2008, twenty-five Texas law firms were compared regarding the characteristics of their profitableness. These law firms were ranked according to their attributes of profitability, from the highest profitability to the

* U.S. Department of the Interior, "Profitability of Offshore Petroleum Ventures and Operations."

† Chabot, Kellet, and Saulnier, "Defining Advanced Wind Energy Tariffs Systems."

‡ Knight, "Customer Profitability Analysis."

lowest profitability, as a method of determining whether "equity partners" were receiving compensation that was "more or less than the average revenue brought into the firm."* Further, based on the profitability indices, it was determined that nineteen of the firms demonstrated some level of profitability, whereas six demonstrated unprofitability.

These uses of the profitability index demonstrate its robustness as a financial analysis tool among a myriad of domains. Although this profitability analysis method incorporates the time value of money in its mathematical construct, it does not consider the chronological attributes of time that may affect the rendering of a capital budgeting decision. Therefore, its use is limited solely to considerations of profitability. However, it may be used as a supplement or a complement to other methods of capital budgeting analysis. Overall, it is an appropriate method of facilitating the rendering of human decisions regarding potential capital initiatives.

8.3 Profitability Index (PI) Method

The PI is a capital budgeting tool that is primarily used to determine the potential profitability of capital investments through time. The period of time may be either strategic or tactical. Regardless, the basic concepts of the PI are applicable within both situations. The PI method incorporates the time value of money within its basic, mathematical construct. Therefore, it is indicative of monetary value equivalencies through time.

The concept underlying the PI method is quite basic and is easily understood. This concept involves the manifestation of a ratio between the present values of the anticipated cash flows versus the initial investment costs of the considered initiative. This concept manifests few variables within the mathematical relationship comprising the PI method. The following variables are used to delineate the mathematical entities that exist within the mathematical construct of the PI method:

- PI Profitability index
- P Period of time considered
- A_P Annual cash flow value
- ΣA_P Present monetary value of the summation of annual cash flow values
- V_I Cost of initial investment value

The following formula expresses the mathematical basis and primary construct of the PI method:

* Jeffreys, "Who's really making money?"

$$PI = \left(\frac{\sum_{P=1}^{P} A_P}{V_I} \right) \tag{8.1}$$

8.4 Application of the PI Method

From the perspective of rendering a capital budgeting decision, the PI method demonstrates a superior approach than is demonstrated through the processes necessitated within the payback time method. The PI does not ignore the time value of money but incorporates the time value of money within its mathematical construct. Through the use of the PI method, organizational leaders gain a perspective of profitability influences that impact decisions concerning potential investment initiatives. Unlike the payback time method, which ignores any cash flows that exist after a payback time threshold is established, the PI method examines all anticipated future cash flows that are specified through time.

Although the PI method incorporates the time value of money in its mathematical construct, it only presents a perspective regarding the profitability characteristics of future cash flows. Therefore, it does not directly consider the characteristics of time limitations that may impact the rendering of a capital budgeting decision. Hence, it is recommended that the PI method be applied, in conjunction with the payback time method, the net present value method, and the internal rate of return method, as a complementary and supplementary analysis of capital budgeting initiatives.

The application of the PI method may be viewed from multiple perspectives. The first perspective involves a consideration of only one project that is being contemplated. Another perspective involves the concept of mutual exclusion—the selection of one, and only one initiative, from multiple capital initiatives. An additional perspective involves the selection of two (or more) projects from many projects. The example problems of this chapter demonstrate the PI method calculations that are applicable among each of these situations.

Although the outcomes of the PI method present quantitative findings, the outcomes must be interpreted. The rules governing the interpretation of the PI outcome are quite basic:

1. Accept the capital initiative if the value of the calculated PI outcome is greater than the value of 1.0.
2. Reject the capital initiative if the value of the calculated PI outcome is lower than the value of 1.0.
3. When the conditions of mutual exclusion govern the problem domain, select the capital initiative that demonstrates the highest PI outcome.

These rules provide the basis for judging a project as either acceptable or unacceptable, with respect to an analysis of cash flows, through time. However, other factors exist that may influence the rendering of a capital budgeting decision. Even though the PI method outcome may be greater than the value of 1.0 and may indicate that a project should be accepted, the ultimate decision to accept or reject a project is rendered by humans. Humans must also incorporate the characteristics of the domain environment that influence the decision process. Factors such as time, organizational politics, contribution to organizational value, and the availability of necessary resources also contribute toward the rendering of capital budgeting decisions. Therefore, regardless of any PI method outcome, the decisions to accept and to pursue capital initiatives are subject to a variety of influences.

EXAMPLE 8.1: SOLITARY PROJECT

A basic example of the PI concept may be used to show how data is processed within its mathematical construct. A single capital initiative may be considered. The following capital initiative data may be used to demonstrate the primary concept of the PI method:

Anticipated initiative period: 4 years
Specified financial rate: 4.7%
Initial cost of the initiative: \$100,000.00
First year cash flow: \$84,000.00
Second year cash flow: \$93,000.00
Third year cash flow: \$101,000.00
Fourth year cash flow: \$110,000.00

Given this data, the following questions may be posed:

Question 1: What is the Profitability Index (PI) of the above situation?
Question 2: Based on the calculated PI value, should this initiative be accepted?

Solution Overview of Example 8.1

An initial observation of this data set yields immediate values that may be identified. The values of the following variables are provided within the given data set:

$P = 4$ years
$V_I = \$100,000.00$

The value representing the sum of the anticipated cash flows, ΣA_P, in the terms of current monetary value must be derived. The value of ΣA_P is found through using the current monetary value formula, given in Chapter 4, to determine the contemporary monetary value of the anticipated cash flows through time. These substitutions are accomplished as shown in Table 8.1:

When substituted appropriately into the current monetary value formula, the resulting summation of current monetary values outcome, A_P, is \$344,605.75. This specification of the value of the variable representing the

Table 8.1 Determination of Current Monetary Values

Period	Cash Flow	Substitution	A_P
0	($100,000.00)	N/A	($100,000.00)
1	$84,000.00	$84,000.00/(1.0 + 0.047)^1	$80,229.23
2	$93,000.00	$93,000.00/(1.0 + 0.047)^2	$84,837.84
3	$101,000.00	$101,000.00/(1.0 + 0.047)^3	$87,999.73
4	$110,000.00	$110,000.00/(1.0 + 0.047)^4	$91,538.96

present monetary value of the anticipated cash flows, A_P, provides enough data to sufficiently determine the profitability index. The value of $344,605.75, representing A_P, and the value of the initial cost of capital investment, $100,000.00, V_I, may be substituted into the profitability index method. These substitutions, the appropriate calculations, and the resulting outcome are given as follows:

$$PI = \left(\frac{\sum_{P=1}^{P} A_P}{V_I} \right)$$

$$PI = \left(\frac{\$344{,}605.75}{\$100{,}000.00} \right)$$

$$PI = 3.45$$

Solution for Example 8.1: Capital Budgeting Decision

The resulting outcome, representing the value of the calculated profitability index, P_I, is 3.45. This outcome may be considered from the perspective of the given problem statement. The first question of the problem statement queried the value of the profitability index. The preceding calculations determined the value of the profitability index, P_I, to be 3.45. The second question of the problem statement queried whether the considered capital initiative should be either accepted or rejected. Based on the selection rules governing the determination of acceptance regarding the profitability index method outcome, the resulting P_I value, 3.45, is deemed to be acceptable. Therefore, this capital initiative should be recommended for acceptance and potential pursuance through time.

EXAMPLE 8.2: PI METHOD AND MUTUAL EXCLUSION

The following example again examines the cash flows of the hypothetical example introduced in Chapter 5. The problem domain of this example is representative of the mutual exclusion condition. The problem statement is given as follows:

Last year, a tornado destroyed the police training facility of an urban area. The damages were sufficient enough to warrant the total loss of the building and its supporting infrastructure. After the devastating event occurred, the city council approved a measure to erect a new police training facility. The destroyed facility served as a training institute for regional first responders, among the four bordering states, whose functions included the provision of emergency services during both natural and man-made disasters. Therefore, it is imperative that this facility be restored.

Table 8.2 Cash Flows of Example 8.2

Period	Contractor A	Contractor B	Contractor C
0	($291,000.00)	($293,000.00)	($295,000.00)
1	$109,527.00	$110,527.00	$108,000.00
2	$129,034.00	$125,034.00	$127,000.00
3	$135,068.00	$133,368.00	$129,068.00
4	$148,927.00	$148,927.00	$135,000.00
5	$159,000.00	$159,000.00	$147,000.00
6	$168,000.00	$168,000.00	$155,000.00
7	$174,980.00	$174,980.00	$159,980.00

The training tuition dollars of local personnel were provided by the devastated city. However, any nonlocal personnel were responsible for providing their own tuitions (e.g., self-pay, sponsor pay, grants). Because it was a regional training facility, the majority of the trainees were not local personnel. Therefore, this training facility provided a source of revenue for the city and its police department.

A combination of monies—to be obtained via taxation, city bond investments, a limited insurance policy, loans, and goodwill and charitable donations—are proposed to fund the initial costs of the capital investment. Through time, additional debt payments are to be made from the revenue stream of the restored facility.

Three contractors submitted bids for the rebuilding project. The bids of the contractors were $291,000.00, $293,000.00, and $295,000.00. The rates associated with these values, respectively, are 4.30%, 4.57%, and 5.00%. Regardless of which contractor is selected, the pursued course of rebuilding must return an amount of at least $500,000.00.

Because of other obligations, these contractors are unable specify identical dates to begin the construction of the new facility. Therefore, these time differences may offset the estimated cash flows of the facility. Further, because of existing debt obligations, the city must begin paying its debt within the next two years.

Based on the listing of anticipated cash flow values in Table 8.2, what are the PI outcomes of each of the proposals? Based on the PI method outcomes, which contractor is the recommended entity? Based on the calculated PI method values, is it feasible and advisable for the city to pursue this proposed course of action?

Solution Overview of Example 8.2

This problem considers capital budgeting decisions from the perspective of mutual exclusion. Within the context of mutual exclusion, one, and only one, capital initiative may be recommended for pursuance through time. Although multiple PI method outcomes may qualify as acceptable because they surpass the stated profitability threshold value of 1.0, only one initiative is to be recommended for acceptance and pursuance through time. This example demonstrates the use of the PI method with respect to this constraint.

Example 8.1 provided a demonstration of solving PI method problems manually. Because of the tediousness of solving current monetary situations manually, the ΣA_P values, demonstrated within this example, are solved using

Table 8.3 Variable Values and Calculations of Contractor A

Period	Contractor A	Current Monetary Value
0	($291,000.00)	N/A
1	$109,527.00	$105,011.51
2	$129,034.00	$118,613.89
3	$135,068.00	$119,041.82
4	$148,927.00	$125,845.07
5	$159,000.00	$128,817.71
6	$168,000.00	$130,497.87
7	$174,980.00	$130,316.15
	A_P Summation:	$858,144.02

Table 8.4 Variable Values and Calculations of Contractor B

Period	Contractor A	Current Monetary Value
0	($293,000.00)	N/A
1	$110,527.00	$105,696.66
2	$125,034.00	$114,344.14
3	$133,368.00	$116,635.38
4	$148,927.00	$124,550.37
5	$159,000.00	$127,163.24
6	$168,000.00	$128,489.20
7	$174,980.00	$127,978.98
	A_P Summation:	$844,857.98

software spreadsheets. The reader may verify the accuracy of these ΣA_P outcomes manually through the use of spreadsheets or through the use of a financial calculator. If solved manually, this problem involves the same method of systematically and methodically deriving ΣA_P values for each of the stated contractor entities. After these ΣA_P values are determined, they are used to determine the IP method outcome for each capital investment initiative. Finally, a recommendation of acceptance or rejection is rendered.

When calculated through the use of a software spreadsheet, the following ΣA_P and PI method outcome values may be determined. The following tables show these determinations. For Contractor A, the calculated outcomes are given in Table 8.3. For Contractor B, the calculated outcomes are given in Table 8.4. For Contractor C, the calculated outcomes are given in Table 8.5. These table values show the appropriate current monetary value equivalencies for the A_P variables of Contractor A, Contractor B, and Contractor C. Based on these outcomes, the A_P variable of Contractor A is $858,144.02, the A_P variable of Contractor B is $844,857.98, and the A_P variable of Contractor C is $785,145.04. These calculated values may be substituted appropriately into the profitability index method formula to determine the profitability index outcomes for all three potential capital initiatives. For Contractor A, the appropriate substitutions are as follows:

Table 8.5 Variable Values and Calculations of Contractor C

Period	Contractor A	Current Monetary Value
0	($295,000.00)	N/A
1	$108,000.00	$102,857.14
2	$127,000.00	$115,192.74
3	$129,068.00	$111,493.79
4	$135,000.00	$111,064.83
5	$147,000.00	$115,178.35
6	$155,000.00	$115,663.39
7	$159,980.00	$113,694.80
	A_P Summation:	$785,145.04

$$PI_A = \left(\frac{\sum_{P=1}^{P} A_P}{V_I} \right)$$

$$PI_A = \left(\frac{\$858,144.02}{\$291,000.00} \right)$$

$$PI_A = 2.95$$

For Contractor B, the appropriate substitutions are as follows:

$$PI_B = \left(\frac{\sum_{P=1}^{P} A_P}{V_I} \right)$$

$$PI_B = \left(\frac{\$844,857.98}{\$293,000.00} \right)$$

$$PI_B = 2.88$$

For Contractor C, the appropriate substitutions are as follows:

$$PI_C = \left(\frac{\sum_{P=1}^{P} A_P}{V_I} \right)$$

$$PI_C = \left(\frac{\$785,145.04}{\$295,000.00} \right)$$

$$PI_C = 2.66$$

Solution for Example 8.2: Capital Budgeting Decision

These outcomes may be considered from the perspective of the problem statement. The first question queried the PI method outcomes for each of the capital initiatives. These calculated PI method outcomes demonstrate profitability index outcome values for the capital initiatives of Contractor A, Contractor B, and Contractor C. The PI method outcome of Contractor A, PI_A, is 2.95. The PI method outcome, of Contractor B, PI_B, is 2.88. The PI method outcome of Contractor C, PI_C, is 2.66.

The second question of the problem statement queries the identity of the recommended contracting agency. Based on the PI method outcomes, each of the potential capital initiatives demonstrated a PI method outcome that exceeded the value of 1.0. Therefore, each of the capital initiative qualifies for acceptance. However, within the problem statement, the rules of mutual exclusion were specified as a characteristic of the problem domain. Therefore, only one initiative may be recommended for acceptance regardless of the outcomes of the PI method calculations. Because Contractor A demonstrated a PI method outcome of 2.95, it is the preferred agency.

The third question of the problem statement queries whether it feasible and advisable for the city to pursue this proposed course of action. Although the PI method outcome of 2.95, associated with Contractor A, is preferable, this recommendation is incomplete without a stronger analysis of the problem domain. However, based solely on the outcome of the PI method, it is recommended that the city consider this course of action. This solution only considers the outcome of the profitability index method. It does not incorporate any facets of the chronological requirements that may limit the scope of acceptances, does not consider the perspective of cash flow analysis via the net present value method, and does not consider the rate perspective of the internal rate of return. Therefore, it is also recommended that any capital budgeting decision supplement the PI method outcome with other forms of quantitative analysis.

8.5 Accepting Multiple Initiatives

The example of the ABD Criminal Corrections Corporation given in Chapter 5 can again be examined from the perspective of capital budgeting. However, the next examination may be completed through the use of the PI method, and the condition of mutual exclusion may be removed. Therefore, it becomes possible for multiple initiatives to be considered as potential courses of actions. The updated problem statement reflecting the removal of mutual exclusion is given next.

EXAMPLE 8.3: ACCEPTING MULTIPLE PI METHOD OUTCOMES

The following problem statement is adapted from Chapter 5. It demonstrates alterations of the decision domain that allow the acceptance of multiple initiatives during the upcoming fiscal year. In this example, the conditions of mutual exclusion are not applicable. Therefore, the possibility of determining multiple capital initiatives for acceptance recommendations exists.

The ABD Criminal Corrections Corporation, a for-profit entity, is evaluating four potential capital initiatives. Because of funding shortcomings, the organization is unable to pursue all of its possible initiatives. The board of directors indicated that only two initiatives can be pursued during the coming year. Therefore, the organization must select only two projects from among many to pursue as its choice of capital initiatives.

The first project, Initiative A, involves the purchasing and installation of new telephone equipment. This project would update and improve the telephone system of the correctional facility. Through the use of this system, inmates would be charged to make telephone calls (when permitted to do so). The rate associated with this initiative is 4.86%.

The second project, Initiative B, involves the implementation of laundry services for the correctional facility. A private vendor is now used as an outsourced method of providing cleaning services for linens and clothing. However, laundry facilities exist within the correctional infrastructure, and inmates could perform such duties. If this project is selected, then the correctional facility would annually save money via the use of prisoner labor. The rate associated with this initiative is 4.25%.

The third project, Initiative C, involves the potential replacement of food services from a private contractor. The current food service provides prepacked meals that are sufficient for breakfast, dinner, and supper meals in the facility. However, the correctional facility is considering the development and implementation of its own agricultural program, and inmates could grow their own food and prepare their meals. If this option is selected, then cost saving could be manifested through the use of prisoner labor. The rate associated with this initiative is 4.62%.

The fourth project, Initiative D, involves the development and implementation of newspaper services. The corrections facility would serve as an outsourcing agent for the newspapers of the surrounding townships. The correctional facility houses a printing area, and the use of prisoner labor could be leveraged to provide writing and printing services. These services would have a subscription fee and would provide a source of revenue for the corporation. The rate associated with this initiative is 3.99%. The anticipated annual cash flows and the investment costs of each project are given in Table 8.6.

These four initiatives are all acceptable ideas. However, because of security, financial, and control concerns, the board of directors agreed that only two capital initiatives can be considered for the coming fiscal year. Based on the use of the PI method, which projects are recommended for acceptance? Based on these PI outcomes, which projects should be pursued?

Table 8.6 Values for Example 8.3

Period	Initiative A (Telephones)	Initiative B (Laundry)	Initiative C (Food)	Initiative D (Printing)
0	($1000.00)	($13,200.00)	($3000.00)	($12,000.00)
1	$500.00	$1272.00	$800.00	$1700.00
2	$200.00	$2122.00	$950.00	$2400.00
3	$300.00	$2534.00	$1300.00	$3100.00
4	$600.00	$2900.00	$1700.00	$3300.00
5	$700.00	$3400.00	$1900.00	$3700.00
6	$800.00	$3770.00	$2500.00	$4600.00
7	$900.00	$3400.00	$2900.00	$5300.00

Table 8.7 PI Outcomes for Example 8.3

Period	Initiative A (Telephones)	Initiative B (Laundry)	Initiative C (Food)	Initiative D (Printing)
0	($1000.00)	($13,200.00)	($3000.00)	($12,000.00)
1	$500.00	$1272.00	$800.00	$1700.00
2	$200.00	$2122.00	$950.00	$2400.00
3	$300.00	$2534.00	$1300.00	$3100.00
4	$600.00	$2900.00	$1700.00	$3300.00
5	$700.00	$3400.00	$1900.00	$3700.00
6	$800.00	$3770.00	$2500.00	$4600.00
7	$900.00	$3400.00	$2900.00	$5300.00
Rate	4.86%	4.25%	4.62%	3.99%
PI	3.21	1.22	3.24	1.68

Solution Overview of Example 8.3

This problem considers capital budgeting decisions from the perspective of accepting multiple initiatives. Therefore, more than one capital initiative may be recommended for pursuance through time. This example demonstrates the use of the PI method with respect to such conditions.

Example 8.1 provided a demonstration of solving PI method problems manually. Because of the tediousness of solving current monetary situations manually, the PI method outcome values demonstrated in this example are solved using software spreadsheets. The reader may verify the accuracy of these PI method outcome values manually through the use of spreadsheets or a financial calculator. If solved manually, this problem involves the same method of systematically and methodically deriving PI method outcome values for each of the stated contractor entities. After these PI method outcome values are determined, they are used to compare the PI method outcomes for each capital investment initiative. Finally, a recommendation of acceptance or rejection is rendered.

When calculated through the use of a software spreadsheet, the PI method outcome values shown in Table 8.7 are manifested.

Solution for Example 8.3: Capital Budgeting Decision

Now that these PI method outcomes are determined, enough data exists to facilitate the rendering of a human decision regarding potential, strategic courses of actions. Given the content of the problem statement, the condition of mutual exclusion is not applicable. Therefore more than one contractor may be selected as the entity that shall facilitate the rebuilding effort. The ranked PI outcomes may be examined to determine which contractor is the primary choice for the rebuilding efforts. These capital initiatives are ranked according to precedence, from highest value to the lowest value, as follows:

PI_C: 3.24
PI_A: 3.21
PI_D: 1.68
PI_B: 1.22

The two highest PI outcomes were manifested by Initiative A, telephone services, and Initiative C, food services. Respectively, these PI method outcome values are 3.21 and 3.24. The two lowest PI outcomes were manifested by Initiative B, laundry services, and Initiative D, printing services. Respectively, these PI method outcome values are 1.22 and 1.68.

The first question of the problem statement is concerned with the recommendation of potential initiatives. Each of the PI method outcomes of these potential initiatives is greater than the value of 1.0. Therefore, each of these initiatives may be retained for consideration as acceptable capital initiatives. The second question is concerned with which initiatives should be pursued. Based on the requirements governing PI outcome selection and the restrictions of the problem domain, only two initiatives may be recommended for acceptance. With respect to the tenets of the PI method and the characteristics of the problem domain, Initiative A, telephone services, and Initiative C, food services, qualify as acceptable capital investments because, when ranked, their PI outcomes represent the two highest manifested outcomes.

8.6 Advanced PI Considerations

The discussions and examples contained in this text serve as an introduction to the PI method concept. This introduction considers examples that are relatively understandable and require only the implementation of the basic PI method construct for their solution. Regardless of the period of time considered, the basic PI method concept may be applied to any specific, anticipated cash flows to examine their relevancy within the context of capital budgeting decisions.

Other considerations of the PI method involve the existence of multiple instances of PI method outcome values spawned from irregularities within cash flows through time. It is beyond the scope and magnitude of this introductory text to address such issues. However, extended discussions may be found among the writings of contemporary financial management texts.

Some initiatives may require periods that are longer than those that are considered in this text. When these situations occur, it is recommended that PI method calculations be performed through the use of software spreadsheets, proprietary software, or financial calculators.

8.7 Chapter Comments and Summary

This chapter introduced the profitability index (PI) method of capital budgeting. The methods of capital budgeting encompass perspectives of time, cash value, rate, and profitability potential. The PI is indicative of a profitability-based perspective regarding the rendering of capital budgeting decisions. Further, the PI method incorporates the time value of money within its primary construct. However, although it incorporates the time value of money, it ignores the direct considerations of time. Derivation of the PI method may occur through algebraic manipulation of the net present value formula that is given in Chapter 6.

The PI method is common among a variety of domains. Its use allows humans to compare and contrast the profitability characteristics of potential capital initiatives. Within this chapter, examples of the PI method were considered from the profitability contexts of law firm analysis and loan rate effects through time. Such analysis contributes toward the rendering of human decisions regarding the acceptance or rejection of potential capital investments. Through such analysis, humans may facilitate the informed undertaking of capital initiatives.

The application of the PI method may be viewed from multiple perspectives. The first perspective involves a consideration of only one project that is being contemplated. Another perspective involves the concept of mutual exclusion—the selection of one, and only one initiative, from multiple capital initiatives. An additional perspective involves the selection of two (or more) projects from many projects. The example problems of this chapter demonstrate the PI method calculations that are applicable among each of these situations.

Although the outcomes of the PI method present quantitative findings, the outcomes must be interpreted. The rules governing the interpretation of the PI outcome are quite basic:

1. Accept the capital initiative if the value of the calculated *PI* outcome is greater than the value of 1.0.
2. Reject the capital initiative if the value of the calculated *PI* outcome is lower than the value of 1.0.
3. When the conditions of mutual exclusion govern the problem domain, select the capital initiative that demonstrates the highest *PI* outcome.

These rules provide the basis for judging a project as either acceptable or unacceptable with respect to an analysis of cash flows, through time. However, other factors exist that may influence the rendering of a capital budgeting decision. Even though the PI method outcome might be greater than the value of 1.0 and indicate that a project should be accepted, the ultimate decision to accept or reject a project is rendered by humans. Humans must also incorporate the characteristics of the domain environment that influence the decision process. Factors such as time, organizational politics, contribution to organizational value, and the availability of necessary resources also contribute toward the rendering of capital budgeting decisions. Therefore, regardless of any PI method outcome, the decisions to accept and to pursue capital initiatives are subject to a variety of influences.

8.8 Formulas

Profitability Index Concept

$$PI = \left(\frac{\sum_{P=1}^{P} A_P}{V_I} \right)$$

8.9 Terminology

Acceptance
Capital budgeting
Capital budgeting decision
Capital investment
Cash flow
Constraints
Current monetary value
Discount rate
Equivalency
Future monetary value
Initial investment cost
Internal rate of return
Limitations
Monetary equivalency
Monetary value
Profitability index
Rate
Required rate
Rejection

8.10 Thought and Discussion Questions

Based on the examples given in this chapter, the following situation provides a description for consideration:

The hypothetical Country Law Enforcement Training School (CLETS) is a for-profit training organization that supplies a variety of training materials and courses among law enforcement environments and their served communities. Their services include the provision of combatives and weapons safety courses among both urban and rural communities. The CLETS operations were successful during the last few years, and now the firm seeks to grow its operations.

The CLETS organization is considering expanding its operations into three new locations. However, it has a restriction in that it may pursue no more than three investments during the upcoming years. Table 8.8 shows the anticipated costs of investments and the anticipated cash flows that are affiliated with each of the potential capital investment initiatives. Regardless of the initiative(s) selected, the capital investment must recover its investment costs within a period of four years. Further, the rates of each capital investment differ. The following rates are applicable to the considered capital investments:

Table 8.8 CLETS Expansion Options

Period	Initiative A	Initiative B	Initiative C	Initiative D	Initiative E
0	($21,000.00)	($16,200.00)	($3000.00)	($12,000.00)	($12,000.00)
1	$3000.00	$2534.00	$800.00	$1700.00	$2000.00
2	$3700.00	$2900.00	$950.00	$2400.00	$2150.00
3	$3925.00	$3400.00	$1300.00	$3100.00	$2750.00
4	$4125.00	$3770.00	$1700.00	$3300.00	$3000.00
5	$4400.00	$3400.00	$1900.00	$3700.00	$3500.00
6	$4675.00	$3925.00	$2500.00	$4600.00	$4000.00
7	$4825.00	$4750.00	$2900.00	$5300.00	$4700.00
8	$4850.00	$5150.00	$2975.00	$5400.00	$4775.00
9	$4875.00	$5200.00	$2900.00	$5500.00	$4800.00
10	$4900.00	$5300.00	$2955.00	$5600.00	$5000.00

Initiative A: 4.36%
Initiative B: 4.25%
Initiative C: 4.23%
Initiative D: 4.41%
Initiative E: 4.12%

1. Using the PI method, calculate the appropriate PI outcomes for each of the initiatives.
2. Based on Table 8.8 and descriptions, if the concept of mutual exclusion is not applicable, which of the initiatives may be recommended for pursuance during the upcoming year? Use the PI method to determine the appropriate outcome
3. Based on Table 8.8 and descriptions, if mutual exclusion is applicable, which of the above initiatives may be recommended for pursuance during the upcoming year? Use the PI method to determine the appropriate outcome.

Bibliography

Alaska State Legislature. "Action Narrative: Tape 04-32, Side A." January 12, 2004. Accessed August 10, 2010: http://www.legis.state.ak.us/basis/folioproxy.asp?url=http://www.legis.state.ak.us/cgi-bin/folioisa.dll/CM23/query=*/doc/{t11888}/pageitems={body}?.

Chabot, Bernard, P. Kellet, and B. Saulnier. "Defining Advanced Wind Energy Tariffs Systems to Specific Locations and Applications: Lessons from the French Tariff System and Examples." Paper presented at Global Wind Power Conference, April 2002. Accessed August 12, 2010: http://webcache.googleusercontent.com/search?q=cache:IpTnreEV-cwJ:www.wind-works.org/FeedLaws/France/ADEME%2520advanced%2520wind%2520energy%2520tariffs%2520Chabot.doc+%22profitability+index%22+Canadian&cd=21&hl=en&ct=clnk&gl=us.

Jeffreys, Brenda. "Who's Really Making Money?" *Texas Lawyer: Texas Parte Blog.* May 20, 2008. Accessed August 12, 2010: http://texaslawyer.typepad.com/texas_lawyer_blog/2008/05/whos-really-mak.html.

Knight, Robert. "Customer Profitability Analysis—Part I: Alternative Approaches Toward Customer Profitability," *Federal Reserve Bank of Kansas City Monthly Review*, April 1975. Accessed August 12, 2010: http://www.kansascityfed.org/PUBLICAT/ECONREV/EconRevArchive/1975/2q75knig.pdf.

U.S. Department of the Interior, Bureau of Ocean Energy Management, Regulation and Enforcement (BOEMRE). "Profitability of Offshore Petroleum Ventures and Operations: Empirical Evidence from Oil and Gas Lease Sales and Development on the Gulf of Mexico OCS, 1983–1999." June 2007. Accessed August 11, 2010: http://www.gomr.mms.gov/PI/PDFImages/ESPIS/4/4253.pdf.

Putting It All Together! Let's Make a Decision

9

A system of capitalism presumes sound money, not fiat money manipulated by a central bank. Capitalism cherishes voluntary contracts and interest rates that are determined by savings, not credit creation by a central bank.*

Congressman Ron Paul

9.1 Objectives

The objectives of this chapter are to:

- Understand multiple perspectives of financial decisions
- Understand the complementary functions of capital budgeting methods
- Understand the rendering of financial decisions using multiple analytical methods

9.2 Introduction

The methods of capital budgeting encompass perspectives of time, cash value, rate, and profitability potential. Examining projects from these perspectives involves the use of quantitative tools through which projects may be judged and selected as either acceptable or unacceptable. The preceding chapters introduced four capital budgeting methods, the payback time method (PTM), the net present value (NPV) method, the internal rate of return (IRR) method, and the profitability index (PI) method, through which such decisions may be explored. Respectively, these methods involved perspectives of time, cash flow analysis, rate analysis, and profitability analysis.

Each of the preceding chapters, with respect to the topics and concepts of basic capital budgeting methods, involved a limited perspective of the decision domain and a limited consideration of rendering human capital budgeting decisions. Each chapter was devoted to only a solitary method of analysis that involved limited decision perspectives of the payback time method, the net present value method, the internal rate of return method, and the

* Paul, Ron, "Money Quotes," Brainy Quote, http://www.brainyquote.com/quotes/keywords/money_6.html (accessed July 11, 2011).

profitability index method. Although these methods may be used alone to perform a capital budgeting analysis or to facilitate the rendering of a human decision, their solitary, separate implementations provide only a consideration of only a portion of the capital budgeting analysis perspective that are possible. Therefore, this chapter combines and integrates these functions and provides a multifaceted approach to examining problem domains and the rendering of capital budgeting decisions.

Through such integration, a robust perspective of the decision domain is gained among humans who must render capital budgeting decisions. This robustness encapsulates and integrates the perspectives of the payback time method, the net present value method, the internal rate of return method, and the profitability index method. As a result, humans have more than a single perspective of the decision domain to consider when rendering decisions regarding the pursuance of capital initiatives. (See Figure 9.1.)

In the last few chapters, the same problem domains were examined from different perspectives. Each perspective provided only a glimpse of the capital budgeting characteristics of the problem domain. However, this chapter integrates each of the previously defined and examined capital budgeting methods to the same problem domains. Therefore, readers may now see how each of the materials of the preceding chapters complements and supplements the capital budgeting decision process toward the rendering of a human decision regarding the pursuance of capital initiatives.

Because of the tediousness of solving capital budgeting problems manually, the capital budgeting analysis outcome values demonstrated in this chapter are solved using software spreadsheets. The reader may verify the accuracy of these outcomes manually through the use of spreadsheets or a financial calculator. If solved manually, the solutions of the problems of this chapter involve the same methods of systematically and methodically deriving the capital budgeting analysis values for each of the stated problem domain entities that were delineated among the manual solutions of the preceding chapters. After these outcomes are determined, they are used to determine the integrated capital budgeting analysis outcome values for each of the considered capital investment initiatives. Finally, based on this integrated perspective, a recommendation of acceptance or rejection is rendered.

EXAMPLE 9.1: SOLITARY PROJECT

A basic example of the integrated capital budgeting analysis concept may be used to show how data is processed within its mathematical construct. A single capital initiative may be considered. The following capital initiative data may be used to demonstrate the primary concept of the integrated capital budgeting analysis method:

Anticipated initiative period: 4 years
Specified financial rate: 4.7%

Figure 9.1 Military base realignment and closure necessitates a plethora of financial decisions. Jackie Flowers, a budget analyst with U.S. Army Forces Command G8, discusses the Homeowners Assistance Program (HAP) with the Savannah District Office of the U.S. Army Corps of Engineers, September 20, 2010. Flowers, a member of the FORSCOM Torch Party preparing for the October arrival of the command's advance echelon, says that the HAP process is very complex, and she stands ready to assist other members of the headquarters who will, like her, use the program as they move from their homes in the Atlanta, Georgia area to the Fayetteville/Fort Bragg, North Carolina area as directed by the 2005 Base Realignment and Closure legislation. (Courtesy of the U.S. Army, http://www.army.mil/media/150567.)

Initial cost of the initiative: $100,000.00
First year cash flow: $84,000.00
Second year cash flow: $93,000.00
Third year cash flow: $101,000.00
Fourth year cash flow: $110,000.00

Given this data, the following questions may be posed.

Question 1: What are the payback threshold period, the net present value (NPV), the internal rate of return (IRR), and the profitability index (PI) of the situation?

Question 2: Based on the capital budgeting method values calculated in Question 1, should this initiative be accepted?

Solution Overview of Example 9.1

The preceding chapters considered solutions that examined only a limited, solitary approach to the capital investment decision. These limitations involved examining the problem domain from only a single perspective of capital budgeting. These single perspectives involved the payback time method (i.e., time), the net present value (i.e., cash flow analysis), the internal rate of return (i.e., rate analysis), and the profitability index method (i.e., profit potential analysis). These individual methods embellished the rendering of a capital investment decision. However, the integrated outcomes of these decisions may be considered cumulatively to further embellish the rendering of a capital budgeting decision. Therefore, the approach demonstrated in this chapter involves the integration of time analysis, cash flow analysis, rate analysis, and profitability analysis to yield a recommendation regarding the considered capital investment.

The examples of the preceding chapters provided a demonstration of solving this problem manually. Because of the tediousness and impracticality of solving this problem again manually, the PTM value, NPV outcome value, IRR outcome value, and PI method value demonstrated in this example are solved using software spreadsheets. The reader may verify the accuracy of these outcomes manually, through the use of spreadsheets, or through the use of a financial calculator. If solved manually, this problem involves the same method of systematically and methodically deriving capital budgeting analysis outcome values that were presented within the preceding chapters.

Based on the spreadsheet calculations, the following outcomes are derived from the separate events of capital budgeting analysis:

Payback time method: 1.17 years
Net present value method: $244,605.75
Internal rate of return method: 83.00%
Profitability index method: 3.45

These outcomes are demonstrative of an integrated perspective of the characteristics of the problem domain. Within the domain of the considered capital investment, a period of 1.17 years is required for payback to occur through time. From the perspective of cash flows, the potential financial benefits of the capital initiative, in the terms of the equivalent, current monetary value, would be worth $244,605.75. The calculated rate is 83.00%. Further, the outcome of the potential profitability analysis is 3.45. These calculated values provide sufficient outcomes to facilitate the rendering of a capital budgeting decision.

Solution for Example 9.1: Capital Budgeting Decision

The integrated outcomes provide a sufficient array of information to facilitate the rendering of a human decision regarding this potential capital investment. The salient requirements were given within the statement of the problem:

Initiative repayment period: 4 years
Specified financial rate: 4.7%

Based on the outcome of the payback time method of analysis, a period of 1.17 years is required for payback to occur through time. This payback period of 1.17 years is less than the stated requirement of a period of four years. Therefore, the outcome of the payback time method is sufficient to recommend that the potential capital initiative be considered for acceptance.

From the perspective of cash flows, the outcome of the net present value analysis is \$244,605.75. The initial cost of the investment is \$100,000.00. The calculated NPV outcome is a positive value (i.e., greater than a value of zero) is determined to be \$244,605.75 and surpasses the initial cost value of \$100,000.00. Therefore, the outcome of the NPV method is sufficient to recommend that the potential capital initiative be considered for acceptance.

The calculated outcome of the rate analysis is 83.00%. In the statement of the problem, the stated financial rate is 4.7%. The calculated IRR outcome value of 83% significantly exceeds the required rate value of 4.7%. Therefore, the outcome of the IRR method is sufficient to recommend that the potential capital initiative be considered for acceptance.

Finally, the outcome of the potential profitability analysis is 3.45. According to the acceptance rules of the profitability index method of analysis, any outcomes that are greater than the value of 1.0 should be recommended for acceptance. Therefore, the outcome of the PI method is sufficient to recommend that the potential capital initiative be considered for acceptance.

Individually, the outcomes of the payback time method, the NPV analysis, the IRR analysis, and the PI method analysis each suggest that the considered capital initiative may be recommended for acceptance. When integrated, these considerations combine to provide a robust perspective of the problem domain. Cumulatively, when considering the integration of these separate analysis outcomes, the considered capital initiative may be recommended for acceptance.

EXAMPLE 9.2: PI AND MUTUAL EXCLUSION

The following example again examines the cash flows of the hypothetical example introduced in Chapter 5. The problem domain of this example is representative of the mutual exclusion condition. The problem statement is given as follows:

Last year, a tornado destroyed the police training facility of an urban area. The damages were sufficient enough to warrant the total loss of the building and its supporting infrastructure. After the devastating event occurred, the city council approved a measure to erect a new police training facility. The destroyed facility served as a training institute for regional first responders, among the four bordering states, whose functions included the provision of emergency services during both natural and man-made disasters. Therefore, it is imperative that this facility be restored.

The training tuition dollars of local personnel were provided by the devastated city. However, any nonlocal personnel were responsible for providing their own tuitions (e.g., self-pay, sponsor pay, grants, etc.). Because it was a regional training facility, the majority of the trainees were not local personnel. Therefore, this training facility provided a source of revenue for the city and its police department.

A combination of monies—to be obtained via taxation, city bond investments, a limited insurance policy, loans, and goodwill and charitable donations—is proposed to fund the initial costs of the capital investment. Through time, additional debt payments are to be made from the revenue stream of the restored facility.

Three contractors submitted bids for the rebuilding project. The bids of the contractors were \$291,000.00, \$293,000.00, and \$295,000.00. The rates associated with these values, respectively, are 4.30%, 4.57%, and 5.00%. Regardless of which contractor is selected, the pursued course of rebuilding must return an amount of at least \$500,000.00.

Table 9.1 Cash Flows of Example 9.2

Period	Contractor A	Contractor B	Contractor C
0	($291,000.00)	($293,000.00)	($295,000.00)
1	$109,527.00	$110,527.00	$108,000.00
2	$129,034.00	$125,034.00	$127,000.00
3	$135,068.00	$133,368.00	$129,068.00
4	$148,927.00	$148,927.00	$135,000.00
5	$159,000.00	$159,000.00	$147,000.00
6	$168,000.00	$168,000.00	$155,000.00
7	$174,980.00	$174,980.00	$159,980.00

Because of other obligations, these contractors are unable specify identical dates to begin the construction of the new facility. Therefore, these time differences may offset the estimated cash flows of the facility. Further, because of existing debt obligations, the city must begin paying its debt within the next two years. However, the selected initiative must generate sufficient cash flows to reimburse its investment costs within three years and must demonstrate the potential of being profitable through time.

Based on the listing of anticipated cash flow values in Table 9.1, what are the PTM, NPV, IRR, and PI outcomes of each of the proposals? Based on these outcomes, which contractor is the recommended entity? Based on the characteristics of the recommended course of action (if any), is it feasible and advisable for the city to pursue this proposed course of action?

Solution Overview of Example 9.2

This problem considers capital budgeting analysis decisions from the perspective of mutual exclusion. Within the context of mutual exclusion, one, and only one, capital initiative may be recommended for pursuance through time. Although multiple, analytical method outcomes may qualify the capital initiatives as acceptable, only one initiative is to be recommended for acceptance and pursuance through time. This example demonstrates the use of the integration of the separate capital budgeting outcomes with respect to this constraint of mutual exclusion.

The preceding chapters provided a demonstration of solving capital budgeting problems manually. Because of the tediousness of solving this problem manually, the capital budgeting analysis outcome values demonstrated in this example are solved using software spreadsheets. The reader may verify the accuracy of these outcomes manually through the use of spreadsheets or through the use of a financial calculator. If solved manually, this problem involves the same method of systematically and methodically deriving the capital budgeting analysis values for each of the stated contractor entities. After these outcomes are determined, they are used to determine the integrated capital budgeting analysis outcome values for each capital investment initiative. Finally, based on this integrated perspective, a recommendation of acceptance or rejection is rendered.

When calculated through the use of a software spreadsheet, the following capital budgeting analysis method outcome values may be determined. With respect to the potential capital initiative of Contractor A, the following values are determined:

Payback time method (PTM): 2.38
Net present value (NPV): $567,144.02
Internal rate of return (IRR): 41.51%
Profitability index (PI): 2.95

With respect to the potential capital initiative of Contractor B, the following values are determined:

Payback time method (PTM): 2.43
Net present value (NPV): $551,857.98
Internal rate of return (IRR): 40.88%
Profitability index (PI): 2.88

With respect to the potential capital initiative of Contractor C, the following values are determined:

Payback time method (PTM): 2.46
Net present value (NPV): $490,145.04
Internal Rate of Return (IRR): 38.75%
Profitability Index (PI): 2.66

For each of the potential capital initiatives, these outcomes are demonstrative of an integrated perspective of the characteristics of the problem domain. Therefore, an integrated perspective of each of the individual capital investments may be derived from these calculated capital budgeting analysis outcomes.

Solution for Example 9.2: Capital Budgeting Decision

These calculated outcomes may be compared to the data given in the problem statement to determine whether a recommendation of acceptance may be given to any of the considered courses of actions. Such a comparison provides the basis of benchmarking these calculated outcomes, with the limitations and requirements provided in the statement of the problem, regarding the attributes that define the qualities of capital initiatives that are deemed as acceptable. However, unlike the solitary considerations of evaluation that were presented and discussed in the preceding chapters, the integrated capital budgeting decision must incorporate each of the perspectives of time, cash flow analysis, rate, and profitability toward the rendering of a human decision regarding the potential investment initiatives.

The first question of the problem statement necessitated the calculation of mathematical value outcomes for the variables associated with an integrated capital budgeting function.

For the payback time method outcomes, the synopsis of the calculated outcomes is given as follows:

Contractor A: 2.38 years
Contractor B: 2.43 years
Contractor C: 2.46 years

For the NPV outcomes, the synopsis of the calculated outcomes is given as follows:

Contractor A: $567,144.02
Contractor B: $551,857.98
Contractor C: $490,145.04

For the IRR outcomes, the synopsis of the calculated outcomes is given as follows:

Contractor A: 41.51%
Contractor B: 40.88%
Contractor C: 38.75%

For the PI method outcomes, the synopsis of the calculated outcomes is given as follows:

Contractor A: 2.95
Contractor B: 2.88
Contractor C: 2.66

The integrated capital budgeting decision first involves the qualification of potential capital initiatives as being classified as either acceptable or unacceptable. This task may be accomplished through examining the PTM, NPV, IRR, and PI method outcomes with the requirements given within the statement of the problem. Given the integrated nature of the capital budgeting decision, any calculated outcome that is deemed unacceptable shall disqualify the project from any further evaluation regarding its acceptance potential.

According to the problem statement, the debt repayments must begin within two years. However, the selected capital initiative must generate sufficient cash flows to compensate for its investment costs within three years. With respect to the integrated capital budgeting decision, the former consideration is immaterial, whereas the latter consideration is pertinent. The latter consideration of time regarding cash flows that are sufficient to compensate for the costs of investment within the three-year period is required of the selected initiative. A consideration of the PTM outcomes indicates that all three of the potential capital investments satisfy this requirement. Therefore, based solely on the chronological perspective, all three initiatives are deemed as acceptable.

According to the problem statement, the amount of at least $500,000.00 must be returned from the selected capital initiative. A consideration of the NPV outcomes indicates that the capital initiatives of both Contractor A and Contractor B satisfy this requirement. However, the capital initiative of Contractor C does not satisfy this requirement. The NPV outcomes of Contractor A and Contractor B, respectively, are $567,144.02 and $551,857.98. Both of these outcomes surpass the stated minimum requirement of $500,000.00 and are categorized as acceptable. The NPV outcome of Contractor C is $490,145.04, and it does not surpass the mandated, minimum value of $500,000.00. Therefore, the initiative of Contractor C may be immediately disqualified and discarded from any further evaluation. Hence, only the initiatives of Contractor A and Contractor B remain for further evaluation.

According to the problem statement, the rates affiliated with Contractor A, Contractor B, and Contractor C, respectively, are 4.30%, 4.57%, and 5.00%.

Any selected initiative must surpass these specified rates. The preceding NPV evaluation disqualified Contractor C from further competition. Therefore, only the rates of Contractor A and Contractor B are considered in the IRR evaluation. The calculated IRR value of Contractor A, 41.51%, surpasses the stated minimum rate of 4.30%. The calculated IRR value of Contractor B, 40.88%, also surpasses the stated minimum rate of 4.57%. Therefore, the initiatives of both Contractor A and Contractor B are retained for additional analysis.

The final evaluation involves a consideration of profitability. According to the problem statement, the selected initiative must demonstrate some potential of being profitable through time. Based on the outcomes of the PI method calculations, the initiatives of both Contractor A and Contractor B satisfy this requirement of potential profitability. Respectively, the PI outcomes of Contractor A and Contractor B are 2.95 and 2.88. With respect to the profitability index method rules governing the qualification of capital initiatives, because both values surpass the value of 1.0, both initiatives manifest some potential of profitability. Therefore, both the initiatives of Contractor A and Contractor B are retained for further evaluation.

The qualification of the considered capital initiatives is completed. Two potential initiatives remain as candidates for further evaluation: Contractor A and Contractor B. Although both initiatives show promise as courses of actions, the stipulation regarding mutual exclusion, given in the statement of the problem, disallows the accepting of both initiatives. Therefore, only one initiative may be accepted regarding the rebuilding efforts. Hence, a comparison must be made between the characteristics of these projects with respect to the requirements given in the statement of the problem. Table 9.2 shows the individual characteristics of the capital budgeting analysis outcomes and the stated requirements of the problem statement.

The selection rules of each of the separate capital budgeting methods must be considered from the overall perspective of the integrated decision. Both separately and cumulatively, these selection rules necessitate the selection of the initiative that demonstrates the greatest potential value for the organization. This consideration must be observed when evaluating the remaining initiatives of Contractor A versus Contractor B.

The second question of the statement of the problem with respect to the established condition of mutual exclusion queries the identification of the preferred initiative. Within the preceding table, the capital budgeting analysis outcomes are presented for both Contractor A and Contractor B. An evaluation of the PTM values indicates that the initiative of Contractor A may be completed in less time than the initiative of Contractor B. An evaluation of the NPV outcomes indicates that the initiative of Contractor A provides a greater cash flow value than the initiative of Contractor B. An evaluation of the IRR outcomes indicates that the initiative of Contractor A provides a higher rate of

Table 9.2 Integrated Mutual Exclusion Selection

Method	Contractor A	Contractor B	Stated Minimum
PTM	2.38 years	2.43 years	3.00 years
NPV	$567,144.02	$551,857.98	$500,000.00
IRR	41.51%	40.88%	4.57%
PI	2.95	2.88	1.0

return than the initiative of Contractor B. An evaluation of the PI outcomes indicates that the initiative of Contractor A demonstrates a greater potential of profitability than the initiative of Contractor B. Therefore, given the integration of these observations, it is observed that the initiative of Contractor A is superior to the initiative of Contractor B. Hence, it is recommended that the initiative of Contractor A be qualified as the acceptable choice regarding the rebuilding efforts.

The third question of the problem statement queries whether it is both feasible and advisable to pursue the course of action that is commensurate with the selected capital budgeting initiative. The need to rebuild is obvious given the necessity of providing training functions among law enforcement entities. Therefore, a capital initiative must be pursued to restore the training regimens that were eradicated because of the natural disaster. Hence, from this perspective, the pursuit of the initiative of Contractor A may be advocated. Further, from the perspective of the mathematical outcomes, the initiative of Contractor A satisfies the established requirements, mathematically, for pursuing the anticipated rebuilding effort. Therefore, quantitatively, it is feasible to pursue the initiative of Contractor A. Hence, given these observations, it is feasible to pursue the course of action that is associated with the capital initiative proposed by Contractor A.

The third question also queries the advisability of pursuing the course of action that is commensurate with the initiative of Contractor A. Providing a definitive response to this question is difficult given the myriad of influence that may impact the actual pursuit of the capital initiative. Organizational politics and government policies may impact the rebuilding effort. The availability of resources, such as labor and building materials, may also affect the rebuilding effort. Such considerations are not uncommon and must not be dismissed as immaterial concerns. Therefore, such considerations must be incorporated within the decision to pursue rebuilding efforts. However, given the lack of information regarding these issues within the statement of the problem, based solely on the stated requirements and calculated capital budgeting outcomes, it is advisable to pursue the rebuilding initiative.

9.3 Accepting Multiple Initiatives

The usefulness of the integrated capital budgeting decision process is also applicable regarding the acceptance of multiple capital initiatives. The example of the ABD Criminal Corrections Corporation given in Chapter 5 may again be examined from the perspective of capital budgeting. However, the next examination may be completed through the use of the integration of the capital budgeting methods, and the condition of mutual exclusion may be removed. Therefore, it becomes possible for multiple initiatives to be considered as potential courses of actions within the context of the integrated capital budgeting decision. The updated problem statement reflecting the removal of mutual exclusion is given next.

EXAMPLE 9.3: ACCEPTING MULTIPLE OUTCOMES

The following problem statement is adapted from Chapter 5. It demonstrates alterations of the decision domain that allow the acceptance of multiple initiatives during the upcoming fiscal year. In this example, the conditions of mutual exclusion are not applicable.

The ABD Criminal Corrections Corporation, a for-profit entity, is evaluating four potential capital initiatives. Because of funding shortcomings, the organization is unable to pursue all of its possible initiatives. The board of directors indicated that only two initiatives may be pursued during the coming year. Therefore, the organization must select only two projects from among many to pursue as its choice of capital initiatives. Any selected project must return its investment cost within a period of four years. Also, any selected initiative must demonstrate some potential of generating financial benefit for the organization through time.

The first project, Initiative A, involves the purchasing and installation of new telephone equipment. This project would update and improve the telephone system of the correctional facility. Through the use of this system, inmates would be charged to make telephone calls (when permitted to do so). The rate associated with this initiative is 4.86%.

The second project, Initiative B, involves the implementation of laundry services for the correctional facility. A private vendor is now used as an outsourced method of providing cleaning services for linens and clothing. However, laundry facilities exist within the correctional infrastructure, and inmates could perform such duties. If this project is selected, then the correctional facility would annually save money via the use of prisoner labor. The rate associated with this initiative is 4.25%.

The third project, Initiative C, involves the potential replacement of food services from a private contractor. The current food service provides prepacked meals that are sufficient for breakfast, dinner, and supper meals within the facility. However, the correctional facility is considering the development and implementation of its own agricultural program, and inmates could grow their own food and prepare their meals. If this option is selected, then cost saving could be manifested through the use of prisoner labor. The rate associated with this initiative is 4.62%.

The fourth project, Initiative D, involves the development and implementation of newspaper services. The corrections facility would serve as an outsourcing agent for the newspapers of the surrounding townships. The correctional facility houses a printing area, and the use of prisoner labor could be leveraged to provide writing and printing services. These services would have a subscription fee and would provide a source of revenue for the corporation. The rate associated with this initiative is 3.99%.

The anticipated annual cash flows and the investment costs of each project are given in Table 9.3.

These four initiatives are all acceptable ideas. However, because of security, financial, and control concerns, the board of directors agreed that only two capital initiatives may be considered for the coming fiscal year. Based on the use of the payback time method, the NPV method, the IRR method, and the PI method, which projects are recommended for acceptance? Based on these capital budgeting analysis outcomes, which projects should be pursued?

Table 9.3 Values for Example 9.3

Period	Initiative A (Telephones)	Initiative B (Laundry)	Initiative C (Food)	Initiative D (Printing)
0	($1000.00)	($13,200.00)	($3000.00)	($12,000.00)
1	$500.00	$1272.00	$800.00	$1700.00
2	$200.00	$2122.00	$950.00	$2400.00
3	$300.00	$2534.00	$1300.00	$3100.00
4	$600.00	$2900.00	$1700.00	$3300.00
5	$700.00	$3400.00	$1900.00	$3700.00
6	$800.00	$3770.00	$2500.00	$4600.00
7	$900.00	$3400.00	$2900.00	$5300.00

Solution Overview of Example 9.3

Within the context of integrated capital budgeting methods, this problem considers capital budgeting decisions from the perspective of accepting multiple initiatives. Therefore, more than one capital initiative may be recommended for pursuance through time. This example demonstrates the use of the capital budgeting methods with respect to such conditions.

The preceding chapters provided a demonstration of solving capital budgeting problems manually. Because of the tediousness of solving this problem manually, the capital budgeting analysis outcome values demonstrated in this example are solved using software spreadsheets. The outcomes of the capital budgeting analysis functions are commensurate with the equivalent function values of the preceding chapters. The reader may verify the accuracy of these outcomes manually through the use of spreadsheets or a financial calculator. If solved manually, this problem involves the same method of systematically and methodically deriving the capital budgeting analysis values for each of the stated contractor entities. After these outcomes are determined, they are used to determine the integrated capital budgeting analysis outcome values for each capital investment initiative. Finally, based on this integrated perspective, a recommendation of acceptance or rejection is rendered.

Solution for Example 9.3: Capital Budgeting Decision

The first question of the statement of the problem queried the values of the capital budgeting analysis outcomes. The use of electronic spreadsheets may be used to calculate the values of the capital budgeting functions regarding time, cash flow analysis, rate analysis, and profitability index. Table 9.4 provides a synopsis of these outcomes.

Table 9.4 Comparison of Integrated Outcomes (Multiple)

Method	Initiative A	Initiative B	Initiative C	Initiative D
PTM	3.00	5.30	2.96	4.40
NPV	$2214.70	$2903.18	$6723.37	$8143.17
IRR	41.99%	9.16%	39.11%	17.36%
PIM	3.21	1.22	3.24	1.68

The condition of mutual exclusion is removed concerning the problem domain. Therefore, based on the outcomes of the capital budgeting analysis functions, more than one capital initiative may be recommended for acceptance (if necessary). The qualification(s) of these capital initiatives may occur through the integrated consideration of the outcomes of the capital budgeting functions.

An examination of the PTM category may qualify for acceptance the outcomes of the time perspective of capital budgeting. According to the problem statement, any initiative must return its cost of investment within a period of four years. Respectively, the PTM outcome values of Initiative A, Initiative B, Initiative C, and Initiative D are 3.00, 5.30, 2.96, and 4.40. Only two of these capital budgeting PTM analysis outcomes satisfy the requirement of the four-year limitation regarding the compensation of investment costs: Initiative A and Initiative C. The PTM analysis outcome value of Initiative A is 3.00, and the PTM analysis outcome value of Initiative C is 2.96. Therefore, both Initiative B and Initiative D are recommended for rejection, whereas both Initiative A and Initiative C are recommended for acceptance.

A consideration of the NPV analysis outcomes may further examine the qualification potential of the remaining initiatives. The NPV analysis outcome of Initiative A is $2214.70 and the NPV analysis outcome of Initiative C is $6723.37. With respect to the NPV selection rules, both of these outcomes are greater than the value of zero. Therefore, from the NPV perspective, both initiatives qualify for acceptance. However, these outcomes must also be considered from the perspective of the problem statement. According to the statement of the problem, any selected initiative must demonstrate some potential of generating financial benefit for the organization through time. Because the NPV analysis outcomes of both considered initiatives are greater than the value of zero, they demonstrate the potential of manifesting financial value through time. Therefore, with respect to the requirement of the statement of the problem, both Initiative A and Initiative C qualify for acceptance.

A consideration of the IRR analysis outcomes may further examine the qualification potential of the remaining initiatives. The IRR analysis outcome of Initiative A is 41.99%, whereas the IRR analysis outcome of Initiative C is 39.11%. With respect to the IRR selection rules, these outcomes must be compared with their respective rates of investment. According to the statement of the problem, the investment rate of Initiative A is 4.86%, and the investment rate of Initiative C is 4.62%. With respect to Initiative A, the IRR analysis outcome value of 41.99% surpasses the required rate value of 4.86%. With respect to Initiative C, the IRR analysis outcome value of 39.11% surpasses the required rate value of 4.62%. Because both of these IRR analysis outcome values exceed the required rates given in the statement of the problem, both Initiative A and Initiative C qualify for acceptance.

A consideration of the PIM analysis outcomes may further examine the qualification potential of the remaining initiatives. The PIM analysis outcome of Initiative A is 3.21. The PIM analysis outcome of Initiative C is 3.24. According to the selection rules of the PIM concept, initiatives whose PIM outcomes are greater than the value of 1.0 may be recommended for acceptance. Because both of the PIM analysis outcomes of Initiative A and Initiative C exceed the value of 1.0, both Initiative A and Initiative C may be recommended for acceptance.

Separately, the use of the individual capital budgeting functions disqualified two potential initiatives: Initiative B and Initiative D. However, the use of these functions also generated the recommendation of acceptance for Initiative A and Initiative C. The remaining initiatives may be considered from the perspective of the integrated capital budgeting decision. According to the problem statement, any initiative must have the capacity to recover the costs of investment within four years and must demonstrate some potential of profitability. Based on the combined considerations of the PTM analysis outcomes, the NPV analysis outcomes, the IRR analysis outcomes, and the PIM analysis outcomes, both Initiative A and Initiative C may be recommended for acceptance.

The statement of the problem does not involve mutual exclusion. Therefore, multiple initiatives may be recommended for acceptance. The statement of the problem also indicates that no more than two initiatives may be pursued. Because Initiative B and Initiative D were eliminated, only two candidate initiatives remained for consideration: Initiative A and Initiative C. Both Initiative A and Initiative C also satisfied the requirements of the capital budgeting functions and the requirements of acceptance delineated within the statement of the problem. Therefore, Initiative A and Initiative C are both recommended for acceptance and pursuance.

9.4 Advanced Capital Budgeting Considerations

The discussions and examples contained in this text serve as an introduction to the capital budgeting methods concept. This introduction considers examples that are relatively understandable and that require only the implementation of the basic capital budgeting methods and constructs for their solution. Regardless of the period of time considered, the basic capital budgeting methods and concepts may be applied to any specific, anticipated cash flows to examine their relevancy within the context of capital budgeting decisions.

Other considerations of the capital budgeting methods involve the existence of multiple instances of capital budgeting methods outcome values spawned from irregularities within cash flows through time. It is beyond the scope and magnitude of this introductory text to address such issues. However, extended discussions may be found among the writings of contemporary financial management texts.

Some initiatives may require periods that are longer than those that are considered in this text. When these situations occur, it is recommended that capital budgeting analysis calculations be performed through the use of software spreadsheets, proprietary software, or financial calculators.

9.5 Chapter Comments and Summary

The preceding chapters involved discussions of the separate functions of capital budgeting analysis. These functions examined capital investment decisions from the perspectives of time, cash flow, rate, and profitability potential. Respectively, these perspectives are representative of PTM analysis, NPV analysis, IRR analysis, and PIM analysis. However, these individual examinations provided only a limited perspective of the considered problem domains. Although the use of the individual perspectives contributed toward the rendering of a capital budgeting decision, this decision was rendered with only a subdued understanding of the problem domain. In some instances, the effects of the time value of money were not applicable regarding the capital investment decision.

However, the use of the integrated perspective regarding multiple facets of the problem domain provides a robust approach to the rendering of capital investment decisions. The use of the integrated method incorporates the concurrent attributes of time, cash flow, rate, and profitability, which describe the decision domain, to facilitate the rendering of a capital investment decision. This integrated form of decision analysis provides a stronger decision outcome than would be derived from the use of a solitary method of capital budgeting analysis. In the integrated method, the uses of analytical methods that observe the effects of the time value of money are complemented through the use of analytical methods that ignore the effects of the time value of money.

The use of this combined approach embellishes the analytical potential of humans who render financial management decisions. Through the use of the full range of capital budgeting concepts, humans gain the ability to recognize and acknowledge multiple facets of the decision domain, identify potential courses of strategic actions, select the desired capital initiatives, and pursue appropriately the necessary courses of action(s). Therefore, the use of the full range of capital budgeting methods provides a strategic benefit for the organization through time.

Within the context of law enforcement and criminal justice entities, the use of capital budgeting has strategic implications through time. Capital budgeting analysis provides the tools through which analytical evaluations occur to rendering decisions regarding the investment uses of limited monetary funds. As an example, through the use of capital budgeting analysis, organizational leaders may choose between erecting new jail facilities or purchasing a set of vehicles. Further, the use of capital budgeting techniques assists in maintaining the sanctity of the fiduciary obligation of rendering decisions that are in the best interests of the organization, any shareholders, any stakeholders, and society. Therefore, the soundness of the principal–agency relationship may be maintained through time, and appropriate decisions may be offered regarding the pursuit of capital initiatives.

9.6 Formulas

Profitability Index Concept

$$PI = \left(\frac{\sum_{P=1}^{P} A_P}{V_I} \right)$$

Net Present Value Concept

$$NPV = \left(\sum_{P=1}^{P} \frac{A_P}{\left(R_{per} + 1.0\right)^P} \right) - V_I$$

Internal Rate of Return Concept

$$NPV = 0.00 = \left(\sum_{P=1}^{P} \frac{A_P}{(IRR + 1.0)^P} \right)$$

9.7 Terminology

Acceptance
Capital budgeting
Capital budgeting decision
Capital investment
Cash flow
Constraints
Current monetary value
Discount rate
Equivalency
Future monetary value
Initial investment cost
Integrated method
Internal rate of return
Limitations
Monetary equivalency
Monetary value
Profitability index
Rate
Required rate
Rejection

9.8 Thought and Discussion Questions

Based on the examples given in this chapter, the following situation provides a description for consideration:

The hypothetical Country Law Enforcement Training School (CLETS) is a for-profit training organization that supplies a variety of training materials and courses among law enforcement environments and their served communities.

Table 9.5 CLETS Expansion Options

Period	Initiative A	Initiative B	Initiative C	Initiative D	Initiative E
0	($21,000.00)	($16,200.00)	($3000.00)	($12,000.00)	($12,000.00)
1	$3000.00	$2534.00	$800.00	$1700.00	$2000.00
2	$3700.00	$2900.00	$950.00	$2400.00	$2150.00
3	$3925.00	$3400.00	$1300.00	$3100.00	$2750.00
4	$4125.00	$3770.00	$1700.00	$3300.00	$3000.00
5	$4400.00	$3400.00	$1900.00	$3700.00	$3500.00
6	$4675.00	$3925.00	$2500.00	$4600.00	$4000.00
7	$4825.00	$4750.00	$2900.00	$5300.00	$4700.00
8	$4850.00	$5150.00	$2975.00	$5400.00	$4775.00
9	$4875.00	$5200.00	$2900.00	$5500.00	$4800.00
10	$4900.00	$5300.00	$2955.00	$5600.00	$5000.00

Their services include the provision of combatives and weapons safety courses among both urban and rural communities. The CLETS operations were successful during the last few years, and now the firm seeks to grow its operations.

The CLETS organization is considering expanding its operations into three new locations. However, it has a restriction in that it may pursue no more than three investments during the upcoming years. Table 9.5 shows the anticipated costs of investments and the anticipated cash flows that are affiliated with each of the potential capital investment initiatives. Regardless of the initiative(s) selected, the capital investment must recover its investment costs within a period of four years. Further, the rates of each capital investment differ. The following rates are applicable to the considered capital investments:

Initiative A: 4.36%
Initiative B: 4.25%
Initiative C: 4.23%
Initiative D: 4.41%
Initiative E: 4.12%

1. Using the integrated capital budgeting analysis methods of PTM, NPV, IRR, and PIM, calculate the appropriate analysis outcomes for each of the initiatives.
2. Based on Table 9.5 and descriptions, if the concept of mutual exclusion is not applicable, which of the initiatives may be recommended for pursuance during the upcoming year? Use the integrated capital budgeting methods to determine the appropriate outcome.
3. Based on Table 9.5 and descriptions, if mutual exclusion is applicable, which of the initiatives may be recommended for pursuance during the upcoming year? Use the integrated capital budgeting methods to determine the appropriate outcome.

Day and Night Shifts
Integrating the Concepts 10

When the federal government spends more each year than it collects in tax revenues, it has three choices: It can raise taxes, print money, or borrow money. While these actions may benefit politicians, all three options are bad for average Americans.*

Congressman Ron Paul

10.1 Objectives

The objectives of this chapter are to:

- Understand the significance of capital budgeting techniques
- Introduce advanced forms of rendering financial decisions
- Understand making financial decisions using integrated techniques

10.2 Introduction

The basic methods of capital budgeting encompass the perspectives of time, cash value, rate, and profitability potential. Examining projects from these perspectives involves the use of quantitative tools through which projects may be judged and selected as either acceptable or unacceptable. The preceding chapters introduced four capital budgeting methods, the payback time method (PTM), the net present value (NPV) method, the internal rate of return (IRR) method, and the profitability index (PI) method, through which such decisions may be explored. Respectively, these methods involved perspectives of time, cash flow analysis, rate analysis, and profitability analysis.

These perspectives and their associated capital budgeting tools assist humans in identifying the salient characteristics of the problem domain. They also provide the basis of approaching capital investment problems from a methodical, systematic approach to facilitating the rendering of strategic decisions quantitatively. In order to have a robust knowledge and sound understanding of the problem domain, organizational leaders must use these perspectives and tools concurrently. Although each capital

* Paul, Ron, "Ron Paul Quotes," Brainy Quote, http://www.brainyquote.com/quotes/quotes/r/ronpaul401775.html (accessed on July 11, 2011).

budgeting method when used alone may contribute toward the rendering of a human decision, it is through the combination of all of these methods that a strong decision may be rendered. Within the context of the decision domain, the integration of these capital budgeting methods facilitates the incorporation of perspectives that both ignore and include the principles of the time value of money.

The use of the capital budgeting paradigm provides additional benefit among organizations. Through the use of the capital budgeting paradigm, organizational leaders gain the ability to efficiently and effectively render decisions via quantitative analysis. Because of the quantitative attributes of the capital budgeting analysis, the justifications of decisions and the pursuance of courses of actions are easier to rationalize, explain, and defend. Further, through the use of capital budgeting, organizational leaders are better able to fulfill their roles and responsibilities within the context of the principal–agency relationship. Capital budgeting provides the means through which the highest and best investments may be identified among an array of possible capital investment endeavors. Strategically, the use of capital budgeting allows organizational leaders to delineate and express the potential, long-term commitments of time, resources, and monies that contribute toward the pursuit of mission and the achieving of vision.

The initial chapters of this text indicated that cash flow is the lifeblood of any organization and stressed the necessity of properly implementing sound financial management practices among organizational settings. The use of capital budgeting functions contributes toward the activities, goals, and objectives of sound financial management. Although capital budgeting provides a method of examining the potential benefits and value capacities of possible investment initiatives, capital budgeting techniques are not the sole methods through which financial management functions may be embellished. (See Figure 10.1)

Capital budgeting provides a perspective of the time required to pay back the investment costs of a potential capital initiative, but it does not consider the threshold period when the mathematical basis of break-even profitability occurs. Capital budgeting provides a perspective of current monetary values versus future monetary values, but it does not necessarily consider any form of what-if variations that may impact cash flows and investment rates. Capital budgeting may reveal which capital investment initiatives may provide the greatest financial value, through time, for an organization, but it does not determine whether capital assets must be leased or purchased. Capital budgeting innately incorporates rate risk within its rate computations but does not directly consider the fluctuations among rates that may yield a myriad of classifications of risk outcomes. Given these notions, it is determined that capital budgeting provides a sound method of facilitating human decisions with respect to a single instantiation of domain variables

Figure 10.1 Financial decisions have long-term and short-term effects. CPT Philip Kaberline, the commander of Delta Detachment, 106th Finance Management Company, and SFC Class Charles Moten, the noncommissioned officer in charge of the detachment, case the unit's guidon in preparation for the unit's deployment to Kuwait in support of Operation New Dawn. The unit will be deployed for one year. (Photo by SGT Fay Conroy, 21st TSC Public Affairs. Courtesy of the U.S. Army, http://www.army.mil/media/151790.)

but does not directly accommodate multiple variations of variable values that may affect a single instantiation of the problem domain through time. Therefore, capital budgeting paradigms, though powerful quantitative tools, are limited with respect to other factors that impact the analysis of financial decisions through time.

The use of the capital budgeting paradigm provides financial managers with a robust array of quantitative tools that allows humans the ability to render investment decisions. However, variations of potential outcomes regarding such potential investment decisions must be considered through the use of additional, quantitative techniques. These techniques are advanced forms of financial analysis, and they also contribute toward the strengthening of human financial management decisions strategically.

Among these advanced tools are concepts of benefit–cost examinations, leasing versus purchasing considerations, different aspects of scenario analysis, examinations of the dynamics of change that involve sensitivity analysis, and examinations of chronological attributes of profitability regarding break-even analysis. Each of these concepts provides an additional measure of quantitative evaluation through which capital investment decisions may be examined, facilitated, and rendered to provide strategic benefits among organizational settings.

10.3 Benefit–Cost Ratio Concepts

According to the federal Office of Management and Budget (OMB), the benefit–cost (B/C) concept is defined as the "systematic, quantitative method of assessing the desirability of government projects or policies when it is important to take a long view of future effects and a broad view of possible side-effects." This assessment is expressed through the mathematical derivation of the B/C ratio. Further, according to the OMB, the B/C method is "recommended as the technique to use in a formal economic analysis of government programs or projects."*

The concept of the B/C ratio encompasses a monetary value perspective of potential capital initiatives and incorporates the use of the time value of money. The B/C ratio facilitates an understanding of whether a considered capital initiative is worth pursuing through time and contributes toward the rendering of a human decision regarding the pursuance of the considered capital initiative. This concept is expressed as a ratio between the overall benefits of an initiative versus its investment costs. According to the U.S. Department of Transportation (DOT), the purpose of B/C analysis is to identify "all benefits and costs accruing to society from a project or course of action, regardless of which particular party realizes the benefits or costs, or the form these benefits and costs take," and also identifies "the economically efficient investment alternative, i.e., the one that maximizes the net benefits to the public from an allocation of resources."†

According to the DOT, the B/C analysis method encompasses the following steps:‡

1. Establish objectives
2. Identify constraints and specify assumptions
3. Define base case and identify alternatives
4. Set analysis period
5. Define level of effort for screening alternatives
6. Analyze traffic effects
7. Estimate benefits and costs relative to base case
8. Evaluate risk
9. Compare net benefits and rank alternatives
10. Make recommendations

Within the B/C ratio relationship and its analytical processing, both monetary variables of investment costs and possible benefits must be

* Office of Management and Budget, "Guidelines and Discount Rates."

† U.S. Department of Transportation, "Economic Analysis Primer."

‡ Ibid.

discounted to express their values in the terms of current monetary values. Normally, both the investment costs and possible benefits are examined throughout the anticipated life cycle of the considered capital initiative. According to the DOT, the B/C ratio may be used when restrictions and limitations of cash flows are manifested. The DOT indicates that the B/C analysis begins with the application of a "discount rate to the benefits and costs incurred in each year of the project's life cycle" and culminates in the identification of "one or more alternative measures of a project's economic merit."*

Similar to the concept of capital budgeting, the use of human judgment, influenced by the mathematical outcomes of B/C analysis, is necessary to determine whether a potential initiative is either acceptable or unacceptable. The B/C ratio produces a quantitative outcome numerically. With respect to the characteristics of the considered problem domain, the outcome value of the B/C ratio analysis may be assessed as follows:

If the value of the B/C ratio outcome is less than the value of 1.0, then reject the initiative.
If the value of the B/C ratio outcome is greater than the value of 1.0, then accept the initiative.

A variety of practical uses of the B/C ratio are easily identifiable among public sector settings. According to the City of Glendale, California, "Benefit/cost analysis is used in natural hazards mitigation to show if the benefits to life and property protected through mitigation efforts exceed the cost of the mitigation activity," and may be used to "assist communities in determining whether a project is worth undertaking now, in order to avoid disaster related damages later." Further, regarding this context, the use of "benefit/cost analysis is based on calculating the frequency and severity of a hazard, avoided future damages, and risk."† Because many law enforcement entities are first-responder entities in such emergencies, these notions are salient concerning preventive measures and operational capacities of law enforcement organizations. Through the use of the B/C technique, law enforcement entities gain the perspective of which investments are strategically lucrative for both societal benefit and organizational benefit.

Similarly, in Arkansas the use of B/C analysis provides a method of analyzing which transportation infrastructure projects must be undertaken. According to the Arkansas State Highway and Transportation Department (ASHTD), the B/C analysis method is useful regarding considerations of highway bypass infrastructures. According to the State of Arkansas, the B/C

* U.S. Department of Transportation, "Economic Analysis Primer."
† City of Glendale, California, "Appendix C."

method was used to examine a comparison between a proposed bypass "as an Interstate-type toll facility with the existing four-lane divided Highway 71 facility for the first twenty years the facility is open (2013 through 2033)." This B/C analysis examined benefits versus costs regarding the following scenarios: "(1) Building the Bypass as a toll facility, and (2) No-Build for the Bypass, where motorists would continue to use existing Highway 71." The B/C ratio outcome for this Arkansas initiative was 1.26. The financial assessment determined that a total of approximately $108 million would be manifest in cost savings.* Based on the preceding tenets that govern initiative acceptance from the perspective of the B/C ratio, this proposed initiative qualifies for acceptance.

This Arkansas capital initiative has implications regarding law enforcement entities. The construction of the bypass must incorporate regular highway patrolling by law enforcement entities. Therefore, law enforcement entities along the proposed stretch of bypass must accommodate the needs of societal public service. Within their budgeting analysis and requirements, additional costs of manpower, fuel, training, vehicles, maintenance, and other pertinent line items must be incorporated. Given the inclusion of such additional variables and their associated financial expenses, the rendering of strategic financial management decisions, facilitated through capital budgeting techniques, must also be inclusive of such additional resources.

The B/C ratio provides a powerful form of analysis that supplements capital budgeting decisions regarding potential financial investment initiatives. Through the use of the B/C analysis method, organizations gain the capacity to determine, economically, whether a capital initiative is a worthwhile endeavor necessitating the rendering of long-term, strategic financial investments involving the implementation of capital budgeting techniques. If a potential capital investment initiative is deemed as acceptable, then additional analysis, involving the integration of multiple techniques of capital budgeting, may be mandated regarding the rendering of financial decisions strategically.

10.4 Leasing versus Purchasing Concepts

A lease is defined as the "non-permanent disposition, of an interest in real property, including but not limited to, leases, permits, licenses and temporary easements."† Usually, the leasing relationship is expressed formally through a written, legal agreement between the parties of interest. Leasing involves the rental, possession, and use of assets, over time, in exchange for some

* Arkansas State Highway and Transportation Department, "Benefit Cost Analysis."
† City of St. Petersburg, Florida, "Municipal Charter."

form of compensation. However, owning represents an equity investment, in addition to the functions of possession and use, of an asset. These concepts, underlying the question of leasing versus purchasing, are salient concerns of law enforcement entities. Law enforcement entities may elect to purchase or lease physical infrastructures, equipment, or supplies.

Decisions to lease or purchase assets are not uncommon among law enforcement entities. The Woodburn (Oregon) Police Department during 2010 issued a call for proposals soliciting leasing bids, from any interested vendors, regarding the leasing of "up to nine (9) full-size four-door 'police package' sedans for a three-year period."[*] Other considerations include the leasing of city-owned property as a method of generating additional cash flow streams. During 2010, the City of New Brighton, Minnesota, announced that space was available for lease within its city hall building.[†] The benefit of leasing city property is manifested through revenue streams that may be funneled to compensate for the costs of city operations, including policing services.

Decisions to purchase assets also provide law enforcement entities with a myriad of benefits and tools. After 2002, the Satsuma (Alabama) Police Department purchased "police vehicles, mobile data transmitters (lap top computers) and digital recording camera systems" using monies obtained through the seizing of "drug funds."[‡] Among smaller towns and rural areas, purchasing decisions may be financed through the use of grant funding. The Libby (Montana) Police Department, during its 1990s growth stages, leveraged grant funding to purchase patrol bicycles, and leveraged financial resources to purchase surplus patrol vehicles from the Montana Highway Patrol.[§]

However, when considering the issues associated with the questions of leasing versus purchasing, the use of quantitative analysis facilitates the rendering of human decisions. This form of analysis involves a consideration of analyzing cash flows through time. Therefore, the analysis of leasing versus purchasing incorporates the principles of the time value of money. The lease versus purchase analysis "compares the cost of each alternative by considering the timing of the payments, the tax benefits, the interest rate on a loan, the lease rate and other financial arrangements" in conjunction with "assumptions about the economic life of the equipment, salvage value and depreciation."[¶] It is not uncommon to embellish these financial calculations through the uses of finance calculators, financial tables of future monetary value and current monetary value equivalencies, and the use of software spreadsheets.

[*] City of Woodburn, Oregon, "Request for Proposal."
[†] City of New Brighton, Minnesota, "Home Page."
[‡] City of Satsuma, Alabama, "Police Department."
[§] City of Libby, Montana, "A Brief History."
[¶] University of Missouri, "Lease vs. Purchase Considerations."

A variety of factors influence the decision to either lease or purchase an asset. The implementation of a leasing mechanism may facilitate additional budgetary considerations of the financial requirements of an asset among organizational budgets. With purchasing options, cash monetary down payments may be required to secure assets (e.g., vehicles, buildings, land), whereas such down payment requirements may be immaterial within a leasing relationship. Some localities might necessitate voter referendums or approvals of significant financial purchases, whereas the leasing arrangement may not require such considerations of the constituency. Depending upon the contractual terms, lease payments may be negotiated to determine the frequency, monetary amounts, and types of payments that are due through time. Further, lease arrangements may include a cancellation clause or may not require renewal should the law enforcement entity no longer need or desire the use of the leased asset(s). However, such leasing arrangements may include fees for early termination.

Other considerations may include the maintenance costs and issues associated with the utilization and upkeep of assets. Additional considerations include the length of time required for the asset, the considerations of depreciation, the considerations of appreciation, the potential impacts of any salvage values, and considerations of obsolescence. Within the context of law enforcement entities, the aspects of overall societal benefit must also be included in the decision domain.

Given these notions, the decision to either lease or purchase assets is subject to numerous influences. Such decisions must neither be regarded lightly nor understated. Regardless, the decision concerning leasing versus purchasing is highly unique and situational. Each organization has its innate requirements for equipment, real estate, vehicles, and so forth that impact the rendering of human financial decisions strategically. Therefore, the decision that is appropriate for one organization may be completely inappropriate for another organization. Hence, each situation must be evaluated according to its own merits and characteristics, and each organization must evaluate its unique advantages and disadvantages regarding the leasing versus purchasing decision.

10.5 Scenario Analysis Concepts

Within the financial management domain may be many possible courses of actions, a myriad of combinations, and various permutations of possible outcomes associated with the rendering of human financial decisions strategically. Therefore, when contemplating the strategic investment of financial funds strategically, organizational leaders may consider an array of possible, multiple outcomes that may be generated from the rendering of a solitary financial decision. The use of analysis may also be appropriate to examine courses of action and their associated potential outcomes from nonfinancial contexts.

These considerations of potential, multiple outcomes are expressed through the notion of scenario analysis. Scenario analysis involves the mathematical delineation of multiple scenarios that are indicative of the best case, most likely case, and worst case situations that may be generated from the rendering of a human decision through time. The use of risk determination may separate and distinctly identify these specific outcomes mathematically. Although these three categories represent the primary anticipated situations that may arise from the rendering of human decisions, many other scenarios may be generated through the changing of the probability value used to examine the potential future outcome.

The use of scenario analysis among law enforcement entities or within the criminal justice system is not uncommon regarding the possible consequences and ramifications of rendering human decisions. The nonfinancial applications of scenario analysis include a variety of endeavors that affect society. According to the DOT, various considerations exist regarding the "safety of commercial heavy trucks, and particularly questioning if changing truck sizes and weights would alter roadway safety." Additional vehicular considerations involve the use of scenario analysis within the context of safety analysis and performance analysis.*

With respect to considerations of risk, examinations of transnational criminal activity may be facilitated through the use of scenario analysis. According to Caliber Associates, the use of scenario analysis may facilitate the identification of "best practices in responding to transnational crime from actual cases handled by local and state law enforcement" through placing student personnel "in the role of decision makers, asking them to distinguish pertinent from peripheral facts, to identify central alternatives among several issues competing for attention, and to formulate strategies and policy recommendations." This form of analysis improves the ability of humans to render decisions. Such improvements are manifested through the learning of roles and responsibilities, the realism of scenarios and the cooperativeness among personnel, and the determination of effective responses concerning the characteristics of the considered scenarios.† These lessons may be applied to rendering decisions of financial management given the risks involved with financing law enforcement organizations and the risks associated with both tangible and intangible value that may be generated from law enforcement activities and endeavors.

Further considerations involve the financial aspects of scenario analysis. The use of scenario analysis may be used to detect various characteristics of

* U.S. Department of Transportation, "Western Uniformity Scenario Analysis."

† Caliber Associates, "State and Local Law Enforcement Response."

money laundering through an examination of financial records. According to Elwart et al., the use of scenario analysis may be applied to examinations of possible outcomes of investing grant funding concerning domestic abuse programs.* From the perspective of threat analysis and disaster planning, monetary savings are considered by Tijan, Kos, and Ogrizović.† Many other monetary applications may be considered from the perspective of scenario analysis.

Given the preceding examples of financial and nonfinancial applications, implementations of scenario analysis may incorporate various facets of risk and the time value of money during its analysis of future, potential implications regarding current financial decisions. Through the use of scenario analysis, humans gain the advantage of considering multiple perspectives of possible outcomes that may result from the rendering of a financial decision strategically. Therefore, the use of scenario analysis contributes toward the rendering of strengthened and more robust decisions through time.

10.6 Sensitivity Analysis Concepts

The use of scenario analysis examines a variety of possible outcomes, quantitatively, that may represent future states of existences regarding the implications of the rendering of human decisions during current periods. However, regardless of the probability used to generate these possible outcomes, scenario analysis is relatively a static method of examining projected scenarios through time. Therefore, although it does consider the potentials of future states of being, scenario analysis does not directly consider changes among variables that may impact the future state of existence regarding a single instantiation of a given scenario. Hence, despite its potential concerning examinations of possible future outcomes, scenario analysis fails to answer a solitary question regarding these possible future states of being: What if?

Many strategic connotations may be associated with such a simple question. What if fewer or greater quantities of officers are assigned patrol duties during peak crime hours? What if societal demographics show either increasing or decreasing crime trends over time? What if work hours are assigned via rotating swing shifts among patrol officers? Certainly, many other questions may be posed. Further, such questions may be examined from both the perspectives of financial outcomes and nonfinancial outcomes depending on the needs of the law enforcement entity.

Similar to scenario analysis, the use of sensitivity analysis is not uncommon within the context of law enforcement entities. With respect to the Los Angeles Police Department, sensitivity analysis was used to examine facets

* Elwart et al., "Increasing Access to Restraining Orders."

† Tijan, Kos, and Ogrizović, "Disaster Recovery and Business Continuity."

of "sensitivity of the conclusion that the 10-percent expansion of the police force in Los Angeles" would satisfactorily fulfill the requirements of a cost/benefit test.* Cartwright implements sensitivity analysis testing to examine financial attributes of "drug addiction and treatment costs over one year are estimated from interviews of police officials and program administrators."† Günal, Onggo, and Pidd consider sensitivity analysis regarding improvements within policing control areas.‡ Each of these instances shows the diversity of the sensitivity analysis approach to facilitating human decisions.

Given the preceding examples of financial and nonfinancial applications, implementations of sensitivity analysis may incorporate various facets of risk and the time value of money during its analysis of future potential implications regarding current financial decisions. Through the use of sensitivity analysis, humans gain the advantage of considering multiple perspectives of possible outcomes that may result from the rendering of a financial decision strategically. However, unlike the method of scenario analysis, the sensitivity analysis paradigm incorporates the dynamics of change that affect variables within the problem domain. Therefore, the use of sensitivity analysis contributes to the rendering of strengthened and more robust decisions through time.

10.7 Break-Even Analysis Concepts

Another salient method of embellishing human decisions is through the use of break-even analysis. This form of analysis provides an additional method of analyzing the decision domain with respect to its chronological attributes. Unlike the payback time method of capital budgeting, which calculates the required period that is necessary for a capital investment to return its costs of investment, the break-even approach examines the period of time that is necessary for an investment to become theoretically profitable. Through the use of the break-even analysis method, humans gain the advantage of using an additional method of chronologically examining the decision domain strategically. The time factor is not the only method of examining the problem domain through the implementation of the break-even analysis. Instead, other variables may be considered as categories through which break-even thresholds may be established. Examples include sales quantities, financial amounts, or any other measureable characteristics of the problem domain.

The use of the break-even analysis paradigm is not uncommon among law enforcement and criminal justice settings. Through the use of this method,

* Heaton, "Hidden in Plain Sight."
† Cartwright, "Cost-Benefit Analysis."
‡ Günal, Onggo, and Pidd, "Improving Police Control Rooms."

organizations may determine the quantities of a certain characteristic or events that are necessary to become profitable regarding various attributes of the problem domain. The RAND Corporation considers the use of the break-even approach as a method of systematically querying "how much a new domestic intelligence agency would have to reduce terrorism risk—given a presumed level of threat and estimates of agency cost—to justify creating it."* Break-even analysis facilitated examinations of communications infrastructures in the Maryland State Highway Administration to determine the period of time that was necessary to establish a break-even threshold regarding the proposed communications initiative.†

The City of Huron, Ohio, considers the use of break-even analysis regarding examinations of estimates concerning "parking and commuting costs using police vehicles." Regarding this implementation, the "break-even distance for subsidized commuting using this approach is in the range 7 to 14 miles," and indicates that "it may be less expensive for the city to provide in-city parking for officers who live more than this many miles beyond city limits." Further considerations included the notion that "If the city were to use other criteria for setting policy, the city might decide to subsidize commuting for all (or most) of the officers with assigned cars."‡ The outcome of this situation yielded a recommendation that police personnel should be allowed to take home their assigned vehicles.

The preceding examples demonstrate the robustness and variability of the break-even paradigm regarding both nonfinancial and financial decisions. Regardless of the type of decision, the break-even method provides humans with the ability to determine the threshold quantity of units that are necessary to justify the pursuance of a capital investment. Given this notion, the break-even paradigm is another complement to the methods of capital budgeting that influence the rendering of human financial decisions strategically.

10.8 Complements, Not Competitors

The basic methods of capital budgeting described in this text provide humans with the capacity to perceive financial problem domains from the perspectives of time, cash flows, rates, and profitability. Although these perspectives provide a sound, robust basis for facilitating the rendering of human decisions, other methods exist that strengthen the scope and magnitude of these human decisions. Therefore, the additional, analytical methods of lease versus

* Leuschner, "Research Brief."

† Gianni and Moore, "Intelligent Transportation System (ITS) Telecommunications Analysis."

‡ ICMA Consulting Services, "Data and Operational Analysis Report."

purchase analysis, benefit–cost analysis, sensitivity analysis, scenario analysis, and break-even analysis complement the traditional functions of capital budgeting.

The decision to pursue a capital investment involves the rendering of a strategic decision, which requires a dedicated, unequivocal commitment of resources through significant periods of time. Such decisions must not be taken lightly or understated regarding their consequences and ramifications. Only through a thorough examination of the characteristics of the problem domain should recommendations of acceptance regarding potential capital investment initiatives be offered among organizational leaders. Although the use of the integrated techniques of capital budgeting provides a method through which various facets of the problem domain may be examined, the use of the additional financial techniques given in this chapter strengthen the financial decisions rendered by humans.

The use of the integrated capital budgeting methods is advantageous in that it presents a well-rounded perspective of financial value. However, the use of the additional methods given in this chapter presents an additional consideration of economic value analysis. Therefore, when combined, both approaches provide a consideration of financial value and resource allocation perspectives. Hence, this combination of analytics provides organizational leaders with a strong set of tools through which capital investment issues may be strongly examined.

10.9 Chapter Comments and Summary

This chapter concludes the introductory discussions of basic capital budgeting. The perspectives of time analysis, cash analysis, rate analysis, and profitability analysis comprise the basic four functions of capital budgeting analysis methods. Respectively, these functions are commensurate with the quantitative models of the payback time method, the net present value method, the internal rate of return method, and the profitability index method. Although they may be implemented solitarily, these methods may be combined to perform a robust, integrated capital budgeting function when considering capital investment decisions strategically.

Whether they are deployed solitarily or through an integrated fashion, the four capital budgeting models present a perspective of financial value strategically. Therefore, they are concerned with the financing of long-term, capital-intensive investments through time. However, they are not necessarily concerned with an economic perspective of capital investing regarding the worthiness of resource allocation strategically.

Given such a notion, additional methods of analysis may be used to further examine capital investment decisions strategically. These methods consist of lease versus purchase analysis, benefit–cost analysis, sensitivity analysis, scenario analysis, and break-even analysis. Through the use of these additional methods, the functions of capital budgeting are quantitatively complemented to yield stronger analytical examinations of the considered problem domain. Therefore, it may be stated that additional methods exist through which the rendering of human decisions may be embellished and strengthened.

Because this text is an introductory discussion of the application of capital budgeting methods, an extensive delineation of the complementary analytical methods is beyond the scope and magnitude of this manuscript. Therefore, specific formulas and mathematical models are not described in this book. However, other texts fully consider these complementary methods and demonstrate their applications within the context of rendering long-term, strategic decisions regarding potential capital initiatives. Regardless of the approach selected, all capital investment decisions must be considered through the use of some systematic, methodical model through which human decisions may be facilitated.

10.10 Terminology

Benefit–cost analysis (BCA)
Benefit–cost ratio (B/C)
Break-even analysis (BEA)
Capital budgeting
Capital investment
Complementary methods
Compounding
Current monetary value
Discounting
Economic analysis
Economics
Finance
Financial analysis
Future monetary value
Internal rate of return (IRR)
Lease
Net present value (NPV)
Payback time method (PTM)
Profitability index method (PIM)
Purchase
Scenario analysis
Sensitivity analysis
Strategic decision
Time value of money

10.11 Thought and Discussion Questions

1. Define the terms *finance* and *economics.* Discuss their commonness and their differences. Further, within this discussion, consider the notion that finance is a subset of economics and substantively argue that financial management decisions are essentially economic decisions.
2. Compare and contrast the methods of the payback time method and the break-even analysis method. Within this discussion, consider the

aspects of financial analysis and economic analysis that impact capital investment decisions strategically.

3. Compare and contrast the methods of sensitivity analysis and scenario analysis. Further, within this discussion, consider the notion that scenario analysis is a subset of sensitivity analysis and substantively argue the justification of this relationship between these two analytical methods.
4. The four basic methods of capital budgeting and the complementary methods of analysis given in this chapter all improve the capacity of humans to render long-term, strategic decisions regarding capital initiatives. However, these methods are not the only methods available that may be applied to capital investment domains. What other approaches exist to facilitate the rendering of capital investment decisions?

Bibliography

Arkansas State Highway and Transportation Department. "Benefit Cost Analysis." Accessed August 25, 2010: http://www.arkansashighways.com/BVB/BenefitCost_Analysis.pdf.

Caliber Associates. "State and Local Law Enforcement Response to Transnational Crime—Task Order T-046 Final Report." Prepared for U.S. Department of Justice, March 2, 2005.

Cartwright, William. "Cost-Benefit Analysis of Drug Treatment Services: Review of the Literature." *The Journal of Mental Health Policy and Economics*, 3 (2000): 11–26.

City of Glendale, California. "Appendix C—Economic Analysis of Natural Hazard Mitigation Projects." Accessed August 25, 2010: http://www.ci.glendale.ca.us/HMP_Apndx-C_Economic%20Analysis.asp.

City of Libby, Montana. "A Brief History of the City of Libby Police Department." 2009. Accessed August 26, 2010: http://www.cityoflibby.com/police.html.

City New Brighton, Minnesota. "Home Page." Accessed August 26, 2010: http://www.ci.new-brighton.mn.us/.

City of Satsuma, Alabama. "Police Department." Accessed August 26, 2010: http://www.cityofsatsuma.com/PoliceDepartment.html.

City of St. Petersburg, Florida. "Municipal Charter." March 2007. Accessed August 26, 2010: http://www.stpete.org/pdf/citycharter.pdf.

City of Woodburn, Oregon. "Request for Proposal—Vehicle Lease Proposal." Police Department home page. Accessed August 26, 2010: http://www.ci.woodburn.or.us/police/.

Elwart, Liz, Nina Emerson, Christina Enders, Dani Fumia, and Kevin Murphy. "Increasing Access to Restraining Orders for Low-Income Victims of Domestic Violence: A Cost-Benefit Analysis of the Proposed Domestic Abuse Grant Program." Prepared for State Bar Association of Wisconsin, December 2006. Accessed August 26, 2010: http://www.wisbar.org/am/template.cfm?template=/cm/contentdisplay.cfm&contentid=63633.

Gianni, Ben and Alisoun Moore. "A Case for Intelligent Transportation System (ITS) Telecommunications Analysis. Maryland State Highway Administration ITS Telecommunications Study." U.S. Department of Transportation, 1997. Accessed August 26, 2010: http://www.fhwa.dot.gov/tfhrc/safety/pubs/its/resourceguides/itscase.pdf.

Günal, Murat, Stephan Onggo, and Mike Pidd. "Improving Police Control Rooms Using Simulation." *Journal of the Operational Research Society*, 59 (2008): 171–181.

Heaton, Paul. "Hidden in Plain Sight: What Cost-of-Crime Research Can Tell Us about Investing in Police." RAND Center on Quality Policing, 2010. Accessed August 27, 2010: http://health.rand.org/pubs/occasional_papers/2010/RAND_OP279.pdf.

ICMA Consulting Services. "Data and Operational Analysis Report: Public Safety Services (Police/Fire/EMS)—Huron, Ohio." City of Huron, 2009. Accessed August 27, 2010: http://www.cityofhuron.org/huron/pdf/ICMA%20Public%20Safety%20Study.pdf.

Leuschner, Kristin J. "Research Brief: Should the United States Establish a Dedicated Domestic Intelligence Agency for Counterterrorism?" RAND Corporation, 2008. Accessed August 26, 2010: http://www.rand.org/pubs/research_briefs/RB9369/index1.html.

Office of Management and Budget. "Guidelines and Discount Rates for Benefit–Cost Analysis of Federal Programs." OMB Circular A-94, October 29, 1992. Accessed August 25, 2010: http://www.whitehouse.gov/sites/default/files/omb/assets/a94/a094.pdf.

Tijan, Edvard, Serdo Kos, and Dario Ogrizović. "Disaster Recovery and Business Continuity in Port Community Systems." *Scientific Journal of Maritime Research*, 23 (2009): 243–260. Accessed August 26, 2010: http://www.google.com/url?sa=t&source=web&cd=117&ved=0CDEQFjAGOG4&url=http%3A%2F%2Fhrcak.srce.hr%2Ffile%2F60323&rct=j&q=%22scenario%20analysis%22%20%20police%20money&ei=r254TI38NoSclgezwqywCg&usg=AFQjCNGqKTIK736sIEcb-54HJeckp-zDGg&cad=rja.

University of Missouri. "Lease vs. Purchase Considerations." 2008. Accessed August 26, 2010: http://www.missouribusiness.net/sbtdc/docs/lease_vs_purchase.asp.

U.S. Department of Transportation. "Economic Analysis Primer: Benefit–Cost Analysis." Accessed August 23, 2010: http://www.fhwa.dot.gov/infrastructure/asstmgmt/primer05.cfm.

U.S. Department of Transportation. "Western Uniformity Scenario Analysis." April 2004. Accessed August 27, 2010: http://www.fhwa.dot.gov/policy/otps/truck/wusr/chap07.htm.

The Slammer
Concuding Remarks
11

Giving money and power to government is like giving whiskey and car keys to teenage boys.*

P. J. O'Rourke

11.1 Objectives

The objective of this conclusion is to emphasize the importance of rendering informed financial decisions.

11.2 Financial Commentary

Parole is defined as a "promise made with or confirmed by a pledge of one's honor; especially the promise of a prisoner of war to fulfill stated conditions in consideration of his release" or "a conditional release of a prisoner serving an indeterminate or unexpired sentence."† Parole involves the desires, hopes, and dreams of freedom from confinement. Those who are incarcerated count the days until their anticipated date of release arrives and relish the day when their freedom is granted.

However, freedom is not free. There is always a cost associated with freedom. From the contexts of history and modern American security, the lives of many military personnel and civilians were sacrificed to ensure future generations enjoyed the benefits of freedom. No dollar amounts are equivalent to the blessings and vibrancies of human life and freedom. Modern America owes much to its contemporary military personnel and civilians, and also to those of previous generations.

From a qualitative perspective, such sacrifices were both priceless and emotionally costly. However, from a quantitative perspective, the prices of these engagements were quantifiable and remain quantifiable during modern times. During the authorship of this book, America continues its struggles against terrorism. According to Belasco, such costs are summarized as follows:

* O'Rourke, P. J., "P. J. O'Rourke Quotes," Brainy Quote, http://www.brainyquote.com/quotes/authors/p/p_j_orourke.html (accessed June 2, 2011).

† *Merriam-Webster Dictionary*, "Parole."

> With enactment of the sixth FY2011 Continuing Resolution through March 18, 2011, (H.J.Res. 48/P.L. 112-6) Congress has approved a total of $1.283 trillion for military operations, base security, reconstruction, foreign aid, embassy costs, and veterans' health care for the three operations initiated since the 9/11 attacks: Operation Enduring Freedom (OEF) Afghanistan and other counter terror operations; Operation Noble Eagle (ONE), providing enhanced security at military bases; and Operation Iraqi Freedom (OIF). This estimate assumes that the current CR level continues through the rest of the year and that agencies allocate reductions proportionately. Of this $1.283 trillion total, CRS estimates that Iraq will receive about $806 billion (63%), OEF $444 billion (35%) and enhanced base security about $29 billion (2%), with about $5 billion that CRS cannot allocate (1/2%). About 94% of the funds are for DOD, 5% for foreign aid programs and diplomatic operations, and 1% for medical care for veterans.*

Such costs are considerable and show the investment decisions that are necessary to facilitate the safety and security of the American nation. Military police (MP) units are important components of such operations, and both their activities and personnel require funding through time. Fielding such MP units involves numerous costs that include recruiting, training, uniforms, weapons, logistics, lodging, pay, benefits, foodstuffs, vehicles, fuel, maintenance of equipment, and a variety of other financial investments. The costs of such operations are satisfied through the provision of funding that is obtained through tax dollars and other government financing mechanisms. These decisions must be made to yield the highest and best use of such funds while simultaneously facilitating outcomes that are in the strategic and tactical interests of the United States.

Similarly, numerous costs are associated among civilian law enforcement entities. Civilian law enforcement agencies are primary components of homeland security operations within the United States. According to the Department of Homeland Security, numerous programs, operations, and entities exist through which homeland security functions occur. Examples include federal air marshals; law enforcement partnerships among federal, state, and local agencies (e.g., training centers, 287(g) program); canine programs; fraud investigations; immigration operations; fugitive operations programs; and protective missions (e.g., Secret Service).† Again, many costs are involved including recruiting, training, uniforms, weapons, logistics, lodging, pay, benefits, foodstuffs, vehicles, fuel, maintenance of equipment, and a variety of other financial investments. Protecting American society is not inexpensive, and such costs are justified to provide safety and security within the American populace.

* Belasco, "The Cost of Iraq."

† U.S. Department of Homeland Security, "Home Page."

Popular and familiar American landmarks are now potential terrorist targets because of their "symbolic value." Because of the threats of terrorism, increased financial investments are necessary to protect America's landmarks annually. According to the National Parks Conservation Association (NPCA), "places like Mount Rushmore, the Washington Monument, and the St. Louis Arch" must be protected. However, because of difficulties regarding the allocation of resources and personnel, the NPCA indicates that "when rangers from parks such as Rocky Mountain and Shenandoah are sent to guard the Statue of Liberty during times of heightened security, dams, and porous international park borders, their positions remain unfilled." As a result of such altered duties and increased responsibilities, annual park service budget requirements, solely for unfunded homeland security functions, are approximately $43 million.*

The costs of providing law enforcement and security services among national parks are high. The NPCA estimated that the costs of recent security enhancements, solely for Independence Hall, were approximately $5 million. Further, the NPCA indicates that a "30-mile-long vehicle barrier at Organ Pipe Cactus cost approximately $14 million to build, but the Park Service doesn't have enough money to maintain it, which park staff fear may lead to breaches." Although the government has invested much money to bolster parkland security, the NPCA indicates that "funding for law enforcement personnel and equipment in most parks is included as part of the operating budget, which research has shown to be short by more than $600 million annually."†

These considerations are indicative of the basic question of economics: how does one satisfy the unlimited wants and needs of humans through the availability, provision, and allocation of scarce resources? When considered from the national parks perspective of law enforcement homeland security functions, those who contemplate this basic, economic query also must be mindful of the need to maintain efficiency and effectiveness of ensuring the safety of American landmarks and members of society. Given these notions, a conundrum is quickly apparent. The threats against the American populace and national landmarks are great, resources to deter such threats are limited, and the security and safety of both landmarks and humans must be maximized unceasingly. Therefore, financial decisions must be rendered with respect to the considerations of threat assessments, symbolic value, visitor throughput, location, personnel, equipment, feasibility, and an array of other factors. This conundrum becomes increasingly complex because perfect solutions are nonexistent. The NPCA is not ignorant of these issues:

* National Parks Conservation Association, "Perilous Parkland."

† Ibid.

> As homeland security needs have increased, many park managers have had to reallocate existing resources to law enforcement to the detriment of other park programs such as interpretation and maintenance. In 2000, Organ Pipe Cactus, for example, had 31 full-time equivalent employees (FTEs); it now has 39. But over the same six years, the Maintenance Division has lost 3 FTEs; Interpretation (public education) lost 3 seasonal interpreters; and the Natural Resources team lost one position. This has had a significant impact on the park's ability to protect park resources and serve and inspire more than 280,000 visitors annually.*

Although the effects of such financial decisions are intended to bolster the security of American parklands, they also diminish the cultural experience of park visitors. In some cases, certain park areas and exhibits may be closed to the public because of the inability to financially provide personnel and resources for their maintenance and operations. These shortcomings demonstrate the complexities of rendering law enforcement financial decisions that benefit the American nation.

Within an operational context of the National Park Service, such considerations of financial decisions balance the servicing of society with the provision of security. Concentrating heavily on the provision of security missions reduces the funding and personnel that are available for public interactions and service. Concentrating heavily on the provision of public service reduces the funding and personnel that are available for security missions. Therefore, the rendering of financial decisions must carefully contemplate the advantages and disadvantages of ranking service obligations and pursuing financial investments through time.

These notions are not limited solely to the National Park Service. These same concerns are found among the law enforcement agencies of local communities throughout the United States. According to the Northwest Tribal Emergency Management Council (NWTEMC), similar concerns are also applicable within the context of community-oriented policing. The NWTEMC exists as a nonprofit "consortium of Tribes in the Northwest region of Washington State to help Tribes participate in Homeland Security and Emergency Management preparedness efforts."† These efforts also include financial decisions about implementing community-oriented policing functions and activities. Among these efforts are the initiatives of the Tulalip Police Department of Tulalip, Washington.

The Tulalip Police Department expresses the contemplation of funding decisions through the following observations:

* National Parks Conservation Association, "Perilous Parkland."

† Northwest Tribal Emergency Management Council, "Home Page."

Chiefs consistently say the Community Policing is a good philosophy but, because of the expense, not something that can be done accomplished given current fiscal constraints. If Chiefs don't focus on more personnel, then they discuss the various amounts of hardware, including mini-stations, mobile precincts, and other pieces of equipment that must be obtained before Community Policing can even be contemplated. This preoccupation with funding and equipment actually impedes an agency's transition to a Community Policing philosophy and slows police administrators planning."*

The Tulalip Police Department also notes that:

The bottom line is that there is not enough money in the world to pay for Community Policing. Community Policing is a value driven philosophy and—like human affection or friendship—it cannot be bought. It must come from within, and officers involved in it must believe it is the right thing to do and must want to do it. By controlling officers' time and allowing them to experience Community Oriented Policing it has been repeatedly because of ownership and the positive response they get when working with the community. This is not to say that Community Policing does not take an enhanced level of resources, but, again, all the resources in the world will not cause Community Policing to happen. Administrators should focus on innovative ways to accomplish it by freeing their officers' time up to work in the communities. Once the officers problem solve with the community, organizational changes will occur and the organizational culture will be changed. Administrators can then focus on what is really needed to further the transition to Community Policing. They may find that the answer isn't funding for a new mini-station or new officer after all—perhaps it consists of improving training or giving supervisory support to officer initiatives. The answer will be somewhat different for each department, but it can only be measured if administrators come down off the fundraising stump and find ways to put officers and community members together to solve problems.†

Again, the contemplating of financial investments affects the rendering of decisions regarding the allocation of resources. In this instance, financial decisions have the capacity to affect the implementing of a community-oriented policing program. This decision is also one of multiple perspectives in that it also demonstrates the arguments of operational capacity and mission versus public service and interaction. Further, the limited aspect of funding is acknowledged and addressed in the preceding commentaries of the Tulalip Police Department. Therefore, law enforcement leaders and city administrators must carefully and deliberately consider the investing of

* Tulalip Office of Neighborhoods, "How Much Does Community Policing Cost?"

† Ibid.

financial funds to yield the highest and best outcomes associated with the prevention of crime and the maintaining of order.

The limited aspect of available funding is an issue that pertains to all law enforcement entities and all facets of the criminal justice system. Although the primary chapters of this text discussed the methods through which such organizations are funded, the secured funds are limited. Therefore, financial decisions must be cautiously considered and courses of actions must be pursued appropriately.

Additional methods of funding the criminal justice system and law enforcement agencies may be unique and varied. The Alabama State Legislature is examining additional technology fees and charges through which additional cash flows may be procured to finance its justice system and affiliated agencies. According to the Homeland Security Newswire, this scenario is expressed as follows:

> The Alabama State Legislature is currently considering a bill that proposes adding a $10 technology fee to court costs in Chilton County; the fee is aimed at offset the rising technology costs of local law enforcement agencies; local police departments are struggling to comply with state mandates that require local agencies to electronically file tickets and other reports; the state has not provided funding to help departments pay for the operation and maintenance of computer systems; if the fee had been in place last year, it would have generated approximately $90,000."*

This method of potentially funding organizational monetary requirements provides a means through which additional cash flows may be established and exploited. Public tax dollars must be used to fund a variety of functions other than law enforcement and justice systems. Therefore, law enforcement entities and the criminal justice system receive only allocations of designed financial resources within their annual budgets. There is no guarantee that a sufficient supply of monies will exist to completely fund all of the endeavors and activities that are sponsored by law enforcement entities and within the criminal justice system.

This constant struggle for dollars and the decisions regarding their use are endless. It pervades all levels of public service encompassing both for-profit and nonprofit entities within the law enforcement domain and within the criminal justice system. It affects the provision of law enforcement and legal services in society, which may fluctuate with the amounts of monies that are allocated for their implementation. It affects the provision of government functions through which the security of society is annually facilitated. From a quantitative perspective, these notions are expressed within the American

* Homeland Security Newswire, "Alabama Proposes Law Enforcement Technology Fund."

national budget proposal for the 2012 year. According to Pelofsky, such observations are summarized as follows:

> The Obama administration on Monday proposed a nearly 2 percent increase for the U.S. homeland security budget for 2012, one the few areas of the budget that will likely see a boost as the White House battles a ballooning deficit. Its 2012 budget proposal requests $43.8 billion to spend on homeland security across the entire federal government, excluding the Defense Department, up $800 million from 2011. The request for the increase comes as militant groups like the al Qaeda wing based in Yemen have increased their efforts to strike the United States, including plots to blow up bombs on airplanes or in major city centers. The Department of Homeland Security alone would see its budget grow to more than $37 billion, up almost 3 percent over the 2011 budget level, and includes a 4 percent bump up for increasing transportation and border security. While the 2012 budget proposal called protecting the American people President Barack Obama's 'highest priority,' administration officials will likely face close scrutiny by Congress about where and how they spend the money.*

This passage is again indicative of the need for dollars versus the areas in which they are invested. It is also demonstrative of the continuous need to finance programs and entities that facilitate American security. The last sentence is especially notable because it expresses the notions of accountability that were presented within the primary chapters of this text. When rendering financial decisions that affect law enforcement entities and the criminal justice system, those who render such decisions must be accountable to the society from which the affected funds are procured.

Rendered decisions are not always popular or easy to understand. The rendering of financial decisions involves the weighing of costs—both quantitative and qualitative—that affect the serviced society. Balances must be considered among a variety of different, competing factions that include decisions regarding public programs, operational requirements, the types of services rendered among markets, desired benefits, and desired outcomes in the serviced market. Certainly, many others may be identified. From a perspective of financial management, every rendered decision has consequences, both good and bad, that represent the quantitative and qualitative constraints that affect the rendering of human financial decisions. All decisions are costly despite their contributions toward ensuring the safety and the integrity of society. Although the rendering of human decisions may occur with some scope of freedom to choose and pursue a course of action, societal constraints and considerations will always affect the rendering of human financial decisions.

* Pelofsky, "U.S. Homeland Security Budget."

The opening section of this conclusion indicated that freedom is not free. From the perspective of national security, this notion is most certainly true—both quantitatively and qualitatively. From the perspective of law enforcement and the criminal justice system, this notion is also true. American society shall never be free of the dangers and threats of crime and its perpetrators. The issues of financing deterring crime and maintaining order are both great and costly.

The preceding discussions and examples are indicative of the notion that dollars are limited, whereas the issues of deterring crime and maintaining order are unlimited. This notion encapsulates the basic theme of economics that has pervaded the entirety of this book: how does one satisfy the unlimited wants and needs of humans through the availability, provision, and allocation of scarce resources? Simply, the needs and wants of deterring crime and maintaining order are unlimited, whereas the available monies to pursue commensurate activities to deter crime and to maintain order are limited and scarce. Therefore, those who are responsible for rendering financial decisions must be mindful of this simple concept.

No panacea exists that will solve this economic conundrum that affects global decisions as well as the decisions of local law enforcement entities. However, through the use of the capital budgeting methods presented among the preceding chapters of this text, humans may render decisions with greater knowledge, confidence, clarity, and certainty. Even when capital budgeting methods are used, there shall always be lingering questions regarding the potency of the decision and the long-term benefits that it may herald through time. Regardless, capital budgeting is a tool that strengthens the ability of humans to render decisions within the law enforcement domain and within the criminal justice system.

Bibliography

Belasco, A. "The Cost of Iraq, Afghanistan, and Other Global War on Terror Operations Since 9/11." Congressional Research Service Report for Congress. Washington, DC: Congressional Research Service, 2011.

Homeland Security Newswire. "Alabama Proposes Law Enforcement Technology Fund." Accessed June 21, 2011: http://www.homelandsecuritynewswire.com/alabama-proposes-law-enforcement-technology-fund.

Merriam-Webster Dictionary. "Parole." Accessed June 2, 2011: http://www.merriam-webster.com/dictionary/parole.

National Parks Conservation Association. "Perilous Parkland: Homeland Security and the National Parks." July 24, 2009. Accessed June 19, 2011: http://www.npca.org/media_center/fact_sheets/security.html.

Northwest Tribal Emergency Management Council. "Home Page." Accessed June 21, 2011: http://www.nwtemc.org/.

Pelofsky, Jeremy. "Update 1—U.S. Homeland Security Budget Gets Small Budget Boost," Reuters News Service. February 14, 2011. Accessed June 21, 2011: http://www.reuters.com/article/2011/02/14/usa-budget-security-idUSN1411205720110214.

Tulalip Office of Neighborhoods. "How Much Does Community Policing Cost?" Accessed June 21, 2011: http://www.google.com/url?sa=t&source=web&cd=2&ved=0CCgQFjAB&url=http%3A%2F%2Fwww.nwtemc.org%2Fblockwatch%2FHowMuchDoesCommunityPolicingCost.doc&rct=j&q=community-oriented%20policing%20costs&ei=Tc3_Ta7UKIby0gHL_5XDDQ&usg=AFQjCNEB6fqidsisz3FYaKrz_dw_hN2syA&cad=rja.

U.S. Department of Homeland Security. "Home Page." Accessed July 10, 2011: http://www.dhs.gov.

Afterword

To the Reader

Thank you for your interest in our work and taking the time to immerse yourself in our writings. It is our sincere hope that you found these materials to be beneficial and meaningful. We are always delighted to answer questions or to further clarify the points of discussion contained within this book, and are certainly open to conversing with our readers and colleagues. We may be contacted by e-mail:

Adrian Doss:	professorbusiness@gmail.com
William "Bill" Sumrall:	bsumrall@belhaven.edu
Don Jones:	djones@belhaven.edu

Thank you for your time, attention, and support.

Adrian Doss, Bill Sumrall, and Don Jones

APPENDIX A: Financial Variables and Symbols

Monetary Value vs. Time

R_{per} Rate factor through time
P Period of time
V_{curr} Current monetary value
V_{futr} Future monetary value

Payback Time Method

T Time required for payback to occur
P Period currently examined within the current payback time method iteration
A_P Annual cash flow value
V_I Value amount of the initial funding
E_R Financial effect of a partial year (if any)
T_P Partial year period (if any)

Net Present Value Method

NPV Net present value
P Period currently examined within the net present value method iteration
R_{per} Rate factor through time
A_P Annual cash flow value
V_I Value amount of the initial funding

Internal Rate of Return Method

IRR Internal rate of return
P Period of time considered
A_P Annual cash flow value
V_I Cost of initial investment value

Profitability Index Method

PI Profitability Index
P Period of time considered
A_P Annual cash flow value
ΣA_P Present monetary value of the summation of annual cash flow values
V_I Cost of initial investment value

APPENDIX B: Financial Formulas

B.1 Mathematical Formulas

The basic methods of capital budgeting encompass the perspectives of time, cash value, rate, and profitability potential. Respectively, these perspectives are commensurate with the formulas of the payback time method (PTM), the net present value (NPV) method, the internal rate of return (IRR) method, and the profitability index method (PIM). Further, with the exception of the PTM, each of these capital budgeting methods incorporates the time value of money within its mathematical model.

With respect to the time value of money, three concepts are salient: current monetary value, future monetary value, and rate. Rates may be categorized as discount rates or compounding rates. When a future monetary value sum is analyzed to yield its current monetary value, in terms of present-day dollars, it is appropriate to implement the stated, accepted discount rate during the mathematical processing of the current monetary value formula. When a current monetary value sum is analyzed to yield its future monetary value, in terms of future dollars, it is appropriate to implement the stated, accepted compounding rate during the mathematical processing of the future monetary value formula. The current monetary value formula and the future monetary value formula may be manipulated to derive most any capital budgeting formula.

The formulas used within this manuscript are demonstrative of these concepts. Such formulas were presented and discussed within their respective chapters regarding capital budgeting applications. For the sake of convenience, these formulas are provided next.

B.1.1 Time Value of Money

The following formulas represent the mathematical foundations of the time value of money:

Future Monetary Value

$$V_{futr} = (V_{curr})(R_{per} + 1.0)^P$$

Current Monetary Value

$$V_{curr} = \frac{V_{futr}}{\left(R_{per} + 1.0\right)^{P}}$$

Rate Determination

$$R_{per} = \left(\sqrt[P]{V_{futr} / V_{curr}}\right) - 1.0$$

Time Period Determination

$$P = \frac{\ln\left(\frac{V_{futr}}{V_{curr}}\right)}{\ln\left(R_{per} + 1.0\right)}$$

B.2 Capital Budgeting Formulas

The following formulas represent the mathematical basis regarding the foundational perspectives of capital budgeting.

B.2.1 Payback Time Method (PTM) Concept

With respect to an overall period of years, the following expression represents the mathematical relationships among the variables that comprise the payback time method:

$$T = \left|\frac{V_I}{\sum A_P}\right|$$

Note: The value of the variable *P* does not exceed the time required for the threshold value to occur.

Further, with respect to a partial period, which is indicative of a period that represents a partial year, the following expression represents the mathematical relationships among the variables that comprise the payback time method:

$$T_P = \left|\frac{E_R}{\sum A_P}\right|$$

Note: The value of the variable P does not exceed the time required for the threshold value to occur.

The concept of the payback time method is fairly straightforward because it is merely the consideration of a ratio between the amounts of financial funds invested versus the amounts of annual cash flows that are necessary to surpass a threshold of compensation regarding the investment costs of the capital initiative. The following section considers the basic premise of the payback time method.

B.2.2 Basic PTM Selection Rule

The accepting or rejecting of any PTM outcome is subjective to the constraints of the problem domain. Users of this formula must specify their qualifications for acceptance, and judge the outcome of this formula against their stated requirements to determine whether an outcome is acceptable.

B.2.3 Net Present Value (NPV) Concept

$$NPV = \left(\sum_{P=1}^{P} \frac{A_P}{\left(R_{per} + 1.0\right)^P} \right) - V_I$$

B.2.4 Basic NPV Selection Rules

Although the outcomes of the NPV method present quantitative findings, the outcomes must be interpreted. The rules governing the interpretation of the NPV outcomes are quite basic:

1. Discard the potential initiative(s) that demonstrate NPV outcomes that are less than the value of 0.00;
2. Retain potential initiatives that have an NPV outcome that is greater than the value of 0.00; and
3. Select the initiative that demonstrates the highest NPV outcome when mutual exclusion, or other limitations, are applicable.

These rules provide the basis for judging a project as either acceptable or unacceptable with respect to an analysis of cash flows through time. However, other factors exist that may influence the rendering of a capital budgeting decision. Even though the NPV outcome may be positive, and may indicate that a project should be accepted, the ultimate decision to accept or reject a project is rendered by humans. Humans must also incorporate the characteristics of the domain environment that influence the decision process. Factors such as time, organizational politics, contribution to organizational value, and the availability of necessary resources also contribute to the rendering of capital budgeting decisions. Therefore, regardless of any NPV outcome, the decisions to accept and to pursue capital initiatives are subject to a variety of influences.

B.2.5 Internal Rate of Return (IRR) Concept

$$NPV = 0.00 = \left(\sum_{P=1}^{P} \frac{A_P}{(IRR + 1.0)^P} \right)$$

B.2.6 Basic IRR Selection Rules

Although the outcomes of the IRR method present quantitative findings, the outcomes must be interpreted. The rules governing the interpretation of the IRR outcome are quite basic:

1. Accept the capital initiative if the value of the calculated IRR outcome is higher than the specified discount rate.
2. Reject the capital initiative if the value of the calculated IRR outcome is lower than the discount rate.
3. When the conditions of mutual exclusion govern the problem domain, select the capital initiative that demonstrates the highest IRR outcome.

These rules provide the basis for judging a project as either acceptable or unacceptable, with respect to an analysis of cash flows, through time. However, other factors exist that may influence the rendering of a capital budgeting decision. Even though the IRR outcome may be positive, and may indicate that a project should be accepted, the ultimate decision to accept or reject a project is rendered by humans. Humans must also incorporate the characteristics of the domain environment that influence the decision process. Factors such as time, organizational politics, contribution to organizational value, and the availability of necessary resources also contribute to the rendering of capital budgeting decisions. Therefore, regardless of any IRR outcome, the decisions to accept and to pursue capital initiatives are subject to a variety of influences.

The solution of problems, involving the IRR method, may occur through the use of spreadsheet software, financial calculators, trial-and-error approaches necessitating the use of mathematical interpolation, or through the use of the Secant method. However, the use of the IRR method may manifest varying levels of difficulty because it necessitates the solution of polynomials of varying degrees. For larger data sets, it is highly recommended that solutions involve the use of financial calculators or software spreadsheets.

B.2.7 Profitability Index Concept

$$PI = \left(\frac{\sum_{P=1}^{P} A_P}{V_I} \right)$$

B.2.8 Basic PI Selection Rules

Although the outcomes of the PI method present quantitative findings, the outcomes must be interpreted. The rules governing the interpretation of the PI outcome are quite basic:

1. Accept the capital initiative if the value of the calculated PI outcome is greater than the value of 1.0.
2. Reject the capital initiative if the value of the calculated PI outcome is lower than the value of 1.0.
3. When the conditions of mutual exclusion govern the problem domain, select the capital initiative that demonstrates the highest PI outcome.

These rules provide the basis for judging a project as either acceptable or unacceptable, with respect to an analysis of cash flows, through time. However, other factors exist that may influence the rendering of a capital budgeting decision. Even though the PI method outcome may be greater than the value of 1.0, and may indicate that a project should be accepted, the ultimate decision to accept or reject a project is rendered by humans. Humans must also incorporate the characteristics of the domain environment that influence the decision process. Factors such as time, organizational politics, contribution to organizational value, and the availability of necessary resources also contribute to the rendering of capital budgeting decisions. Therefore, regardless of any PI method outcome, the decisions to accept and to pursue capital initiatives are subject to a variety of influences.

Index

D

M

N

O

For Product Safety Concerns and Information please contact our EU
representative GPSR@taylorandfrancis.com
Taylor & Francis Verlag GmbH, Kaufingerstraße 24, 80331 München, Germany

www.ingramcontent.com/pod-product-compliance
Lightning Source LLC
LaVergne TN
LVHW011117300926
849160LV00008B/424
* 9 7 8 1 4 3 9 8 9 2 2 3 7 *